Nursing Care
of the Alcoholic
and Drug Abuser

Nursing Care of the Alcoholic and Drug Abuser

Pamela K. Burkhalter, R.N., M.S.N.
Instructor of Nursing
School of Nursing
University of Hawaii

McGRAW-HILL BOOK COMPANY
A Blakiston Publication

New York / St. Louis / San Francisco / Auckland / Düsseldorf / Johannesburg
Kuala Lumpur / London / Mexico / Montreal / New Delhi / Panama / Paris
São Paulo / Singapore / Sydney / Tokyo / Toronto

74-10697

Nursing Care of the Alcoholic and Drug Abuser

2 3 4 5 6 7 8 9 0 DODO 7 9 8 7 6 5

This book was set in Press Roman with Univers
by Allen Wayne Technical Corp.
The editor was Cathy Dilworth;
the designer was Allen Wayne Technical Corp.;
the production supervisor was Sam Ratkewitch.
The printer and binder was R. R. Donnelley & Sons Company.

Library of Congress Cataloging in Publication Data

Burkhalter, Pamela K
    Nursing care of the alcoholic and drug abuser.

    "A Blakiston publication."
    Includes bibliographical references.
    1. Alcoholism. 2. Narcotic habit. 3. Nurses
and nursing. I. Title. DNLM: 1. Alcoholism—
Nursing. 2. Drug abuse—Nursing. WY 156 B959n
RC565.B87   610.73'68   74-10697
ISBN 0-07-009051-3

NOTICE

Medicine is an ever-changing science. As new research and clinical experience
broaden our knowledge, changes in treatment and drug therapy are required.
The editors and the publisher of this work have made every effort to ensure
that the drug dosage schedules herein are accurate and in accord with the
standards accepted at the time for publication. The reader is advised, however,
to check the product information sheet included in the package of each drug
he plans to administer to be certain that changes have not been made in the
recommended dose or in the contraindications for administration. This
recommendation is of particular importance in regard to new or infrequently
used drugs.

To Larry,
My Husband and Best Friend

Contents

Preface

In recent years the health problems associated with alcoholism and drug abuse have assumed epidemic proportions. As members of the health care team, nurses in every area of practice will inevitably be faced with questions, challenges, and problems in dealing with these patients. Therefore, nurses must have adequate information on alcoholism and drug abuse if they are to deliver the highly specialized care required in this field.

As nurses come in contact with the alcoholic and drug abuser with greater frequency, it will become apparent that this population has unique characteristics. These characteristics, whether positive or negative, have direct bearing on the nursing care that is required and delivered. In addition, the needs of the alcoholic and drug abuser can often be extremely demanding of the nurse's attention and creative efforts.

The purpose of this book, therefore, is to provide a foundation of knowledge that will lead to an understanding of these unique people and the role of the nurse in caring for them. The reader will become aware of the vital need for change in many of our present methods of delivering health care to this ever-increasing patient population. At the same time, the reader will learn about many of the new and innovative programs that have been designed to meet the special needs of the alcoholic and drug abuser.

Although *Nursing Care of the Alcoholic and Drug Abuser* has been written primarily for the student of nursing and the nurse practitioner, many professionals in associated health fields will find that the information and suggested approaches contained in the book can be applied to their specific situations.

For the nurse practitioner and student, the book will provide basic and essential information about nursing care as it applies to hospitals, psychiatric areas of practice, and community facilities.

The book is divided into three parts. Part One is concerned with alcoholism, the alcoholic, and the nursing interventions that can be used when caring for the person dependent on alcohol. Part Two concentrates on nursing care as it relates to the drug abuser and includes information on the major drugs of abuse, as well as the role of the nurse in caring for the various patient problems associated with different abused chemicals. Part Three discusses rehabilitation of the alcoholic and drug abuser. Also presented are concepts and trends for future expansion of the role of the nurse in a variety of settings. Although information is presented in three phases, it should be emphasized that there is considerable overlapping of content; i.e., many of the nursing approaches discussed in the care of the alcoholic are also applicable to the care of the person with other drug-dependency problems.

The theme of the book is carried throughout its pages: The nurse in each field of practice has a unique contribution to make to the quality and continuity of care received by the alcoholic and drug abuser. This contribution is invaluable in the total health team approach to the delivery of health care services.

The ultimate objective of the book is to engender an attitude of concern for, and a recognition of, the challenges associated with caring for the alcoholic and drug abuser. It will become clear that these challenges can lead to the creation of new areas of nursing practice as well as personal and professional satisfaction. With the realization of such satisfaction, it is hoped that creativity in devising new and innovative methods of providing meaningful professional nursing care will be introduced.

Pamela K. Burkhalter

Introduction

Throughout the pages of this book a single idea is repeated. That idea has to do with education, specifically the education of practicing nurses and student nurses, on the many diverse aspects of alcoholism and drug abuse. In a recent study completed by this writer, it was found that although many nursing school curricula contain instruction on these topics, the employed registered nurses who completed these courses did not always consider the preparation relevant to the realistic practice of nursing. The implications of this finding to educational efforts within an academic setting as well as in the employment situation are numerous. For nursing educators, it is important that the *method, quality,* and *relevancy* of instructional content be considered, not simply the *quantity* of material presented.

A limited number of nursing schools have implemented multidisciplinary curriculum components on alcoholism nursing. Where possible, similar programs need to be designed and assimilated into other schools of nursing. Nursing education at all academic and nursing service levels must not only recognize the impact of alcoholism on health stability but also seek innovative ways to ensure that students and practitioners are prepared to care for patients with alcohol abuse problems.

While initial strides are being made in the area of alcoholism nursing, evidence of corresponding efforts in the preparation of nurses to care for persons with other serious drug problems is less obvious. It is neither realistic nor practical to neglect drug abuse education while concentrating on the major drug dependence problem in the United States—alcoholism. Both deserve emphasis.

The information contained in this book is aimed at nurses in two phases of development—student and practitioner. In each phase, education plays a major role in the achievement of career goals that focus on improving the quality of health care services received by persons with alcohol and other drug abuse problems. It is hoped that this book will stimulate the interest and commitment of nurses in every field of practice to become engaged in education, research, and care of alcoholics and drug abusers.

REFERENCES

Bosma, G. A.: "Training Professionals for Meeting the Needs of Alcoholics and Problem Drinkers," *Maryland State Medical Journal,* **22**:84–87, November 1973.

Burkhalter, Pamela K.: "Alcoholism, Drug Abuse and Drug Addiction: A Study of Nursing Education." (Study accepted for publication in *The Journal of Nursing Education.*)

Burton, Genevieve: "Nursing Education on Alcoholism," *New York Academy of Sciences (Annals),* 178:48–51, March 29, 1971.

Heinemann, Edith: "Nursing School Offers Unique Alcoholism Study," *Health Science Review,* 3:6–7, University of Washington Health Sciences Center, Seattle, Winter 1974.

Nursing Care
of the Alcoholic
and Drug Abuser

Part One

Alcoholism: Nature, Treatment, and Nursing Care

The abuse of alcohol is this country's most serious and pervasive drug abuse problem. It outranks heroin in the number of people affected and has had a recent upsurge in popularity among the teenage sector of society. For the nurse, these facts point to a predictable increase in the appearance of health problems related to excessive consumption of alcohol. As a result, it is evident that nurses' contacts with the alcoholic, as well as with people whose lives have been affected in some way by alcoholism or severe problem drinking, will also be increased. In order to be able to provide meaningful and effective nursing care to these clients, the nurse must have a degree of understanding about the numerous facets of the disease known as alcoholism. With such knowledge and the understanding that it can engender, the implications for nursing practice can be clearly identified.

In studying alcoholism, it becomes evident that the literature concerned with the subject is extensive. Much of the writing has concentrated on statistics, controlled studies, and proposed methods of treatment, all of which are quite valuable. Unfortunately, the application of such material to the practice of nursing, as well as to many other health professions, has not been dealt with in any depth. Therefore, one of the goals of Part One is to present a summary of the most relevant aspects of this large body of knowledge.

There can be no argument on the importance of nurses learning how they can give quality, professional nursing care to the alcoholic in a variety of settings. However, it must be remembered that the ultimate goal for nursing and other members of the health care team is prevention—the prevention of alcoholism.

Each chapter in Part One deals with information that is directly applicable to nursing practice in many settings. The nurse has an invaluable contribution to make to the care of the alcoholic and his family. The manner in which this contribution is made can serve as a model for other health professions that are struggling with the unique problems related to the delivery of health care to the alcoholic.

Alcoholism nursing is exciting, challenging, and rewarding. As with any specialty area of nursing practice, caring for alcoholics and their families may include varying degrees of frustration and disappointment. On the whole, however, alcoholism nursing presents the nurse with an opportunity to utilize all her knowledge and skill in helping a fellow human being overcome a devastating illness.

Chapter 1

Alcohol, Culture, and Society

For centuries alcohol has been used by man for various and diverse reasons. Before recorded history, there is evidence that alcoholic beverages were used as medicine, as food, and as a required element in certain religious ceremonies. The problems surrounding excessive alcohol use have been known for an equal length of time. According to William James, "The sway of alcohol over mankind is unquestionably due to its power to stimulate the mystical faculties of human nature. . . ."[1] What is there about the substance alcohol that has allowed it to assume such a prominent place in man's life and history? The first step in answering this question will be to investigate the basic chemical characteristics of alcohol.

THE SUBSTANCE ALCOHOL

Alcohol is both a drug and a chemical compound composed of carbon, hydrogen, and oxygen. Depending on the combined quantity of each component, the

[1] William James, *The Varieties of Religious Experience,* Mentor Books, New York, 1958, p. 297.

product may be in the form of methyl alcohol, ethyl alcohol, isopropyl alcohol, or many others. Because ethyl alcohol, almost exclusively, is used in the preparation of alcoholic beverages and the influence of these beverages on the human organism is the subject of this book, the term *alcohol* will denote ethyl alcohol.

Depressant or Stimulant?

Contrary to popular belief, alcohol is not a stimulant. It is a depressant, specifically a depressant to the brain and central nervous system. It is also classified as an anesthetic and can, therefore, intensify the effects of other central nervous system depressants, e.g., hypnotics, tranquilizers, and sedatives.

Absorption and Action

Alcohol is absorbed rapidly and directly through the stomach and small intestine. It is then distributed throughout the body. The rapidity with which this absorption takes place is influenced by several factors:

1 *Concentration of alcohol.* Peak blood-alcohol levels are reached more rapidly with beverages containing high concentrations of alcohol. High concentrations also increase the rate of absorption.

2 *Presence of nonalcoholic substances.* The rapidity with which the beverage is absorbed is related to the quantity of nonalcoholic substances, in addition to alcohol, contained in the drink.

3 *Presence of food in the stomach.* The less food in the stomach, the more rapid the absorption of alcohol. Peak blood-alcohol levels can be diminished by as much as 50 percent when food is combined with alcohol intake.

4 *Drinking rate.* When alcoholic beverages are ingested very rapidly, peak blood-alcohol levels are attained quickly. Thus, if one drinks slowly, intoxicating effects are slower to appear.

5 *Stomach-emptying time.* When the time it takes to empty the stomach is decreased, absorption of alcohol will increase. Factors influencing emptying time include stress, fear, anger, nausea, anxiety, and the condition of the gastric mucosa.

6 *Body weight.* The rapidity with which a specified amount of alcohol is absorbed is directly related to the body weight. Thus, a heavily built person will not feel the intoxicating effects of alcohol as readily as a person of smaller stature.

The most effective and prevalent route of administration of alcoholic beverages is by mouth. After ingestion, the alcohol is absorbed via the digestive tract into the circulatory system.

Action of Alcohol

The action of alcohol on the central nervous system and brain brings about the major behavioral and performance changes that are observed when one becomes intoxicated, e.g., clumsy gait, loss of coordination, lessened self-confidence, euphoria, and decreased concern.

The effects of alcohol on the digestive system range from nausea, vomiting, and diarrhea to ulceration and hemorrhage of the gastric mucosa. The severity of these conditions is related to the amount of alcohol ingested, the pattern of drinking maintained, and the stability and intactness of the digestive tract.

The cardiovascular system responds to alcohol primarily by peripheral vasodilatation. Vasodilatation does not include the coronary arteries, however. Claims that the consumption of alcoholic beverages decreases anginal pain are unfounded. The seeming effectiveness of the alcohol is due to its central nervous system depressant action, which decreases the *perception* of pain.

The action of alcohol on other organ systems includes its effect on the kidneys and lungs. Alcohol acts on the pituitary gland to suppress the release of antidiuretic hormone, thus enhancing water diuresis via the kidneys. The lungs respond to alcohol with a slight increase in respiratory rate. As intoxication progresses, however, it exerts a depressant effect on respiratory reflexes. Respiratory rate decreases, and ultimately apnea can result from excessively high levels. (See Table 1-1 for a summary of the acute effects of alcohol.)

Table 1-1 Primary Response of Various Organs and Systems to Alcohol

Organ or system	Response
Brain and central nervous system	Depressant Behavioral changes Lack of control
Digestive system	Irritant Increased gastric secretions
Cardiovascular system	Peripheral vasodilator Decreases perception to pain
Kidneys	Suppressant to release of ADH Promotes water diuresis

Lungs	Alters respiratory rate;
	  Slight intoxication—slight
	    increase in respiration
	  Heavy intoxication—decrease
	    in respiration
	  Profound intoxication—
	    decreased respiration—apnea

Metabolism

Alcohol is primarily metabolized in the liver, producing water, which is excreted by the kidneys, and carbon dioxide, which is exhaled by the lungs. A small amount is excreted directly via the kidneys and exhaled by the lungs. Energy in the form of heat is produced in the process of metabolizing alcohol. This ability of alcohol to be used by the body as a food to produce a source of energy is severely abused by the person who drinks to excess. As a result, the alcoholic gradually decreases his food intake and over time relies more and more on alcohol to supply energy.

Frequency and Population

It is estimated that there are between nine and ten million alcohol-dependent persons in the United States. This condition is considered to be the fourth major health problem when ranked with heart disease, cancer, and mental illness. The population affected ranges from young adults to the aged, male and female, and to some degree all ethnic and cultural groups. Dependence on alcohol is extremely rare in the young person under the age of twenty.

Although the alcoholic is generally depicted as being male, there is a significant female population as well. At least one alcoholic in five is a woman. While males must face the community and employment outside the shelter of the home, many females can use this home shelter to mask the problem from family and friends. Also, there is often a tendency among family members to protect the wife-mother from identification as an alcoholic. Identification of the elderly alcoholic poses similar problems. This health problem may come to light only when the elderly person seeks assistance for another reason—perhaps an underlying medical condition or traumatic injury.

The most startling statistics surrounding excessive use of alcohol are the ones that indicate the number of people affected either directly or indirectly by the alcoholic's behavior. For every known alcoholic, a minimum of four other persons is affected to some degree. As previously stated, the estimated number of alcoholics ranges from nine to ten million. Multiply this figure by four and the total number of people involved in some way with alcoholism becomes astronomical. Thus, alcoholism has a profound influence on many more lives than simply that of the user.

Why Is Alcohol Used?

Beverage alcohol has often been called the great equalizer, the leveler, and the catalyst to relaxed social interaction. Its ability to lessen inhibitions and promote fellowship is well known and appreciated. Aside from this major reason for using alcohol (not necessarily to excess), additional reasons can be cited. Drinking practices are often culturally defined and regulated by tradition. In order to be accepted by a group, a person participates in the appropriate drinking tradition. Closely related to this concept of group acceptance is the use of alcoholic beverages as a status symbol: a symbol of adulthood, of a certain social class, of prosperity, and of personal success.

The adolescent often uses alcohol in order to appear sophisticated and to "outsmart the law." The adolescent who possesses the means of obtaining it achieves a degree of status within the peer group. And, in spite of the accelerating use of drugs among young people, alcohol continues to remain the cheapest and most easily accessible drug available. It is still *the* drug of abuse.

Alcoholic beverages, then, are extensively used in American society. Obviously, all those who consume such beverages are not alcoholics, nor are they all likely to become alcoholics. We must keep in mind, however, that a highly significant number of those who begin to drink socially and casually do progress over a period of time to alcoholism.

THE LAW AND THE ALCOHOLIC

Historically, the law has been unsympathetic to the alcoholic. It has viewed alcoholism as a "self-inflicted condition for which criminal sanctions ought to be imposed."[2] This attitude has come about partially as a response to the problems of chronic public drunkenness, most often associated with the lower socioeconomic groups and especially skid row inhabitants. (Of importance is the fact that less than 5 percent of the alcoholic population lives on skid row.) The public disturbances these people cause are visible and usually defined as unsightly and repugnant to society. In response to society's demand and needs, laws were passed to remove the alcoholic offender from public view.

Recently the courts have acknowledged that alcoholism is an illness. Therefore, incarcerating a person for behavior related to his illness is not only contradictory to the goals of treating illness but also can prove harmful to him. With this reasoning in mind, in 1966 several decisions concerning public intoxication were handed down. Instead of confining the offending alcoholic, referrals to medical facilities were made. As this trend became accepted, treatment facilities were inundated with requests for care and rehabilitation.

Due in part to the lack of sufficient treatment facilities, significant court decisions were subsequently handed down in which convictions for public intoxication were upheld. Thus, the dilemma of who, where, and how to handle the problem of chronic alcoholism in the form of public intoxication and drunkenness was referred back to the health professions. It is clear that this problem can be solved only by a joint, concentrated effort on the part of all health team members (nurses, physicians, social workers, psychologists, etc.) to devise

[2] Frank P. Grad et al., *Alcoholism and the Law,* Oceana Publications, Inc., Dobbs Ferry, N.Y., 1971, p. xiv.

methods of care that can meet this identified need. Because the nurse is an essential member of the health team, it becomes imperative that she seek ways to stimulate interest in this problem as well as help find solutions and appropriate methods to implement them.

CORRECT AND INCORRECT USE

The passage of the Eighteenth Amendment in 1919 was undoubtedly the outstanding effort in this century to control alcoholism. The contradiction posed by Prohibition was that it attacked alcohol rather than alcoholism by prohibiting the wholesale production and sale of beverage alcohol. Fortunately, with the repeal of the Eighteenth Amendment and the appearance of Alcoholics Anonymous in the 1930s, the attack was shifted to alcoholism.

The manner in which alcoholic beverages are used in American society is characterized by such contradictions. On the one hand, a person is expected to participate in the correct, socially defined drinking patterns in order to be a part of the group. On the other hand, he is frowned upon if he habitually overindulges. As a result, the person who establishes a pattern of overindulgence at social gatherings or in public runs the risk of group rejection. However, if the member is highly valued by the group, the group will rationalize his inappropriate behavior. It would almost seem that if the group members were to overtly identify the chronic overindulger as exhibiting the signs of an illness—alcoholism—they would be "pointing the finger" at themselves, i.e., they too could be potential alcoholics. The thought that *anyone* could become an alcoholic is highly threatening and generally avoided. Therefore, the potential or emergent alcoholic group member is sheltered and not urged to seek treatment. This inability in our society to confront alcoholism and its stereotypes ultimately leads to ostracism of the alcoholic member when the illness approaches chronic proportions.

This inconsistent behavior must be changed if true control and treatment of alcoholism is to become a reality. Society must not only "say the right words" but also internalize and assimilate the basic beliefs about this illness. Hopefully people will then hesitate less to confront the threat of alcoholism wherever it may be encountered.

D.W.I.: DRIVING WHILE INTOXICATED

The contradictions surrounding correct and incorrect use of alcohol have created a major health problem within our society: the operation of automobiles while under the influence of alcohol. The intoxicated driver includes those people who drink only periodically as well as alcoholics. Approximately 50 percent of all traffic accident deaths are attributed to or associated with alcohol. Knowledge of this fact should theoretically motivate people not to drive while intoxicated. However, it appears that a double standard exists: while driving after drinking is overwhelmingly disapproved of by society, people continue to do it, perhaps rationalizing that "it won't happen to me." The problems created by the drunk driver will not be solved until society, and specifically each person, resolves the contradiction it has apparently been willing to accept.

REFERENCES

Auerback, Alfred: "Alcoholism: Its Present Legal and Medical Status," *California Medicine,* **110**:250–252, March 1969.
Bacon, Margaret, and Mary B. Jones: *Teen-Age Drinking,* Thomas Y. Crowell Company, New York, 1968.
Carroll, Charles R: *Alcohol: Use, Nonuse and Abuse,* Wm. C. Brown Company, Dubuque, Iowa, 1970.
Chafetz, Morris E.: "A Bill of Rights of Alcoholic People," *Journal of the American Medical Association,* **219**:1471, March 13, 1972.
Chafetz, Morris E., and Harold W. Demone, Jr.: *Alcoholism and Society,* Oxford University Press, New York, 1962.
Cohen, Sidney: "Metabolism and Pharmacology," in Max Hayman (ed.), *Alcoholism Mechanism and Management,* Charles C Thomas, Springfield, Ill., 1966.
Committee on Alcoholism and Drug Dependence, "Alcohol and Society," *Journal of the American Medical Association,* **216**:1011–1013, May 10, 1971.
Fort, Joel: *Alcohol: Our Biggest Drug Problem,* McGraw-Hill Book Company, New York, 1973.
Grad, Frank P., Audrey L. Goldberg, and Barbara A. Shapiro: *Alcoholism and the Law,* Oceana Publications, Inc., Dobbs Ferry, N.Y., 1971.
Kinsey, Barry A.: *The Female Alcoholic: A Social Psychological Study,* Charles C Thomas, Springfield, Ill., 1966.
Mann, Marty: *Marty Mann Answers Your Questions About Drinking and Alcoholism,* Holt, Rinehart & Winston, New York, 1970.
National Institute of Mental Health, *Alcohol and Alcoholism,* Public Health Service Publication No. 1640, Washington, 1968.
Pittman, David J. (ed.): *Alcoholism,* Harper & Row, New York, 1967.
Rosin, Arnold J., and M. M. Glatt: "Alcohol Excess in the Elderly," *Quarterly Journal of Studies on Alcohol,* **32**:53–59, March 1971.
Ryback, Ralph S.: "The Uniform Alcoholism and Intoxification Treatment Act," *The New England Journal of Medicine,* **287**:911–912, November 2, 1972.

Chapter 2

Alcoholism: Definition, Theories of Causation, and Characteristics

The ability of the nurse to care for the alcoholic depends not only on her expertise in administering physical care but also on her depth of knowledge and understanding of the disease process. Since alcoholism is frequently an unfamiliar illness to nurses, they may tend to feel uncomfortable when interacting with the alcoholic. It is hoped that the information contained in this chapter will provide the nurse with some of the basics necessary to gain an understanding of this disease.

DEFINING ALCOHOLISM

Difficulty in defining the term *alcoholism* has plagued the behavioral and biological sciences for many years. Although the average citizen can offer a generalized definition of this word, generalizations are of little value to the professional who wishes to determine specific treatment and care modalities.

One of the most widely accepted definitions is the one proposed by Mark Keller of the Center of Alcohol Studies at Rutgers University. This definition is closely allied with that of the World Health Organization.

> Alcoholism is a chronic disease, or disorder of behavior, characterized by the repeated drinking of alcoholic beverages to an extent that exceeds customary dietary use or ordinary compliance with the social drinking customs of the community, and which interferes with the drinker's health, interpersonal relations or economic functioning.[1]

Because this statement is comprehensive enough to embrace the various aspects of alcoholism, as well as allow for behavioral and biological application, it will be the definition referred to in this book.

THEORIES OF CAUSATION

When discussing the cause(s) of alcoholism, only three statements can be made with a degree of certainty:

1 Excessive consumption of alcoholic beverages is the *immediate* cause of alcoholism.
2 There is no single motivating factor that induces a person to drink excessively.
3 In order to determine the cause(s) of alcoholism, it is necessary to consider the interdependence of psychological, physiological, and sociological variables.

Several theories of causation have been proposed to explain the mechanism of alcoholism. Each of the biologically based theories will be briefly summarized in this section. Keep in mind that no single cause of alcoholism has been identified to date.

Nutritional Theory

According to this theory, the alcoholic, because of his genetic makeup, is unable to use food. Consequently, he has nutritional deficiencies. As a means of correcting them, the body will crave alcohol. To date, this theory has not been supported by scientific research data and thus is merely one of the many hypothetical proposals under consideration.

Endocrine Theory

It has not been possible to identify a specific endocrine factor in alcoholism. The reason is that it is extremely difficult to separate endocrine causes from

---

[1] National Institute of Mental Health, *Alcohol and Alcoholism*, Public Health Service Publication No. 1640, Washington, 1968, p. 6.

the results associated with endocrine malfunction. However, it is possible that dysfunction within one or more of the endocrine gland networks could bring about a demand for alcohol that would ultimately result in alcoholism.

A second viewpoint considers the possibility that many people suffer from endocrine imbalances that predispose them to alcoholism. Many members of Alcoholics Anonymous believe this theory.

Research into the possible relationship between endocrine function and alcoholism continues to be conducted primarily through animal studies. To date the results have been inconclusive and thus should not be applied to human behavior.

Heredity Theory

The theory of genetic determination of alcoholism has been the subject of considerable research. Results have shown that the normal expectancy of alcoholism among children of one or more alcoholic parents is 20 to 30 percent. For the general population the expectancy is 2 to 3 percent.[2,3] Studies conducted to determine the frequency of alcoholism in families have produced significant results: much higher rates of alcoholism occur among relatives of alcoholics than among the general population.[4]

At this point in time, it is not possible to make conclusive statements about the heredity theory. Yet it is safe to say that genetic makeup, when combined with environmental, psychological, and physiological variables, may very well be a predisposing factor in the development of alcoholism.

Other Theories

The nutritional, endocrine, and heredity theories on the causes of alcoholism have received wide attention and have been the subject of much research. In addition to these theories, three others deserve brief mention:

1 *Allergic response.* According to this theory, the ingestion of alcohol brings about an allergic response which, in some way, creates a need for more alcohol.

2 *Innate properties of alcohol.* Some alcoholic beverages, according to this theory, possess certain properties which in themselves can induce alcoholism when ingested by susceptible people.

3 *Metabolism in the alcoholic and nonalcoholic.* This theory suggests that different metabolizing processes occur in the alcoholic than in the nonalcoholic. For this reason, the alcoholic is more susceptible to the action of alcoholic beverages.

[2] Leonard E. Reaves. "Concepts in the Etiology of Alcoholism," *Journal of Chronic Diseases,* 17:(6)553, 1964.
[3] David J. Pittman (ed.), *Alcoholism,* Harper & Row, New York, 1967, p. 34.
[4] Donald W. Goodwin, "Is Alcoholism Hereditary?" *Archives of General Psychiatry,* 25:545, Dec. 1971.

In the following section, a discussion of the various aspects of the psychological theory of causation will be presented.

ALCOHOLIC PERSONALITY: MYTH OR FACT?

It has been hypothesized that the major cause of alcoholism is a defect in the personality structure of the person. Closely associated with this hypothesis is the concept of the alcoholic personality. The question of vital interest is, Is there an alcoholic personality? The answer, most simply stated, is No. There is no single personality structure that can be described as *the* alcoholic personality. What *has* been identified is a variety of personality patterns or types that can be associated with the alcoholic.

The major difficulty encountered in studying these personality types lies in the old dilemma of which comes first, the personality or the disease. Is the prealcoholic person predisposed to alcoholism due to some innate personality defect, or are personality defects brought about by alcoholism? It is this cause-and-effect question that has prevented the identification of specific personality structures which would allow for early diagnosis and treatment of the prealcoholic.

Although it has not been possible to identify a specific personality type that personifies the alcoholic, it has been possible to identify and describe major personality characteristics. The most significant of these are described below.

Dependency-Independency

A predominant personality characteristic of the alcoholic is a conflict between the need to be independent and the need to be dependent. Of the two needs, dependency is usually most apparent. The alcoholic is unable to confront this conflict. Instead, he either represses independent needs or represses dependent needs—always avoiding the conflict.

For the alcoholic, the conflict arising from the desire to assert independence serves only to increase the need for relief, and alcoholism does provide a degree of relief. However, even though alcohol affords temporary relief, the underlying conflict remains unresolved. As the struggle to maintain dominance while needing to be subservient becomes patterned, the alcoholic's dependency needs increase. He becomes excessively dependent on alcohol, both psychologically and physically.

Anger and Frustration

Anger and frustration are often the result of strong dependency needs. The anger becomes a "fury at the frustration of dependent needs. . . ."[5] Anger also

---

[5] Howard T. Blane, *The Personality of the Alcoholic*, Harper & Row, New York, 1968, p. 39.

arises from the inability to express feelings of worthlessness, failure, and inadequacy. Alcohol allows the expression of rage and offers an excuse for it, i.e., "It wasn't my fault. I was drunk!"

Also characteristic of many alcoholic personalities is a low frustration tolerance. The frustration caused by the inability to cope with daily stress and strain is often the stimulus that leads to continued or resumed drinking.

Feelings of Omnipotence

The desire to feel powerful and in control of his own destiny is expressed through the alcoholic's search for omnipotence. Excessive drinking, and the feelings of power that it can provide, helps to momentarily erase feelings of frustration, guilt, and self-denigration. This basic need to feel important, valued, and respected is in conflict with the alcoholic's behavior. Realization of this inconsistency usually comes the "morning after" when sober thoughts begin to filter through the alcoholic haze. Then feelings of failure and self-reproach come to the fore again and can act as the motivation to once more seek that transitory experience of control afforded by drink.

Depression

The depression that is present in the personality of the alcoholic is self-reinforcing, i.e., it fosters the need for relief and alcohol brings the relief, but the behavior associated with alcoholism creates further depression. The cyclical nature of this depression, then, can be viewed as either:

1   The initial stimulus to drink. In order to self-medicate interolable depression, the alcoholic prescribes increasingly high doses of alcohol. Unfortunately, the self-designed treatment is ineffective, for it serves only to heighten feelings of depression.

2   A result of excessive drinking. As the alcoholic becomes superficially aware that his behavior and relationships with others are changing, and usually for the worse, depressive feelings will intensify. It is this type of depression that promotes denial of the emerging or maturing problem.

3   A reason to continue drinking. In an effort to decrease and mask depression, the alcoholic will seek to drown his awareness of it in alcohol. It is unlikely that these efforts ever succeed. Instead, his depression increases the more he attempts to camouflage it.

Defense Mechanisms

One way of viewing alcoholism is as an expression of the inadequacy of innate coping mechanisms in the face of continued stress. Of the many defense mechanisms that man uses to cope with living, three deserve emphasis when discussing the alcoholic: denial, rationalization, and projection.

Denial, and the rationalization and projection associated with it, is one of the outstanding defense mechanisms of the alcoholic. He will deny that he has any difficulty in controlling the intake of alcohol long after those around him have identified the problem. In many cases, he will exercise absolute denial by claiming that he doesn't drink at all. When he begins to suspect that his behavior is changing, he will often invent reasons for the behavior and try to convince himself that everything is all right. At the same time, he may project blame for his actions on those closest to him. He may blame his wife, employer, or friends, who, in his mind, have driven him to drink.

Thus, the use of defense mechanisms is an important aspect of the personality makeup of the alcoholic. The use of denial, rationalization, and projection allows him not only to continue his behavior but also to justify it.

The concept of the alcoholic personality is of little value to the helping professions as long as it is conceived of as a single entity. Of specific value and relevance, however, to the identification and treatment of those in the pre-alcoholic category is the concept of alcoholic personality characteristics. Several of the most significant of these characteristics have been studied, but continued research into this complex facet of alcoholism is a necessity. Whether through structured research, personal observation, or concentrated study and interaction with the alcoholic, the professional nurse can make a significant contribution to the understanding of the alcoholic's personality characteristics.

CHARACTERISTICS OF ALCOHOLISM

Alcoholism doesn't come about overnight. It takes time, usually many years, before a person reaches that stage. Alcoholism is progressive. It begins with mild drinking and eventually progresses to chronic, excessive drinking, which is indicative of an illness. This progression can be broken down into three stages:

Stage One

In the beginning, the person drinks as a release. He seeks relief or escape from psychologically or physiologically induced stress. Once the person discovers that tension and stress can be decreased or obliterated by high alcohol intake, a pattern becomes established in which:

STRESS - - - - - →   Alcohol Intake - - - - - →   RELIEF

Stage Two

When this behavior is repeated in the face of renewed stress, the person begins to *depend* on alcohol to relieve unpleasant sensations, i.e., psychological dependence develops. As dependency progresses, it becomes intolerable for the person to attempt stressful activities without the drug. Eventually, he will be unable to meet stress without alcohol. Thus:

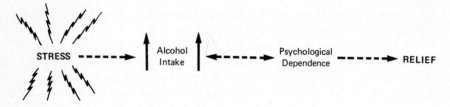

At this point, the person cannot be characterized as a true alcoholic.

Stage Three

If this self-reinforcing pattern continues, the cells of the body begin to adjust to the presence of the drug and more of it is required to create the desired effect. This phenomenon is known as tissue tolerance and is induced by physiological dependence on alcohol.

It is during this third stage that several other significant characteristics become evident. These traits may or may not be apparent in the first two stages. When they do appear, however, it indicates that the person has developed the illness of alcoholism.

Loss of Control Loss of control over the ingestion of alcoholic beverages is perhaps the hallmark of alcoholism. When the person can no longer take a few drinks and stop but must continue to drink until he is satiated or unconscious, he has lost control of his drinking behavior. Over time, this loss of control becomes a patterned behavior.

Craving Craving can be described as an overwhelming and undeniable desire to consume alcohol. It is caused by both psychological dependence and the subsequent compulsion to drink, and the physical dependence associated with tissue tolerance.

Amnesias During a drinking bout, or immediately preceding or following one, the alcoholic is vulnerable to amnesia in the form of blackouts. He is able to perform tasks, converse with others, and generally appear to be aware of his actions. However, the following day he is unable to remember the events that occurred during the blackout. These memory losses are associated with short-term memory retrieval so that events occurring during the immediate past are hazy or forgotten, but long-term memory remains intact. Frequently, memory of the blackout events returns over time.

These blackouts are usually frightening and can form the impetus for seeking help. Seeking help does not indicate, however, that the person is ready to re-nounce his dependence on alcohol.

Withdrawal Syndrome When alcohol intake is either decreased or stopped, physical and psychological withdrawal symptoms appear. The cells of the body, which are accustomed to high alcohol levels, are no longer under the depressant action of alcohol. The resultant rapid increase in cellular activities brings about the withdrawal symptoms. These symptoms may be mild, such as tremulousness and nervousness, or may develop into delirium tremens, a serious physiological condition. Chapter 3 deals with the withdrawal syndrome in greater depth.

These three progressive stages express the sequence in which the major char-acteristics of alcoholism develop. During stages one and two, it is still possible for the drinker to prevent the development of alcoholism. When loss of control becomes apparent, however, choice ceases to be a reality, no matter how much the person insists he can "take it or leave it."

It is during the third stage that the alcoholic develops a vicious cycle in which stress stimulates increased drinking and psychological dependence which in turn brings about physical tolerance, dependence, and craving. Increased al-cohol intake gives a kind of relief, but relief tempered with the knowledge that his behavior is out of control. A self-generated and self-reinforced vicious cycle then becomes established.

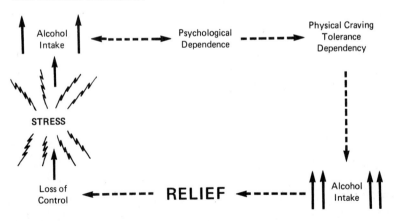

PHYSIOLOGICAL CONSEQUENCES OF ALCOHOLISM

The responses of the body to long-term, excessive intake of alcohol cause sig-nificant and sometimes fatal damage to various organ systems. These responses come from the properties of alcohol as well as the behavior changes caused by alcoholism.

Brain and Nervous System

Alcoholism-related damage to the brain and nervous system has both acute and chronic manifestations. In most cases, acute neurological impairment and associated behavior changes will subside with abstinence and appropriate therapy. For example, the withdrawal syndrome (discussed in Chapter 3) can be successfully treated, and with proper convalescent therapy, full nervous system function will be restored.

Peripheral polyneuritis, a condition in which deficiency of vitamin B_1 brings about defects in nerve conduction, is a common occurrence in the alcoholic. It is a bilateral, symmetrical, and progressive neuritis beginning in the lower extremities and eventually involving the upper extremities. The alcoholic may present with tingling, numb, or prickly sensations distal to the knees. Often complaints of calf muscle and foot pains are described. Changes in gait patterns can be attributed to this peripheral nerve damage.

Besides peripheral polyneuritis, the alcoholic is also quite susceptible to *temporary nerve palsies.* These are usually in the form of radial, ulnar, or common peroneal nerve palsy and are induced by prolonged pressure over the nerve site. Thus, the efficacy of using restraints with alcoholics, a commonly accepted treatment, is dubious.

The physical and psychological manifestations of chronic impairment of brain and nervous system functioning are not likely to respond to treatment efforts. Prominent among chronic permanent manifestations are two types of chronic brain syndrome: *Korsakoff's syndrome* and *Wernicke's syndrome.* These are organically induced examples of brain damage characterized by significant cerebral deterioration and actual brain cell death.

Differentiation between Korsakoff's syndrome (or psychosis) and Wernicke's syndrome is difficult due to the similarity of causative agents. Both are brought about by varying degrees of thiamine and niacin vitamin deficiencies, which cause neuronal degeneration and thus produce the outward signs of the conditions.

When the degenerative processes are largely confined to the cerebrum and peripheral nerves, Korsakoff's syndrome results. Deterioration in the brain stem causes Wernicke's syndrome. Signs and symptoms associated with these syndromes are similar; however specific differences are identifiable:

Korsakoff's syndrome/psychosis—progressive memory loss, disorientation as to time, defective confabulation. Outward appearance is often cheerful, without immediate identification of the damaging results.

Wernicke's syndrome—delirium, emotional lability, moodiness, apathetic behavior, weakness, easy fatigue. Often combined with peripheral polyneuritis. Ocular disturbances are prominent. After vitamin replacement therapy is complete, residual visual impairment may remain.

Myopathy

Alcoholic myopathy can be associated with peripheral neuritis. It is also possible that some existing alcoholic myopathies are unrelated to neural involvement. The clinical portraits are similar for both.

The symptoms of *acute alcoholic myopathy* include cramping and sharp pains in skeletal musculature as well as edema of the lower extremities. Weakness and tenderness of the affected muscles are common. Attacks of alcoholic myopathy usually follow acute drinking bouts. Serum enzymes, specifically the muscle enzymes of CPK, SGOT, and LDH, may become elevated within two or three days of the appearance of symptoms.

The development and progress of *chronic alcoholic myopathy* are often unheralded by prominent external manifestations. Over time, atrophy and wasting of extremity musculature evolves. Weakness of these muscle groups is prevalent. Pain is usually minimal. Occasionally muscle necrosis takes place.

Alcoholic Cardiomyopathy

Due to the interaction and interdependence of body systems, it is extremely difficult to attribute all cardiac changes in the alcoholic to alcohol. Nutritional, metabolic, and concurrent disease states may also contribute to the cardiac damage. Thus, damage to cardiac tissue may result not only from the direct action of prolonged alcohol intake on cardiac cellular activity but also from other systemic sources.

Alcoholic cardiomyopathy is a serious consequence of chronic alcoholism. Vital areas of impairment and damage include:

1 Enlarged heart. An enlarged heart is usually present on x-ray.[7] As long as the alcoholic continues with normal, steady activity levels, the enlarged heart in itself does not compromise circulation. When additional demands are placed on the heart, however, output cannot be maintained. In the late stages of this condition, as the enlarged heart is unable to meet the body's demands, sequelae such as congestive heart failure develop with distended neck veins, increased diastolic blood pressure, and peripheral edema.

2 EKG changes. Significant changes in the electrical conduction system, as measured by the electrocardiogram, include "abnormal P waves, slurred, notched and low-voltage QRS complexes, prolonged Q-T intervals,"[8] and numerous

[6] "'Alcoholic' Myopathy," *The New England Journal of Medicine,* 274:1326, June 9, 1966.

[7] Albert B. Lowenfels, *The Alcoholic Patient in Surgery,* The Williams & Wilkins Co., Baltimore, 1971, p. 120.

[8] George E. Burch and Thomas D. Giles, "Alcoholic Cardiomyopathy," *The American Journal of Medicine,* 50:142, February 1971.

deviations in T-wave pattern. Tachycardia is common. As the myopathy progresses, it is not unusual to find periodic episodes of atrial fibrillation in
addition to the congestive heart failure.

3 Signs and symptoms. Initial complaints may include paroxysmal noc-
turnal dyspnea, weakness, mild, transient chest discomfort, and shortness of
breath. Anginal pain is not usual but can occur with more extensive damage.

Hepatic Disorders

Cirrhosis of the liver is the most conspicuous form of damage to the liver. It
is caused by both the nutritional deficiencies associated with alcoholism and
the direct action of alcohol on liver cells. Not all alcoholics develop cirrhosis,
but most do develop some degree of liver impairment. The most common form
of this impairment is *alcoholic hepatitis,* an inflammation of the liver which is
a precursor to the eventual development of cirrhosis. Progression from mild liver
damage to liver failure can be prevented with early detection and abstinence.
If this regimen is not adhered to, the development of liver failure with ascites,
bleeding tendencies, jaundice, etc., becomes inevitable. Since adequate liver
function is necessary for life, continued heavy drinking when liver damage is
evident will eventually prove fatal.

Pancreatic Disorders

Acute pancreatitis in the form of alcoholic pancreatitis is a frequent consequence
of alcoholism. It is believed that alcohol may act directly on the pancreas,
bringing about the acute inflammatory response, or may induce spasm at the
sphincter of Oddi, thus increasing pressure in the pancreatic duct. Acute pancreatitis is subject to medical and surgical intervention. If acute episodes are
repeated, however, "progressive glandular destruction and insufficiency"[9] will
result in *chronic pancreatitis.* Success in the treatment of chronic pancreatitis
is elusive because drinking is frequently resumed after immediate treatment
efforts are completed.

Hematologic Abnormalities

The hematologic abnormalities associated with alcoholism are numerous. They
are attributed to dietary deficiencies or the direct action of alcohol on blood
cell formation sites.

Iron-deficiency anemia is a frequent finding in the chronic alcoholic. It is
partially due to folic acid depletion and liver damage. The underlying causative
factor is *bone marrow depression.* Alterations in bone marrow function can
begin very early in the alcoholic's drinking career, especially when accompanied
by insufficient nutritional intake.

Thrombocytopenia is also a relatively common occurrence. This marked

---

[9] Lowenfels, op. cit., p. 198.

drop in the platelet count can be directly ascribed to bone marrow depression. Discontinuance of alcohol intake and proper diet therapy will usually normalize platelet counts.

Pulmonary Disorders

Certain behavior patterns, not the direct effect of alcohol on lung tissue and respiratory passages, are responsible for the severe involvement of the respiratory system in chronic alcoholism. For example, excessive use of cigarettes is a prevalent partner to alcoholism. It is not surprising, therefore, that the incidence of chronic obstructive lung diseases is significantly increased in the alcoholic.

Other aspects of chronic alcoholism make it clear why respiratory involvement occurs: diminished cough reflex brought about by central nervous system depression leads to pooling of secretions; the ascites of liver damage *decreases vital capacity;* and prior injury to the rib cage can further decrease chest expansion.[10] All these factors contribute to the increase in susceptibility to *infection* and trauma to the respiratory system.

In addition, the incidence of *tuberculosis* among alcoholics is considerably higher than in the nonalcoholic population. The increased frequency is due in part to: (1) the detrimental lifestyle engendered by chronic alcoholism (lack of personal hygiene, malnutrition, lack of preventive health care, poor living conditions) and (2) the alcoholic's decreased ability to combat infection.

Reproductive System

Recent studies have identified significant harmful effects of alcoholism on the reproductive system of both males and females.[11,12] The male alcoholic is subject to *impotence* of a temporary or permanent nature following excessive chronic alcoholic behavior. With abstinence, normal sexual function can return in many cases. At present, the specific relationship between alcoholism and male impotence has not been isolated. However, suspected causative factors include neurological dysfunction, psychological inhibition, and hormonal malfunction.

Chronic alcoholism in the pregnant woman may have adverse effects on the fetus that result in various types of *malformation.* Such infants may be born with craniofacial, extremity, or cardiovascular defects that are associated with prenatal growth deficiencies and delayed development. The incidence of mal-

[10] Ibid, p. 110.
[11] Frederick Lemere and James W. Smith, "Alcohol-Induced Sexual Impotence," *American Journal of Psychiatry,* 130:212–213, February 1973.
[12] Kenneth L. Jones et al., "Pattern of Malformation in Offspring of Chronic Alcoholic Mothers," *The Lancet,* 1:1267–1271, June 9, 1973.

formed babies delivered of alcoholic mothers is slight because chronic alcoholism is generally less frequent in the woman of childbearing age.

The body's response to chronic alcoholic behavior takes the form of damage to various organ systems. (See Table 2-2 for a summary of the acute and long-term effects of alcoholism.) Many of these resultant conditions could be avoided if the alcoholic received treatment. Therefore, foremost in the minds of nurses and all health workers should be the question, How can I see that the prealcoholic, acute alcoholic, and chronic alcoholic receive vigorous treatment and professional care?

Table 2-2 Effects of Alcoholism on Various Organ Systems

Site	Result

Brain	Acute: Blackouts or amnesias
	Chronic: Chronic brain syndromes—
	    Korsakoff's syndrome/psychosis
	    and Wernicke's syndrome
	Personality changes

Nervous system	Acute: Peripheral polyneuropathy
	    Temporary nerve palsies
	Chronic: Peripheral polyneuropathy with
	    muscle wasting

Musculature	Acute: Alcoholic myopathy Chronic: Chronic myopathy—severe muscle wasting
Heart	Alcoholic cardiomyopathy
Liver	Alcoholic hepatitis Cirrhosis Liver failure

Pancreas	Acute: Pancreatitis—permanent damage
	    unlikely with treatment
	Chronic: Pancreatitis—permanent, progressive
	    damage

Hematologic system	Iron-deficiency anemia Bone marrow depression Thrombocytopenia
Lungs	Decreased vital capacity Respiratory infections Tuberculosis
Reproductive system	Male: Temporary or permanent impotence Female: Potential birth defects

REFERENCES

"Alcohol and the Liver," *The Lancet,* **2**:670–671, September 21, 1968.

"Alcohol-Related Illnesses—Part II," *Maryland State Medical Journal,* **21**:33–36, September 1972.

Alexander, Carl S.: "The Concept of Alcoholic Myocardiopathy," *Medical Clinics of North America,* **52**:1183–1191, September 1968.

Armstrong, John D.: "Alcoholism as a Disease," *Canadian Nurse,* **61**:614–617, August 1965.

Asokan, Sankaran K., Martin J. Frank, and A. Calhoun Witham: "Cardiomyopathy Without Cardiomegaly in Alcoholics," *American Heart Journal,* **84**: 13–18, July 1972.

Bennett, A. E.: "Treatment of Brain Damage in Alcoholism," *Current Psychiatric Therapies,* **1967**:142–146.

Blane, Howard T.: *The Personality of the Alcoholic,* Harper & Row, New York, 1968.

Block, Marvin: *Alcohol and Alcoholism: Drinking and Dependence,* Wadsworth Publishing Company, Inc., Belmont, Calif., 1970.

Carroll, Charles R.: *Alcohol: Use, Nonuse and Abuse,* Wm. C. Brown Company, Dubuque, Iowa, 1970.

Chambers, Francis T.: *The Drinker's Addiction,* Charles C Thomas, Springfield, Ill., 1968.

Cowan, Dale H., and John D. Hines: "Thrombocytopenia of Severe Alcoholism," *Annals of Internal Medicine,* **74**:37–43, January 1971.

Curlee, Joan: "Depression and Alcoholism," *Bulletin of the Menninger Clinic,* Topeka, Kansas, **36**:451–455, July 1972.

Hayman, Max (ed.): *Alcoholism: Mechanism and Management,* Charles C Thomas, Springfield, Ill., 1966.

Helman, Richard A.: "Alcoholic Hepatitis," *Annals of Internal Medicine,* **74**: 311–321, March 1971.

Jones, Kenneth L. et al.: "Pattern of Malformation in Offspring of Chronic Alcoholic Mothers," *The Lancet,* **1**:1267–1271, June 9, 1973.

Kissin, Benjamin, and Henri Begleiter (eds.): *The Biology of Alcoholism Volume 2: Physiology and Behavior,* Plenum Press, New York, 1972.

Lemere, Frederick, and James W. Smith: "Alcohol-Induced Sexual Impotence," *American Journal of Psychiatry,* **130**:212–213, February 1973.

Lieber, Charles S.: "Liver Adaptation and Injury in Alcoholism," *The New England Journal of Medicine,* **288**:356–362, February 15, 1973.

Lisansky, Edith S.: "The Etiology of Alcoholism: The Role of Psychological Predisposition," *Quarterly Journal of Studies on Alcohol,* **21**:314–343, June 1960.

Loehlin, John C.: "An Analysis of Alcohol-Related Questionnaire Items from the National Merit Twin Study," *Annals of the New York Academy of Sciences,* **197**:117–120, May 25, 1972.

McClelland, David C. et al.: *The Drinking Man,* The Free Press, New York, 1972.

Myerson, Ralph M., and Joel S. Lofair: "Alcoholic Muscle Disease," *Medical Clinics of North America,* **54**:723–730, May 1970.

National Institute of Mental Health, *Alcohol and Alcoholism,* Public Health Service Publication No. 1640, Washington, 1968.

Partington, John T., and F. Gordon Johnson: "Personality Types Among Alcoholics," *Quarterly Journal of Studies on Alcohol,* **30**:21–34, March 1969.

Pittman, David J. (ed.): *Alcoholism,* Harper & Row, New York, 1967.

Pittman, David J., and Charles R. Snyder: *Society, Culture, and Drinking Practices,* John Wiley & Sons, Inc., New York, 1962.

Reinert, R. E.: "The Concept of Alcoholism as a Bad Habit," *Bulletin of the Menninger Clinic,* Topeka, Kan., **32**:35–46, January 1968.

Reinert, R. E.: "The Concept of Alcoholism as a Disease," *Bulletin of the Menninger Clinic,* Topeka, Kan., **32**:21–25, January 1968.

Roach, Mary K. et al.: *Biological Aspects of Alcohol,* The University of Texas Press, Austin, 1971.

Wood, Howard P., and Edward L. Duffy: "Psychological Factors in Alcoholic Women," *American Journal of Psychiatry,* **123**:341–345, September 1966.

Chapter 3

Treatment:
What and Where Is It?

As the nurse cares for the alcoholic patient, she soon discovers that it is not realistic to think of treatment in the traditional manner, i.e., diagnosis, treatment, and cure. Each of these terms takes on a different and challenging connotation when the patient is an alcoholic. It is this difference in meaning and its implications for nursing practice that the nurse must assimilate into the care and management of the alcoholic patient. At the same time, the nurse must acquire an understanding and working knowledge of the diverse methods currently being used to treat alcoholism. For this reason, this chapter will describe treatment for alcoholism under a variety of circumstances.

DEFINING TREATMENT

The treatment of alcoholism can best be described as a process, a very long and demanding process. It begins under a variety of circumstances, but generally consists of the following components, not necessarily in this order.

Self-recognition of Alcoholism by the Alcoholic Most alcoholics readily agree that only when the person admits to alcoholism and the absolute necessity for treatment can treatment be a reality. For some persons, being able to admit that a serious drinking problem exists is a major breakthrough. In these cases, although the person has not admitted to alcoholism per se, he still can benefit from treatment.

Seeking Help The manner in which the alcoholic seeks treatment and help varies. He may go to his private physician or arrive at the emergency room of a local hospital. Regardless of the means, he has taken the second step in the treatment process.

It is often possible for the physician, nurse, or other health professional to assist the alcoholic in making these first two steps by offering support, guidance, and acceptance.

Undergoing Withdrawal Each alcoholic, to some extent, must undergo withdrawal from alcohol sometime during treatment. (This aspect of treatment will be discussed later in the chapter.)

It is not always possible for the sequence of these first three components of the treatment process to be maintained. Often the person undergoes withdrawal before he is able to recognize his alcoholism, desire to free himself of dependence, or initiate efforts to seek help. It is important to remember, however, that at some point in the treatment process, all these components must be taken into consideration.

Cure It is not appropriate to use the term *cure* to describe the goal of treatment for alcoholism. More meaningful terms are *improvement, arrest,* or *abstinence.* In reality, the alcoholic cannot drink alcoholic beverages after having achieved abstinence. To do so invites a return to alcoholic behavior. Convincing him of the necessity to maintain abstinence is the core of treatment efforts.

Rehabilitation By the time the alcoholic has sought treatment, his entire lifestyle has been disrupted. His employment and marriage may be greatly altered from what they were before he acknowledged his condition. Thus, in addition to the personal readjustment that he must make, he also must learn to adjust to the pressures and stresses of daily living and decision making.

It is not always possible, nor very likely, that the alcoholic will receive therapy for alcoholism alone. Therefore, besides the basic treatment process, it is also necessary to take into account the treatment for complications of alcoholism.

CATEGORIES OF TREATMENT

The manner in which the alcoholic becomes subject to treatment can be broken down into four categories:

1 Voluntarily seeking treatment specifically for alcoholism
2 Receiving treatment primarily for acute disease or injury
3 Receiving treatment for withdrawal on an involuntary basis
4 Seeking treatment for a chronic condition associated with alcoholism

For some, treatment of alcoholism is not the primary goal but becomes important during the course of therapy for a different condition.

There is a fifth category that focuses on those alcoholics who are repeating treatment—the recidivists or relapsers. Unfortunately, the rate of recidivism or relapse is high and becomes a source of discouragement and frustration to the nurse. As a result, these patients present a major challenge to professional care, treatment, and most of all, patience.

WHERE DOES TREATMENT TAKE PLACE?

Treatment for alcoholism and alcoholism-related conditions usually takes place in one or more of three locations: the general hospital, the psychiatric facility, or the community agency. Where the alcoholic can best be helped is determined by his progress during treatment. When the patient requires acute intervention, the general hospital is most appropriate; when group therapy and personal readjustment to sobriety are required, the psychiatric facility is most appropriate; and when the alcoholic needs transitional support and care during the reentry phase of the treatment process, the community's resources are most appropriate.

Of necessity, this delineation is not restrictive. There is frequently crossover among the three areas with some areas possessing components of another. Brief descriptions of the services available in each setting follow.

General Hospital

The general hospital setting is equipped to provide acute and emergency care for conditions such as withdrawal, trauma, acute illness or infection, and routine medical and surgical intervention. Also, many large general hospitals have acute psychiatric units which may or may not be used, in part, by the alcoholic patient. The ability of the general hospital to offer a wide variety of services is especially relevant to the alcoholic patient population, which may comprise up to 50 percent of the inpatient census.

One of the newer innovations is the detoxification unit. These specialty units are often located in the general hospital. They provide care and services for the acute or toxic episodes associated with withdrawal or detoxification. Some general hospitals also include rehabilitation services within the framework of existing facilities.

Psychiatric Facilities

Many state-supported psychiatric institutions offer acute and chronic care services for alcoholics. Often the state psychiatric facility will be the main center for the custodial care of the alcoholic with organic brain damage. Some of these institutions have expanded their focus to include extensive rehabilitation and intense psychotherapy. For those alcoholics who have an underlying psychiatric illness (approximately 15 percent of the alcoholic population[1]), the psychiatric facility can offer a variety of necessary treatment resources.

Alcoholics who have the requisite financial resources or insurance coverage can utilize private psychiatric facilities. These hospitals or clinics are usually equipped to care for the person from acute withdrawal through intensive psychotherapy.

Each of these settings utilizes a form of psychological or psychiatric intervention to assist the alcoholic in (1) overcoming the desire to drink and (2) learning to confront the problems that led to alcoholic behavior. Depending on the philosophy of the facility, the alcoholic may engage in intensive group therapy or psychiatric therapy on a one-to-one basis with a psychiatrist.

Community Resources

The community offers a wide variety of agencies for the treatment of alcoholism. Resources range from treatment originating in the physician's office to lay organizations such as Alcoholics Anonymous.

Many general hospitals sponsor clinics, some of which specialize in outpatient or day care treatment. These clinics may be the site of medication dispensation or serve as the location for group therapy sessions. In addition, alcoholics often will seek clinic services for any one of numerous alcoholism-related physical complaints.

The Salvation Army has long served as a source of humane and sincere care for the alcoholic, often regardless of whether the person wants help. The offering of food, shelter, and a caring attitude has helped many of the skid row alcoholic population to survive and, in some cases, has served as the stimulus to seek specific treatment. The Salvation Army also provides rehabilitation services through occupational retraining and employment for many recovered

[1] Harvey D. Strassman, "Treatment of the Chronic Alcoholic," GP, 38:89, August 1968.

alcoholics. Such work programs can serve as the catalyst for spiritual and psychological rehabilitation.

Alcoholics Anonymous (AA) has been widely accepted by the helping professions as a very successful approach to the treatment of alcoholism. Its services are utilized by hospitals, clinics, and individual alcoholics. The AA path concentrates on stimulating the development of spiritual awareness and growth within the alcoholic. Goals are based on day-to-day achievement of sobriety. For many alcoholics who have been unable to achieve abstinence in numerous other treatment programs, AA offers a purposeful and meaningful way of life.

In recent years, residential treatment programs and halfway houses have been established in the community for long-term treatment. These facilities are sponsored by public or private agencies. Patients live at the residential centers and participate in diverse therapy groups as well as individual therapy sessions. For many individuals, residing in the halfway house environment provides security and stability during the transitional phase from alcoholism to alcohol-free life.

Although it is not frequently encountered and perhaps is not generally known, a certain number of alcoholics are treated in their homes. When the course of treatment is not expected to be complicated and there are family members who are capable of supporting the alcoholic, treatment in the home can be most appropriate.

Industrial programs have assumed a major role in providing treatment and rehabilitation services to alcoholic employees. Success rates are exceptionally high. (Refer to Part Three, Chapter 1, for more specific, detailed information on industrial rehabilitation programs.)

A portion of the alcoholic population receives treatment while in jail. Treatment can consist of acute detoxification, treatment of complications of alcoholism, and limited rehabilitation.

There are undoubtedly many other treatment sites in addition to those discussed. In one sense, the fact that there is a multitude of available resources is beneficial. It is important to remember, however, that numerous resources create confusion when efforts are not coordinated. For this reason nurses and other health professionals must make themselves aware of the available resources, how contact can be made, and how continuity of care can be maintained at an optimal level.

TREATMENT OF THE WITHDRAWAL SYNDROME

Of vital importance to the alcoholic, as well as to those who care for and treat him, is the aspect of withdrawal. Fear of the withdrawal process often prevents the patient from seeking treatment. At the same time, the feelings and stereotypes adhered to by many in the helping professions, specifically delirium tremens, frequently create negative and at times hostile attitudes toward the alcoholic. For this reason, the nurse must have a basic understanding of the withdrawal syndrome and the accepted methods for treating it. With such an understanding, more positive attitudes and feelings can be generated and reflected in the care the nurse provides.

Goal of Withdrawal

The goal of withdrawal is to end the physical need for alcohol. This must be accomplished before further progress can be made. The withdrawal syndrome is optimally treated in hospital settings where there are facilities for inpatient acute care.

Phases of Withdrawal

Basically withdrawal consists of three phases, usually occurring in sequence and each reflecting the progression in severity from mild to severe symptoms. The phases overlap and are not mutually exclusive.

Tremulousness, or the Shakes The onset for the first phase ranges from three to thirty-six hours after the last drink and is the mildest form of withdrawal. It is characterized by markedly increased psychomotor hyperactivity with tremors, anorexia, insomnia, tachycardia, agitation, hypertension, and acute anxiety. Nausea and vomiting may be present.

Acute Halucinosis Although psychomotor agitation continues, auditory or visual hallucinations assume prominence. Often the hallucinations are of a threatening nature. Appearance of hallucinatory behavior indicates that delirium tremens is impending.

Delirium Tremens The onset is generally twenty-four to seventy-two hours following the last drink. The mortality rate is extremely high—5 to 30 percent.[2] Thus, delirium tremens is the most serious of the withdrawal phases. Disorientation, hallucinations, delusions, and delirium are prominent. Severe agitation continues, accompanied by fever, profuse perspiration, tachycardia, and tachypnea. Seizure activity of the petit mal or grand mal type may begin.

In general, the withdrawal syndrome is of shorter duration and greater severity in the younger alcoholic. The withdrawal process lasts for approximately three to five days.

[2] Richard H. Anderson and Maxwell N. Weisman, *The Alcoholic in the Emergency Room,* The National Council on Alcoholism, Inc., New York, June 1972, p. 3.

Complications of Withdrawal

The most severe complications of the withdrawal syndrome are associated with delirium tremens. The patient who progresses to this phase undergoes tremendous strain on all body reserves and resources. Frequent complications include aspiration pneumonia, peripheral vascular collapse, hyperthermia and infection, myocardial infraction, or self-inflicted traumatic injuries.

Alcoholic Hallucinosis

In addition to the three phases of withdrawal, another condition exists which is often confused with acute hallucinosis. The hallucinations associated with alcoholic hallucinosis are not as severe as the hallucinations of acute withdrawal. Signs of psychomotor hyperactivity are less apparent, and when delusions occur, they are usually associated with the auditory or visual hallucinations characteristic of this experience.

Treatment Regimen for Withdrawal

Treatment of withdrawal comprises drug therapy, correction of fluid and electrolyte imbalances, and supportive and diagnostic measures.

Drug Therapy The goal of drug therapy is to temporarily duplicate the depressant action of alcohol on the central nervous system and thus prevent the occurrence of delirium tremens. When this is not feasible and the patient has progressed to delirium tremens, the goal becomes control of the symptoms and prevention of complications. Following this, use of drugs is decreased and modified as the patient is prepared for ultimate discharge. It is essential to remember that the alcoholic is highly susceptible to dependence on drugs and can easily become dependent if certain drugs are used for prolonged periods of time, for example, barbiturates and sedatives.

A variety of drugs and combinations of drugs are employed in treating withdrawal. Table 3-1 briefly summarizes those drugs commonly used with the realization that individual physician preference is the determining factor in final selection. There is some controversy surrounding the use of certain drugs for withdrawal therapy, e.g., phenothiazines, hypnotics, or barbiturates. Therefore, the summary in Table 3-1 is not meant as an endorsement but rather a listing of some of the drugs currently being used.

Dosages are determined by the severity of the symptoms, the general condition of the patient, the presence or absence of alcohol in the blood, the age of the patient, his reaction to medication, and the addicting qualities of the proposed medications. (For an in-depth discussion of specific drugs, side effects, and contraindications, it is recommended that a text on pharmacology be consulted.)

Table 3-1 Frequently Prescribed Drugs for the Treatment of Withdrawal

Name of drug	Dosage	Route	Frequency	Purpose
Chloral hydrate	0.5–1 gm	PO	At H.S. for sleep	Hypnotic used to produce sedation and sleep. Is habituating. Long-term use can induce dependence. Often used with chlordiazepoxide. The combination induces restful sleep from which the patient is easily aroused.
	1.0–1.5 gm	PO	q6h alternately	Successfully used with paraldehyde on alternating schedule to control delirium tremens.
Chlordiazepoxide (Librium®)	50–200 mg	IM or PO	Initial dose and q6h p.r.n. depending on severity of symptoms	Minor tranquilizer frequently used in the reduction of psychomotor hyperactivity and induction of sedation. Used in combination with antiepileptics or other tranquilizers.
	25–50 mg	PO	TID maintenance dose	
Chlorpromazine (Thorazine®)	25–100 mg	IV, IM, or PO	q3–6h, then p.r.n. when symptoms subside	Major tranquilizer decreasing nausea and vomiting associated with first phase of withdrawal. Also decreases agitation and psychomotor hyperactivity. (Potentiates action of paraldehyde.)
	100–200 mg	PO	q3h p.r.n. depending on severity of symptoms	
Paraldehyde	5–25 cc or 8–15 cc	PO / Deep IM in divided doses not to exceed 5cc per injection site	q1–4h until symptoms are controlled q2–4h p.r.n.	Sedative-hypnotic primarily used for severe withdrawal symptoms, especially delirium tremens. Very pungent odor and bitter taste. Often used in conjunction with other drugs, e.g., chloral hydrate. Is addicting, and thus long-term use is discouraged. Metabolized in liver. Depressed or damaged liver function delays metabolization of paraldehyde. Reacts with most plastics—use glass syringe or nonplastic cups.

Drug	Dosage	Route	Frequency	Description
Promazine Hydrochloride (Sparine®)	25–200 mg	IV, IM, or PO	TID or QID depending on patient's reaction and severity of symptoms	Major tranquilizer which quickly brings about sedation and sleep. Decreases nausea and thus improves appetite. Decreases skeletal muscle tremors. Patient awakens refreshed; low incidence of drug hangover.
Hydroxyzine (Vistaril®)	50–100 mg	IM or PO	q4h schedule or p.r.n.	Minor tranquilizer which is very effective in controlling moderate to severe withdrawal symptoms, especially extreme psychomotor hyperactivity. For severe withdrawal symptoms. Immediate control is possible.
	100 mg	IV	Once as initial dose	
Diphenylhydantoin (Dilantin®)	Dosage and frequency are largely dependent on the extent other drugs are in use and the patient's usual maintenance dose schedule.	IM or PO		Antiepileptic medication often used for control of seizures resulting from delirium tremens or to prevent seizure activity in the known epileptic alcoholic. Also very effective for control of initial tremulousness of withdrawal when used with diazepam.

In addition to the drugs presented in Table 3-1, many physicians utilize diazepam (Valium®), meprobamate, reserpine, phenobarbital, hydrocortisone, or others in varying dosages and in conjunction with the medications in Table 3-1. In rare instances, intravenous administration of solutions containing variable amounts of alcohol has proven successful when sedatives have failed to control severe delirium tremens. Of importance is the fact that there is no single medication schedule used by all physicians or considered to be the "only way" to treat withdrawal.

Correction of Fluid and Electrolyte Imbalances Unless the alcoholic has experienced severe diarrhea, vomiting, and malnutrition preceding hospitalization, he will not be dehydrated. Instead, he will be overhydrated from the increase in total body water caused by continual alcohol ingestion. When the patient is dehydrated, however, oral or parenteral replacement therapy will be started and may include replacement of electrolytes. Frequently prescribed intravenous solutions include 5 percent dextrose in water and 5 to 10 percent glucose or fructose in saline. The amount and type of electrolytes to be added to the solution are determined by the results of blood chemistries.

Supportive and Diagnostic Measures A thorough physical examination is conducted as soon as medication has decreased agitation. The physician usually requests x-rays if there is a question of traumatic injury, especially when the patient's behavior remains bizarre long after ample medication has been administered. Blood work is ordered as needed with concentration on blood glucose levels, liver and kidney function analysis, and determination of the presence of infectious organisms.

Because of the depletion of liver glycogen stores and possible liver impairment, blood glucose levels often are very labile in the alcoholic. In order to prevent hypoglycemic reactions and, at the same time, reduce cerebral edema in the unconscious patient, many physicians administer hypertonic glucose solutions such as 25 to 50 cc of a 50 percent glucose solution diluted in 150 cc of dextrose and water.

Replacement of vitamins usually begins during withdrawal since some of the signs and symptoms of this condition may be caused by vitamin deficiencies. Multivitamin preparations, B-complex vitamins, or vitamin C are frequently prescribed. Along with the prescriptions of vitamins, the initiation of a nutritious diet, is essential.

A decreased magnesium level may in part contribute to the symptoms of withdrawal. For this reason, replacement of magnesium sulfate via the parenteral route may be necessary. Frequently prescribed dosage consists of 2 cc of 50 percent solution IM every three to four hours for four to eight doses.

Orders for bedrest and activity are based on the patient's awareness, physical condition, and reaction to medication. Frequently the patient is allowed activity ad lib as a means of channeling excess agitation and hyperactivity. However, if the patient is debilitated or unable to protect himself from harm, bedrest is most appropriate.

Some of the treatment measures initiated during acute withdrawal are carried on after symptoms have subsided and withdrawal is completed, e.g., diet therapy, moderate amounts of tranquilizers, rest, and vitamin replacement. Complete recovery from delirium tremens with a return to equilibrium does not take place for approximately two to three weeks. By the end of this period, the alcoholic's memory has cleared and he can optimally benefit from continued treatment.

The Comatose Patient

The alcoholic who arrives for treatment in a comatose state presents an emergency situation. Before vigorous therapy can be initiated, the patient must be supported through the acute episode. Intensive treatment and nursing care are concentrated on preventing respiratory depression and circulatory collapse. A thorough physical examination is conducted to rule out traumatic injury, subdural hematoma, skull fracture, etc. The examination, blood analysis, and perhaps gastric analysis are combined with any information obtained from friends or relatives to assist in determining if the alcoholic had taken any drugs with or without alcohol, especially barbiturates. (Barbiturate abuse and alcoholism are frequent companions.)

DISULFIRAM (ANTABUSE®) THERAPY

After the alcoholic has completed withdrawal he is able to consider the merits of Disulfiram therapy. He may be offered this option while still in the general hospital, an outpatient, or as part of a rehabilitation program. Regardless of where this treatment is begun, there are several basic concepts that the patient and the nurse must be aware of prior to beginning such a deterrent program.

Basically, Disulfiram interferes with the metabolism of alcohol and produces a volatile toxic reaction when combined with alcohol. Therefore, when taking Disulfiram on a regular basis, the patient cannot and should not drink. The reaction closely mimics shock with the presence of deep flushing, a sharp rise in blood pressure, spasms of coughing, and feelings of tightening in the throat. Difficulty in breathing, precordial pain, and violent vomiting may follow. It is crucial that the patient be forewarned of the reaction he will have if he drinks while taking the medication.

The patient starts out with a 0.5 gm PO daily dose for five to seven days. Then the dose is decreased to a maintenance level of 0.25 gm or 0.125 gm daily, which can be continued for years.

TREATMENT OF THE COMPLICATIONS OF ALCOHOLISM

Of the many complications of alcoholism, nutritional deficiencies and the sequelae resulting from them (peripheral polyneuritis, Korsakoff's syndrome, Wernicke's syndrome, etc.) cause some of the most severe health disturbances. For this reason diet therapy assumes vital importance in the treatment of such complications. To correct the nutritional deficiencies, a diet high in protein and vitamins is usually prescribed with supplemental feedings as tolerated.

The institution of a nutritious diet in combination with the ongoing replacement of vitamins, adequate rest, and maintenance of fluid and electrolyte balance, contribute to the treatment of most of the remaining complications of alcoholism, i.e., cirrhosis of the liver, the myopathies, pancreatitis. (It is suggested that for a comprehensive presentation of specific treatment measures necessary for these complications, appropriate treatment texts be consulted.)

ONGOING THERAPY MEASURES

Once the alcoholic's acute physical problems have stabilized and the patient is capable of continuing the treatment process, he can begin to participate in some form of long-term therapy. These therapy measures are sometimes carried on in conjunction with other programs and include psychological approaches, rehabilitative programs, and family therapy.

Psychological Approaches

There are several approaches to the treatment of the underlying personality structure and behavior of the alcoholic. Each requires a skilled therapist and revolves around the development of a trusting relationship between patient and therapist. Brief summaries of three of these approaches follow.

Learning Theories Learning theories are based on the premise that behavior can be changed when it is associated with various types of reinforcement. Some schools of thought concentrate on *aversive conditioning* techniques (negative, or punishing, reinforcements) while others concentrate on positive reinforcement techniques (reward).

Aversive conditioning can be accomplished through hypnosis, drugs, or other aversive stimuli. The hypnosis approach uses hypnotic suggestion coupled with the intake of beverage alcohol. The suggestion concentrates on inducing immediate reflex responses of nausea and vomiting whenever alcoholic beverages are ingested.

Use of emeticlike drugs in aversive conditioning has had considerable success although the methods used have been criticized extensively. Emetine hydrochloride has been successful, but its use requires intense observation and the direction of highly skilled therapists, both of which are time-consuming and often costly. Disulfiram therapy is also in this category of aversive conditioning, as discussed on page 35.

Recently, behavioral modification researchers have been attempting to determine successful means of retraining alcoholics to drink in a controlled manner. This approach is not in wide use and requires further study and clarification.

Group Therapies Utilization of one of the group therapy approaches for the treatment of underlying psychological problems and in rehabilitative efforts has been most successful. These groups are usually conducted simultaneously with other treatment measures and rely on skilled therapists, other health professionals, and paramedical personnel. The theoretical basis of the approach is usually eclectic, borrowing from psychoanalytic and learning theories. The emphasis varies widely from orientation to a particular program to role playing and psychodrama.

At this point it must be stated that there is a degree of controversy on the applicability of group therapy techniques to the treatment of alcoholics. Some therapists maintain that the alcoholic is not suitable for group therapy because of his high anxiety level and the tendency toward relapse. For some alcoholics this is undoubtedly true. However, many alcoholics have benefited greatly from participation in group therapy sessions and for this reason it is presented as an acceptable method of long-term treatment.

Psychoanalytic Treatment Psychoanalysis concentrates on assisting the alcoholic in recognizing his unconscious motivations to drink excessively. A second aspect of this approach focuses on the belief that alcoholic behavior is brought about by character disorders. Through long-term therapy, psychoanalysts seek to promote character alteration so that alcoholic behavior will no longer be needed.

Recently there has been an increase in the therapeutic use of LSD in the treatment of alcoholism. The remarkable success rates attributed to the controlled LSD experience has prompted considerable interest in this method. However, controversy surrounds its use and effectiveness and, consequently, it has not been widely accepted as a psychological approach.

There are many other possible variations of psychological approaches to the treatment of alcoholism. This brief summary is by no means intended to represent all the wide and diverse treatment modalities based on psychological theoretical constructs.

Rehabilitation Programs

The goal of most rehabilitation programs is to assist the arrested or recovered alcoholic in the readjustment of his personal and social relationships. The alcoholic comes to treatment, in many instances, in a state of physical, inter-personal, and social bankruptcy. The relationships and hopes that were valued before alcoholism became a reality must be reshaped and internalized so that the person can return to living with realistic goals, renewed self-understanding, and heightened self-respect.

Rehabilitation programs are most frequently based in the community. They can be located in live-in halfway houses and residential centers or in facilities for day care and outpatient treatment to name a few.

Programs for rehabilitation make extensive use of all the members, both professional and lay, of the health team—nurse, physician, social worker, psychologist, counselors, volunteers, etc., and many forms of group therapy are employed. The alcoholic who is a resident in a particular program may participate in activity groups, problem-oriented groups, and self-government groups. Through these activities, the alcoholic has an outlet for the expression of problems and feelings as well as a place in which he can become resocial-ized with people who have similar problems, and with whom he can com-municate openly.

The time spent by the alcoholic in rehabilitation programs or related activities can be as short as a few months to as long as one or two years. Even at the end of the formal rehabilitative phase, however, he may continue to participate in selected aspects of his program.

Family Therapy

As the rehabilitation phase progresses, it is important that the family of the alcoholic or other significant persons be brought into the treatment situation on an active basis. Long before this, however, these people require assistance and guidance in the everyday coping with alcoholic behavior. Those closest to the alcoholic (spouse, children, friends or employer) are under great stress during the time of active alcoholism. The family unit is especially vulnerable to damage and disintegration when a family member suffers from alcoholism.

Informal family therapy can take place in groups such as Al-Anon and Al-Ateen. These lay organizations are composed of relatives and friends of the alcoholic who are seeking understanding of alcoholism and their role in its continuation. A major benefit of these programs is that family members and friends can seek understanding and support even before the alcoholic has realized the problem and sought help. At the same time, family members are able to gain insight into their own behavior and how it relates to the behavior of the alcoholic. This often allows them to cope with alcoholic behavior in more constructive ways.

It is evident that the treatment of the alcoholic has many and varied facets. This chapter represents a summary of the information a nurse must have in order to participate in the treatment of the alcoholic patient. Such information fosters meaningful nursing care and innovative ways of delivering that care. The nursing measures specific to each of the areas described is contained in the following chapters.

REFERENCES

Acton, Conrad: "Detoxification of the Alcoholic Patient," *Maryland State Medical Journal*, 17:123-126, September 1968.

Anderson, Richard H., and Maxwell N. Weisman: *The Alcoholic in the Emergency Room*, National Council of Alcoholism, Inc., New York, June 1972.

Bates, Richard C.: "Dietary Treatment of Alcoholism," *Modern Treatment*, 3: 556-560, May 1966.

Beacham, E. G.: "Management of Acute Phases of Alcoholism, Including Delirium Tremens," *Maryland State Medical Journal*, 18:105-107, March 1969.

Beard, James D.: "Fluid and Electrolyte Abnormalities in Alcoholism," *Psychosomatics*, XI:502-503, September–October 1970.

Blum, Eva Marie, and Richard H. Blum: *Alcoholism: Modern Psychological Approaches to Treatment*, Jossey-Bass Inc., San Francisco, 1967.

Catanzaro, Ronald J. (ed.): *Alcoholism: The Total Treatment Approach*, Charles C Thomas, Springfield, Ill., 1968.

Chafetz, Morris E.: "Drugs in the Treatment of Alcoholism," *Medical Clinics of North America*, 51:1249-1259, September 1967.

Chambers, Joseph F.: "Management of Acute Alcohol Withdrawal Symptoms," *Maryland State Medical Journal*, 15:131-133, June 1966.

Cork, R. Margaret: *The Forgotten Children*, Addiction Research Foundation, Toronto, 1969.

Finer, M. J.: "Diphenylhydantoin in Alcohol Withdrawal," *Journal of the American Medical Association*, 217:211, July 12, 1971.

Golbert, Thomas M. et al.: "Comparative Evaluation of Treatments of Alcohol Withdrawal Syndromes," *Journal of the American Medical Association*, 201:99-102, July 10, 1967.

Greenblatt, David J., and Milton Greenblat: "Which Drug for Withdrawal?", *Journal of Clinical Pharmacology*, 12:429-431, December 1972.

Hoffer, Abram, and Humphry Osmond: *New Hope for Alcoholics*, University Books, Inc., New Hyde Park, N.Y., 1968.

Kissin, Benjamin, and Milton M. Gross: "Drug Therapy in Alcoholism," *Current Psychiatric Therapies*, 10:135-144, 1970.

Knott, David H., and James D. Beard: "Acute Withdrawal from Alcohol," *Emergency Medicine*, 38-41, May 1969.

Knott, David H., and James D. Beard: "A New Approach to the Treatment of Acute Withdrawal from Alcohol," *Psychosomatics*, IX:311-313, November–December 1968.

Knott, David H., and James D. Beard: "Diagnosis and Therapy of Acute Withdrawal from Alcohol," *Current Psychiatric Therapies*, 10:145-153, 1970.

Knott, David H.: "Medical Management of the Alcohol Withdrawal Syndrome," *Psychosomatics*, XI:504-505, September–October 1970.

Leevy, Carroll M. et al.: "Alcoholism, Drug Addiction, and Nutrition," *Medical Clinics of North America,* **54**:1567–1575, November 1970.

Lowenfels, Albert B.: *The Alcoholic Patient in Surgery,* The Williams & Wilkins Co., Baltimore, 1971.

Ludwig, Arnold M., Jerome Levine, and Louis H. Stark: *LSD and Alcoholism,* Charles C Thomas, Springfield, Ill., 1970.

McNichol, Ronald W.: *The Treatment of Delirium Tremens and Related States,* Charles C Thomas, Springfield, Ill., 1970.

McNichol, Ronald W. et al.: "Management of Withdrawal from Alcohol," *American Association of Industrial Nurses Journal,* **16**:19–22, February 1968.

Rodman, Morton J., and Dorothy W. Smith: *Pharmacology and Drug Therapy in Nursing,* J. B. Lippincott Company, Philadelphia, 1968.

Simpson, R. Keith: "Controlling Delirium Tremens and Treating the Alcoholic," *Medical Insight,* **4**:46–53, January 1972.

Who Cares About An Alcoholism Program in the General Hospital?, American Hospital Association, Chicago, 1972.

Chapter 4

Nurses' Attitudes
and the Alcoholic Patient

Attitudes and the values that shape them are major determinants of the response one person will make to another. Values or value systems evolve from upbringing, life experience, education, cultural background, etc., and enable man to interpret his world in a meaningful manner. Unfortunately, value systems can include negative as well as positive components—stereotypes and prejudices.

The stereotypes associated with the alcoholic are well known. They include the comic drunk and the violent drunk, both frequently portrayed in the media, and the skid row bum showed slumped in an alley with a bottle of cheap muscatel. Usually overlooked is the fact that comic and violent alcoholics can be found in any socioeconomic class and form a small percentage of the total alcoholic population. The skid row alcoholic forms 5 percent or less of the alcoholic population. In spite of these facts, many health professionals have based their attitudes toward the alcoholic patient on such negative portrayals.

It must be remembered that values and the attitudes arising from them are formed slowly over time and, thus, awareness of their influence on interpersonal relationships is often masked. Therefore, the nurse, as a health professional who interacts with the alcoholic in a variety of settings, must seek understanding and identification of her attitudes and value systems and how these affect the care this patient receives.

THE IMPORTANCE OF NURSES' ATTITUDES

The scope of nursing practice is continually being refined and extended. At the same time, opportunities for contact with the alcoholic have also broadened. For this reason alone it would behoove nurses to gain insight into their attitudes and feelings toward this large patient population. However, further rationale is offered to explain the importance of the nurse's attitude as it relates to the alcoholic patient.

The Nurse-Patient Relationship

At the center of nursing practice is the nurse-patient relationship. The manner in which this vital relationship is formed and sustained has direct implication for the patient's entire course of treatment. For example, if the nurse projects a negative, stereotyped attitude, the relationship that is established will be clouded by such feelings. Since the alcoholic patient is acutely sensitive to the attitude of others toward him, the nurse-patient relationship in this situation cannot be truly therapeutic or supportive. On the other hand, if the nurse conveys an accepting, sincere, and genuinely caring attitude, the nurse-patient relationship that is established will further patient acceptance and participation in the treatment process. Although the nurse-patient relationship is not solely responsible for the outcome of treatment, it is a significant contributory element. Consequently, nurses must seek ways to increase awareness of their projected and inner feelings.

Personal and Professional Satisfaction

When a nurse or any other person works very hard, often under stressful conditions, the amount of satisfaction she derives must be equal to the challenge. This is especially true with the alcoholic patient, who may require intense, lifesaving care as well as long-term rehabilitative care.

The nurse's identification and understanding of her attitudes toward this particular patient group can help to increase her professional and personal satisfaction. Knowing why a patient behaves as he does and why personal feelings of annoyance and rejection are aroused can serve as the stimulus for reevaluation and realignment of one's responses. Just as this ability is encouraged in the alcoholic, so it must be encouraged in the nurse. Thus the patient benefits from the nursing care given and the nurse benefits from the personal and professional satisfaction engendered by the patient's response.

RESEARCH INTO NURSES' ATTITUDES

Research efforts designed to determine nurses' attitudes toward the alcoholic have largely concentrated on identification and description.[1,2,3,4] Some studies have attempted to measure the effects on patient response of varying approaches while others have concentrated on changing negative attitudes to more positive ones.[5,6] Results of these studies have demonstrated a high degree of similarity of nurses' attitudes toward the alcoholic patient. A summary of the major findings of several research efforts follows.

The Disease Concept of Alcoholism

By far, the majority of nurses and students of nursing have accepted the disease concept of alcoholism. Of interest, however, is an additional finding which indicates that although respondents believed alcoholism to be an illness, they also believed that the alcoholic can cease drinking behavior if he *really* wants to. At the same time, these nurses believed that the illness could be treated.

Ambivalence toward the Alcoholic

Identified nurses' attitudes were characterized by ambivalence. While there appears to be an acceptance of the disease concept, there are expressions of frustration, discouragement, and rejection of the alcoholic patient when his behavior deviates from accepted patterns. The conflicts created by such ambivalence are a source of confusion to the nurse who sees herself in a helping and supporting role to the patients she cares for.

The Nurse's Educational Background and Experience

Those nurses with advanced education in nursing or related fields generally possessed more positive attitudes. Advanced education consisted of formal courses and programs, individual study, or employment-related educational offerings. This finding does not mean that all nurses with basic educational background had negative attitudes. There was, however, a significant direct relationship between the amount of education and the type of attitudes toward the alcoholic patient.

---

[1] Philip M. Moody, "Attitudes of Nurses and Nursing Students Toward Alcoholism Treatment," *Quarterly Journal of Studies on Alcohol,* 32:172–175, March 1971.

[2] Ernest W. Ferneau, Jr. and Elvera L. Morton, "Nursing Personnel and Alcoholism," *Nursing Research,* 14:174–177, March–April 1968.

[3] Edith Heinemann and Robert J. Rhodes, "How Nurses View the Tuberculosis Alcoholic Patient," *Nursing Research,* 16:361–365, Fall 1967.

[4] Marilyn W. Johnson, "Nurses Speak Out on Alcoholism," *Nursing Forum,* 4(4):16–22, 1965.

[5] Ernest W. Ferneau, Jr., "What Student Nurses Think About Alcoholic Patients and Alcoholism," *Nursing Outlook,* 15:40–41, October 1967.

[6] Mark Berke et al., *A Study of the Nonsegregated Hospitalization of Alcoholic Patients in a General Hospital* (Chicago: American Hospital Association, 1959), pp. 10–18, 36–41.

Length and type of work experience with alcoholic patients was also related to the nurses' attitudes. Nurses who had worked longest with alcoholic patients were found to have more negative attitudes. This was in part attributed to the repetitious and demanding nature of the work. Characteristic of some of the findings was the fact that those nurses who came in frequent contact with the alcoholic patient were the ones with more negative attitudes. On the other hand, those nurses with more educational preparation who had more positive attitudes were farthest from the bedside of alcoholic patients and, thus, had the least experience in caring for them.

A Challenge

Although a majority of the nurses measured in these studies expressed positive and negative attitudes in an ambiguous manner, a significant number also viewed their experiences as a challenge. Many felt discouraged and frustrated when first exposed to the care of the alcoholic patient. After working with these patients and receiving additional preparation in their special needs, the nurses expressed very positive attitudes.

Research into the nature of nurses' attitudes toward alcoholic patients has generally succeeded in identifying and describing the major areas of concern. The populations measured in such studies are necessarily small, and therefore the results cannot be universally applied. At this point, the question becomes, Can this research be applied to some extent to current nursing practice? The answer is, of course, Yes and will be discussed in succeeding sections of this chapter.

SOME REASONS FOR NURSES' ATTITUDES

In order to modify attitudes or learn new methods of expressing them, it is necessary to gain an understanding of why the attitudes have taken their present shape. Many of the reasons for the existence of ambivalent attitudes among nurses are directly associated with the characteristics of alcoholism.

The Frequency of Relapse

The nurse may find it difficult to accept the alcoholic who repeatedly "falls off the wagon." Perhaps this particular patient has been admitted several times, treated, and discharged only to be readmitted in two weeks. He then begins the sequence again. Such behavior is understandably discouraging.

The nurse may also view relapse behavior as a negative reflection on her abilities. To rationalize such feelings the nurse may unknowingly justify the failure by conferring blame on the alcoholic, i.e., thinking that he is weak-willed and would stop drinking if he really wanted to.

The Appearance of Recovery

If the treatment is uncomplicated, the alcoholic very quickly attains the appearance of recovery. This superficial manifestation of health can be very deceiving, especially when the seemingly recovered healthy person returns to excessive drinking patterns while still hospitalized or immediately upon discharge. For the nurse who does not realize that this appearance of wellness is external only, such behavior can be extremely frustrating and lead to rejection during future admissions.

Nurses' Expectations of Treatment

Nurses are generally accustomed to seeing a discharged patient not return to the hospital or other treatment site for the same problem unless there is a medical complication or condition that is highly physically stressful. However, this usual sequence of events is not the pattern for most alcoholics and thus can add to the nurse's frustration and dissatisfaction.

Complications of Alcoholism

Long-term, chronic alcoholic behavior inevitably leads to physical complications which are characteristic of alcohol's action of various body systems and organs. Often the nurse finds it difficult to comprehend why the alcoholic continues drinking in view of what it is doing to his body. The nurse's desire to be effective in assisting the patient in ceasing the alcoholic behavior and prevent such complications can be met with resistance and apparent disinterest. It is not surprising that under these circumstances the nurse may reject the alcoholic, label him as a "trouble maker" or "impossible," and generally avoid a close nurse-patient relationship with him.

Nurses' Values

As the nurse views the alcoholic's behavior and how it has affected every aspect of his life, she may experience feelings of disgust and moral condemnation. These feelings reflect her individual value system and may be based at an unconscious level. In any event, they have a profound influence on her attitudes.

SUGGESTED APPROACHES TO THE ATTITUDE PROBLEM

Negative and ambivalent attitudes expressed by the nurse while caring for the alcoholic are a source of discomfort to both parties. Although the attitudes responsible for this problem cannot be changed instantaneously, it is possible to suggest approaches or methods of viewing the alcoholic and the nurses' feelings toward him.

Identification and Acknowledgment of Inner Feelings

In order for the nurse to understand why she feels as she does, it is necessary to look inward. Identifying and analyzing her personal value system as it relates to alcoholism and alcoholics is one way the nurse can gain insight into her attitudes. This introspection must be an ongoing process, one that will continue as long as the nurse comes in contact with alcoholics.

Gaining insight involves asking oneself such questions as, What does the alcoholic *do* that bothers me so much? Is this something contrary to my value system? If so, is it realistic to expect the patient to comply with my values? Do I *really* accept the disease concept of alcoholism? Answering these and related questions contributes to the process of gaining insight. As self-awareness is increased, it then becomes possible to control and modify negative or ambivalent attitudes. The benefits achieved by gaining such insight are quite tangible: the patient benefits from the nurse's genuine approach, and the nurse's feelings of discomfort can be dispelled or decreased.

It would be neither reasonable nor likely that all nurses could change or control all values that conflicted with their ability to care for the alcoholic. It becomes imperative, then, that those nurses who find it continually stressful, discomforting, and distasteful to care for alcoholic patients not seek such contacts.

The Nurse's Level of Emotional Maturity

The nurse who chooses to specialize in one of the areas of practice that concentrates on caring for the alcoholic must be an emotionally mature and stable person. One component of emotional maturity is the ability to accept oneself and others. Much of this maturity is acquired as the nurse seeks insight into her feelings. It is important to remember, however, that emotional maturity does not always coincide with chronological maturity and, thus, the young or novice practitioner may have as much to offer as the more experienced nurse.

The manner in which the nurse is able to accept the alcoholic's behavior, interpret it, and respond consistently and sincerely is in large part a reflection of her emotional maturity. With these qualities, the emotionally mature nurse will feel more comfortable in discussing alcoholism with the patient. She will be less likely to become upset by his challenging and demanding behavior.

Acceptance of the Alcoholic

The nurse's attitude should be dominated by acceptance: acceptance of the alcoholic as a person and as someone who is ill. Acceptance can be conveyed only by a nonpunitive, nonmoralistic, and nonpreaching attitude. A projection of sincerity, caring, and hope is essential.

Acceptance must be realistic. The nurse should always keep in mind the goals of treatment and the nature of alcoholism. The realistic approach does not, however, have to conflict with acceptance. As long as a sincere and consistent attitude is conveyed, without the presence of phoniness, a genuinely meaningful nurse-patient relationship can be maintained.

Improvement, Not Cure

In view of the characteristics of alcoholism and its treatment, the nurse must think of improvement rather than cure. Improvement indicates a positive change, a step in the direction of ultimate well-being. This is a more realistic approach to the care of the alcoholic who may not be able to achieve permanent abstinence following first treatment efforts.

As the nurse integrates this viewpoint into her approach, it will be possible to more readily accept the patient's relapses for what they are: a symptom of a chronic illness, a temporary setback. In this way, the nurse can establish realistic short-term goals. It is a more feasible goal to think of abstinence for a month, especially when the patient has never been able to abstain for more than a week.

Study the Subject of Alcoholism

It is a natural tendency to avoid that which is discouraging or upsetting. One of the basic ways these feelings can be dispelled is through information. For this reason it is vital that the nurse seek more information about alcoholism and its many facets when confronted with ambivalent attitudes. Enlarging one's knowledge becomes a professional nurse's responsibility when, due to lack of information and understanding, she is unable to provide high-quality patient care. Information can be gleaned from the literature, from colleagues, from other professionals, and through employment of community resources. It is an ongoing process since knowledge about the dynamics of alcoholism is continually being expanded and refined.

SUMMARY COMMENT

The character of the nurse's attitude toward the alcoholic has a direct relationship to the type of nursing care received by the patient. It is necessary, then, that the nurse realize what these attitudes are, the reasons for them, and how they might be changed or controlled. Therefore, the suggested approaches to the problems posed by ambivalent or negative attitudes are offered as initial guidelines. The approaches are not mutually exclusive—one or all can be used at the same time.

It is hoped that by understanding personal attitudes and the attitudes of others, it will be possible for nurses who work with alcoholics to increase their professional satisfaction while improving the nursing care given.

REFERENCES

Andruzzi, Ellen A.: "Nursing Care for the Alcoholic," *Maryland State Medical Journal,* **19**:93–94, February 1970.

Berke, Mark et al.: *A Study of the Nonsegregated Hospitalization of Alcoholic Patients in a General Hospital,* American Hospital Association, Chicago, 1959.

Ferneau, Ernest W., Jr.: "What Student Nurses Think About Alcoholic Patients and Alcoholism," *Nursing Outlook,* **15**:40–41, October 1967.

Ferneau, Ernest W., Jr., and Elvera L. Morton: "Nursing Personnel and Alcoholism," *Nursing Research,* **14**:174–177, March–April 1968.

Fowler, Grace R.: "Understanding the Patient Who Uses Alcohol to Solve His Problems," *Nursing Forum,* **4**:(4)6–15, 1965.

Golder, Grace M.: "The Nurse and the Alcoholic Patient," *American Journal of Nursing,* **56**:436–438, April 1956.

Heinemann, Edith, and Robert J. Rhodes: "How Nurses View the Tuberculosis Alcoholic Patient," *Nursing Research,* **16**:361–365, Fall 1967.

Johnson, Marilyn W.: "Nurses Speak Out on Alcoholism," *Nursing Forum,* **4**:(4)16–22, 1965.

Moody, Philip M.: "Attitudes of Nurses and Nursing Students Toward Alcoholism Treatment," *Quarterly Journal of Studies on Alcohol,* **32**:172–175, March 1971.

Queen, Dolores: "Attitudes and Skills of the Nurse in Working With the Alcoholic and His Family," *Maryland State Medical Journal,* **20**:83–85, June 1971.

Tuerk, Isadore: "Attitudes and Alcoholics," *Maryland State Medical Journal,* **17**:110–111, April 1968.

Ujhely, Gertrud: *Determinants of the Nurse-Patient Relationship,* Springer Publishing Company, Inc., New York, 1968.

Weisman, Maxwell N.: "Current Status of the Treatment of Alcoholism," *Maryland State Medical Journal,* **21**:73–76, March 1972.

Chapter 5

Caring for the Alcoholic in the General Hospital

In recent years, many large general hospitals have revised admission policies to include treatment for alcoholism. However, even though the hospital's professional association has not only endorsed admittance of alcoholics but also urges it, a significant number of general hospitals continue to refuse to openly admit the alcoholic for treatment.

Fortunately, one of the major stumbling blocks to alteration of admittance policies has begun to change—insurance coverage. Several of the large insurance carriers now pay benefits specifically for the treatment of alcoholism. Some plans prefer that the general hospital serve as the primary treatment site. With the advent of insurance coverage and the mandate of the courts to provide treatment for alcoholics, general hospitals should no longer refuse admittance to alcoholics. Resolution of this problem is of vital importance to nursing practice. It has a profound influence upon the manner in which nurses can care for the alcoholic patient as well as the quality of professional care that can be given.

REASONS FOR HOSPITALIZATION

Hospitalization of the alcoholic becomes necessary under the following circumstances:

 1 When the patient is severely intoxicated and may develop stupor, coma, or respiratory depression
 2 When withdrawal symptoms are impending or evident
 3 When illness or injury associated with alcoholism is present
 4 When continuous binge drinking cannot be interrupted and the danger of physical or psychological collapse is imminent
 5 When the patient wishes to "dry out" and participate in initial recovery efforts preparatory to long-term treatment and rehabilitation

Because alcoholism does not respect age, sex, socioeconomic status, or cultural background, patients admitted for any of these reasons will be representative of the general hospital population. In addition to the adult patient, the nurse may on occasion care for a child who has inadvertently consumed a large quantity of alcohol. This is an emergency situation and can prove fatal with the advent of uncontrollable convulsions.

A second rare experience for the nurse will be the female alcoholic in labor and delivery. If the mother is acutely intoxicated, the newborn may experience acute withdrawal shortly after birth, since alcohol freely crosses the placental barrier and intoxicates the fetus. This also is an emergency situation in which highly skilled nursing care for the mother and the newborn is required.

ADMITTING POLICIES AND NURSING IMPLICATIONS

Since most general hospitals do not openly or knowingly admit alcoholic patients and many alcoholics desperately need hospital care, it has frequently been necessary, on the part of alcoholics and physicians, to utilize subterfuge and camouflage in admitting these patients. Once admitted to the hospital, however, the patient's true diagnosis poses additional problems.

Known, Communicated Diagnosis

When the diagnosis of alcoholism is clearly and consistently communicated to the nursing staff, the quality and thoroughness of the nursing care and approach are greatly increased.

Known Diagnosis, Not Communicated

For one reason or another, the physician may know that the patient is an alcoholic but not tell the nursing staff. The reason may stem from a patient request, hospital policy, or an unknown physician preference. Regardless of the reason, an uncommunicated diagnosis of alcoholism can disrupt normal activities on the nursing unit. Take the case of a man who was admitted one afternoon with a fractured neck of the femur. He was alert, cooperative, a little nervous (not unusual under the circumstances), and had no odor of alcohol on his breath. He was made comfortable, positioned carefully, and seated. The following morning he was taken to surgery. When he returned to the unit in the early afternoon, the nursing staff learned that he had been combative, loud, and uncooperative in the recovery room. The physician was notified. Shortly thereafter he began to thrash about in bed, tried to get out of bed, and was actively hallucinating. His appearance was florid, his skin was diaphoretic, and he was incontinent and delirious. The nursing staff again consulted the physician. This time they were informed of the patient's alcoholic diagnosis. The anger and frustration experienced by these nurses is easy to comprehend. As this situation illustrates, it is both necessary and advantageous that a patient's alcoholic diagnosis be told to the nursing staff.

Alcoholic, Admitted under Other Diagnosis

The majority of alcoholic patients the nurse sees and cares for are admitted under diagnoses that are either associated with or a direct result of alcoholism. Commonly seen diagnoses include cirrhosis of the liver, pancreatitis, malnutrition, orthopedic and neurological injuries, bleeding disorders, pneumonia, multiple trauma, and many other ailments. The physician will frequently inform the nursing staff of the patient's drinking problem and include appropriate treatment measures in the patient's orders. When this is not done, it is often the nurse who discovers the patient is also an alcoholic. If this occurs, the nurse must immediately inform the physician, who can then reevaluate treatment measures.

Undiagnosed Alcoholism

Alcoholics are highly skilled in denying their illness. They are also often successful in hiding it from others. Thus the nurse may be faced with the undiagnosed alcoholic patient admitted for elective surgery or a medical problem. Much of this patient's behavior closely parallels that of a nervous or highstrung person, one who is afraid of hospitalization. Again, it is usually the nurse who becomes suspicious of the patient's behavior. She then seeks further information from the patient and his family regarding drinking patterns and the possibility of alcoholism. In such inquiries the words "alcoholic" and "alcoholism" need not be used. Often queries about any drinking problems that the patient might have are sufficient to elicit the necessary information.

If the patient is to undergo an elective surgical procedure, he may complain of nervousness and express inordinate fear of the surgical experience. Some of these feelings are genuine. However, the most overriding fear is that the patient's alcoholism will be discovered and he will then be cut off from his supply. He may fear that he will be unable to get a substitute and begin showing withdrawal symptoms. Thus he repeatedly asks for something to calm his nerves or hides a bottle at the bedside.

When this patient returns from surgery, he requests analgesic and tranquilizing medication frequently. (He may also return to the unit in the same condition as in the previous example.) The patient's inability to sleep, increasing tremulousness, and progressive symptoms of withdrawal alert the nurse to the true reason for the behavior. In these cases, the nurse must always investigate other possible causes for the patient's restlessness. For example, the patient's age—elderly patients can become confused and incoherent in unfamiliar surroundings. There may be a reaction to anesthesia, an inability to void or an unstable intake/output pattern with resultant electrolyte imbalance, or possible traumatic injury. In any event, the physician should be notified of the patient's behavior and symptoms.

The patient who is admitted via the emergency room following severe traumatic injury (auto accident, falls, fights, etc.) also fits into this category. The diagnosis of alcoholism is frequently unknown and because of the crisis nature of such situations, discussion with the patient may not be possible. In addition, there is often no one associated with the patient available to consult. It then becomes vital that the nurse closely monitor the patient's behavior and detect those signs and symptoms that are associated with withdrawal.

Once the alcoholic has been admitted, his placement within the hospital structure will vary. Many large general hospitals have detoxification units, some place alcoholics on psychiatric units, and others place them on general medical or surgical units on a nonsegregated basis.

Because nursing care in the detoxification and psychiatric units will be discussed in later chapters, the remainder of this chapter will dwell on the care of the alcoholic on the general medical or surgical unit. Those hospitals that place alcoholics on such units have found that they are no more disruptive than other patients who have periodic episodes of erratic behavior.

THE NURSING ASSESSMENT

The nursing assessment of the alcoholic patient consists of an orderly investigation to determine the nature of the patient problems. These problems relate specifically to the response of the individual patient to alcoholism and its treatment. After the patient problems are identified, the nursing care plan can be formulated.

In assessing the newly admitted alcoholic patient, the nurse takes into account physical, psychological, and social data. Much of the information can be directly recorded on the nursing history format and can be obtained as the nurse admits and assists the patient in getting settled in his room or cubicle. Throughout the patient's hospitalization the nurse can add to her original assessment and modify the care plan accordingly. (See Table 5-1 for a summary of the nursing assessment components.)

Table 5-1 The Nursing Assessment Process for the Alcoholic Patient

Assessment Component	Focus of Assessment
Physical assessment	Vital signs
	Stage of withdrawal
	Nutritional status
	Fluid balance
	Circulatory-respiratory status
	Personal hygiene
Psychological assessment	Orientation and alertness
	Degree of insight into alcoholism
	Nurse-patient relationship
	Motivation for treatment
Social assessment	Identification of existing or potential problems
	Family stability
	Occupational status
	Financial needs
	Need for referrals

Physical Assessment

One goal of the physical assessment is to determine the presence and severity of withdrawal symptoms. A second goal is to assess the patient's overall physical condition in order to identify potential and existing nursing care problems. To achieve these goals, the nurse has to consider the following components of assessment.

Vital Signs The nurse should monitor blood pressure, pulse, respiration, and temperature. The readings give an indication of the extent of psychomotor hyperactivity and, thus, elevations or other abnormal readings must be recorded and reported promptly.

Stage of Withdrawal It is necessary to identify the signs and symptoms of withdrawal. These give an indication of the patient's progression in withdrawal and are a measure of the excitability of the central nervous system. If the patient is experiencing tremulousness, his hands will shake. He will have difficulty in holding and drinking a glass of water steadily. Does he drop cigarette ashes on the floor? His coordination will be decreased. The extent of this incoordination can be observed in his manner of movement and placement of personal belongings in the room. Does he drop objects? Is his gait steady? He will have anxieties, a short attention span, and insomnia. When hallucinations are evident, the patient will be distracted, frightened, and disoriented. He will continue to be anxious, nervous, and excitable. If he has advanced to delirium tremens, his behavior will be characterized by severe psychomotor hyperactivity. The nurse will see the patient in an extremely agitated state. He may be incontinent of urine or stool. He will be uncooperative and confused, and may have no idea where he is or how he got there. Commonly, diaphoresis is present.

Nutritional Status As the nurse assists the patient in undressing and putting on a hospital gown (this may be preparatory to the physical examination), she can observe the patient's gross nutritional status. How is the patient's weight distributed over his body? Are the extremities thin with a loss of muscle tissue? Is the patient overweight? Some alcoholics are able to maintain an adequate food intake, and when this is accompanied by alcoholism, the patient can become obese. Observation of the condition of gum tissue will indicate the presence of gross vitamin deficiencies. Are they dry, bleeding, or cracked? Vitamin and nutritional deficiencies will also be apparent in unhealed sores or cuts.

Fluid Balance Assessment of fluid balance includes examination of mucous membranes of the mouth, testing for skin turgor, and observation of skin moisture. If the patient is dehydrated, mucous membranes will be dry, flaky, and cracked. When the nurse obtains a urine specimen, it should be tested for specific gravity. Odor, color, and clarity should be carefully assessed. High specific gravity, dark color, cloudiness, and foul odor indicate the presence of dehydration, possible infection, or both.

Circulatory-Respiratory Status The nurse can check the patient's lower extremities and sacral area for dependent edema. Quality and rhythmicity of apical pulse can identify the presence of gross arrhythmias, which can be indicative of cardiomyopathy or more advanced withdrawal symptoms. (Patients frequently experience cardiac arrhythmias during advanced withdrawal syndromes, especially premature ventricular contractions and atrial fibrillation.) Assessment of the patient's respiratory status includes observation of breathing pattern, skin color, and listening to the chest for congestion. Observing and reporting the characteristics of the patient's sputum will assist the physician in determining the presence or absence of respiratory infection. Warmth and color of extremities, nailbeds, lips, and ears give an indication of circulatory perfusion and vascular condition.

Personal Hygiene As the nurse assesses the physical status of the alcoholic, close observation of his hygienic status will give clues to recent or chronic drinking patterns. If the patient appears not to have bathed for many days, his fingernails are dry and cracked with dirt beneath them, and his clothing is soiled, he may just have completed an episode of binge drinking. If so, the withdrawal he will experience is likely to be severe. The alcoholic who is clean, shaven, and neatly dressed may not have experienced long-term, chronic alcoholism. This is not a hard-and-fast rule since patients will vary considerably in personal hygiene. However, observation of this aspect of the patient's physical appearance will add data to the overall assessment.

Presence of Trauma The nurse must be especially alert to the presence of traumatic injuries, past or present. Presence of scars, cigarette burns, stains on the hands, bruises, and cuts indicate the need for additional treatment and care. Examination of the head especially should be thorough because alcoholics are highly susceptible to orthopedic and neurological traumatic injuries. Checking pupils for reactivity to light and assessment of strength and equality of hand grasps is vital. The confused, stuporous patient may have had a recent stroke or may be suffering from a cerebral concussion, subdural hemorrhage, fracture, or other injury.

Psychological Assessment

The psychological assessment consists of the data obtained through (1) conversation with the patient and (2) observation of behavior that is indicative of his psychological status.

Orientation and Alertness As the nurse initially interviews the newly admitted alcoholic, she will have ample opportunity to determine alertness, orientation to time, place, and current events, and emotional stability. Is the patient fidgety, nervous, talking incessantly, or very quiet? Is he exhibiting behavior indicative of intoxication? Does he listen and respond to sounds and sights that aren't there, i.e., is he actively hallucinating? Information pertaining to these areas assists in determining the patient's stage of withdrawal.

Degree of Insight into Alcoholism In conversing with the alcoholic, the nurse can assess the degree of insight he possesses toward his alcoholism and his attitude toward the illness and treatment he is to receive. Does he want to discuss his illness? Is he asking questions about it and his treatment program? Does he show an understanding of the disease nature of alcoholism? Does he use the term alcoholic and apply it to himself? Does he express guilt or self-condemnation? Does he deny that he is an alcoholic but admit he has a drinking problem? The patient who demonstrates insight and willingness to undergo treatment needs realistic reassurance and sympathetic support from those caring for him. In order to admit to alcoholism or a severe drinking problem, the person must have undergone great personal and painful self-examination. He now needs to know that his decision was worthwhile. The alcoholic who has not admitted his illness to himself needs an equal amount of support and care if he is to advance to the point where he *can* gain this necessary insight.

All this information will help the nurse in planning teaching sessions as well as in devising a consistent method of approach.

Nurse-Patient Relationship As the nurse interacts with the patient and gathers data on his psychological status, she is also initiating and establishing a nurse-patient relationship. This is possibly one of the most crucial times for this interaction to take place. The newly admitted alcoholic is highly susceptible to intervention at this time, and thus it is important that the nurse initiate interaction on a meaningful basis.

When discussing the reason for hospitalization, the nurse should not probe deeply if the patient does not wish to discuss the subject. As the patient gains comfort and trust in the treatment situation, he will be able to express his feelings with greater ease. The alcoholic is very susceptible to criticism and has thus created strong defense mechanisms as a result. It is necessary for the nurse, therefore, to accept his behavior and be willing to discuss his problems with him when he indicates readiness to do so.

Motivation for Treatment The psychological component of the assessment process would not be complete without consideration of the patient's desire to complete treatment, continue treatment following discharge, and maintain abstinence. Alcoholics are known to be manipulative. Therefore, the nurse should realize that although the patient appears sincere, he may be testing her attitude toward him or her ability to help him. This kind of information has definite implications for the nursing care plan.

Social Assessment

Social assessment consists of the identification of any existing or potential problems that relate to the patient's interactions with others. These include family relationships, living and employment status, and friend or peer relationships.

In talking with the alcoholic or his family, the nurse must gather clues that will indicate the degree of stability within the family unit. Because families with an alcoholic member are frequently disrupted or unstable, identification of such problem areas alerts the nurse to the need for early referral services.

It is not appropriate at this time to make in-depth inquiries about employment status, financial needs, or living conditions unless the patient volunteers the information. It is important, however, that any indication of need for early counseling or referral be made to the appropriate source, i.e., social worker, family counselor, public health nurse, etc.

Alcohol Abuse Progress Sheet

The alcohol abuse progress sheet is used by one hospital as a method of focusing on and recording information that specifically pertains to alcohol abuse and alcoholism. (See Figure 5-1 for an example.[1]) The progress sheet includes a social history profile which aids in determining current living status, demographic information, and the most recent treatment for alcoholism. Alcohol abuse and alcoholism history data specifically pertaining to current patterns are recorded on the second section of the sheet. Current drinking habits are emphasized since the problems being caused by such behavior are what will be dealt with during hospitalization. The third section of the sheet consists of blank space for recording the nurse's progress notes of the patient's behavior as it relates to alcoholism or alcohol abuse. When the patient is discharged, the nurse records the method of follow-up care to be used. Other information concerning patient care and progress continue to be recorded in the regular nurses' notes.

ALCOHOL ABUSE PROGRESS SHEET

SOCIAL HISTORY PROFILE

| | MAIDEN | | STAFF |
NAME: | NAME: | | MEMBER: |

ADDRESS: | PHONE: | CONTACT: |

BIRTHDATE: | PLACE: | SEX: | ETHNICITY: | RELIGION: |

Marital Status: _____   Previous Treatment
Financial Status: _____   for Alcoholism: .... YES_____ NO_____
Education: _____
Employment Status at Present: _____   If YES:
Medical Status: _____   Where? _____
    Admitted: _____   When? _____
    Discharged: _____

ALCOHOL ABUSE AND/OR ALCOHOLISM HISTORY

What problem is drinking causing for you?_____
When did you start drinking?_____
What kind of liquor do you drink?_____ Amount?_____
Consumed day of admission?_____
Longest period of sobriety in last 6 months?_____
How often and how much do you drink at present?_____
Present living environment_____

Figure 5-1

[1] "Alcohol Abuse Progress Sheet," currently in use at St. Francis Hospital, Honolulu, Hawaii.

Depending on hospital policy, the form may be retained in the nursing unit's files or may become a permanent part of the patient's record. In either case, utilizing the information contained on the sheet for current and subsequent admissions allows for greater continuity of patient care. Also, use of such a progress sheet format assists the nurse in concentrating on the alcoholism component of the patient's hospitalization. Too often this component can become buried in the treatment regimen when the patient's medical or surgical problems are highly complex and demanding.

NURSING CARE PLANNING FOR THE PATIENT
EXPERIENCING WITHDRAWAL FROM ALCOHOL

The patient who experiences withdrawal from alcohol presents many immediate and potential nursing care problems. The problems necessitate nursing intervention in order to lessen the symptoms or to prevent development of other symptoms or complications associated with the withdrawal phenomenon.

The nursing care plan format to be presented here is composed of patient problems, goals or objectives for nursing actions, and nursing approaches or action necessary to achieve the identified goal. The fourth component of the nursing care plan is, of course, evaluation. The patient undergoing withdrawal is in a dynamically changing state. Thus, nursing approaches must be continually evaluated on an ongoing basis to ensure that care is appropriate to the patient's most current need. At the same time, the assessment process continues and provides additional information that must be integrated into the care plan. It is apparent, then, that the nursing care plan is a dynamic tool, one that will change as the patient's nursing care needs are modified.

The care plans illustrated here reflect accepted procedures for each phase of withdrawal. Many of the proposed nursing actions are appropriate for more than one phase and are applicable for use in the detoxification unit as well as the general hospital nursing unit. It is important to remember that creativity in devising individualized methods of delivering care is to be encouraged. Therefore, the approaches discussed here are not meant to represent the "one right way" to accomplish the objectives. At all times the nurse must exercise discretion in the selection and implementation of nursing measures.

Tremulous Phase of Withdrawal

Problem Psychomotor hyperactivity causes possible instability of vital signs.

Goal To detect changes in vital signs that indicate increase in agitation or complicating conditions associated with withdrawal.

Approaches

1 Explain procedure to patient. R: Patient may be highly anxious and uncertain of unfamiliar actions.
2 Monitor blood pressure, pulse, respirations, and temperature as ordered.
3 If tremulousness is severe, monitor vital signs every three to four hours.
4 Record vital signs, note presence of trends of abnormal readings, and communicate with physician unusual results promptly.

Problem Psychomotor hyperactivity decreases comfort and relaxation.

Goal Promote comfort, relaxation, and prevent exacerbation of symptoms.

Approaches

1 Provide quiet environment. R: Stress increases the severity of tremors.
2 Permit family and friends to visit (restrict the number visiting at one time). R: Visits from family and friends during this phase is recommended since they help the patient to maintain his orientation and a hold on reality.
3 Administer tranquilizing medications promptly as ordered. R: Early administration of medication can prevent development of more severe withdrawal symptoms.
4 Do not undersedate. R: Administer an adequate amount of sedative or tranquilizing medication. The alcoholic is accustomed to high levels of sedation in the form of alcohol. Seemingly large doses of medication are necessary to duplicate sedation and prevent exacerbation of symptoms.
5 Maintain environment in neat order. R: Disarray of immediate environment with unnecessary objects scattered about contributes to stress.
6 Allow ambulation ad lib if ordered. Carefully evaluate patient's stability.
7 Provide support in ambulation when needed.

Problem Psychomotor hyperactivity makes it difficult to maintain adequate food intake.

Goal Ensure adequate food intake.

Approaches

1 Diet as ordered.
2 Provide frequent, small feedings. R: Often these are more palatable due to decreased appetite.
3 Administer antiemetic medication before mealtime as ordered. R: Nausea and vomiting often accompany withdrawal.

4 Offer favored foods (if included in diet). Consult with the dietician to determine ways of providing favored foods within diet limitations.
5 Assist with eating—patient may require feeding because of tremors. Use straws and arrange food on tray so that it is easily accessible.
6 Administer vitamin preparations as ordered.

Problem Psychomotor hyperactivity decreases the patient's ability to maintain personal hygiene.

Goal (a) To help the patient maintain dignity and pride through optimal personal hygiene and (b) to promote optimal skin care as the first line of defense against infection.

Approaches

1 Assist the patient with his bath and mouth care.
2 Reassure patient that assistance is temporary. R: Self-reproach at lack of interest in and decreased ability to carry out personal hygiene measures is common.
3 If vomiting is present, assist patient in washing and rinsing mouth.
4 Postpone shaving, nail care, and any other measure requiring patient's attention and restriction in movement.

Problem Psychomotor hyperactivity decreases the patient's ability to protect himself from harm.

Goal Promote safety and protection until patient is capable of reassuming these actions.

Approaches

1 Orient patient to room and immediate environment.
2 Ensure that excess equipment not necessary to care of patient is removed from the room. R: Agitation and high doses of medication can decrease patient's perception of environment and thus he can inadvertently harm himself on unfamiliar objects.
3 Do not allow ambulation if the patient is unsteady due to symptoms or medication.
4 If the patient is severely depressed, ensure that environment is free of hazards that might serve as a means to self-inflict injury. R: Severe depression in alcoholics can lead to suicidal behavior.
5 Ensure that medication is taken in nurse's presence. R: Patient who fears withdrawal may try to hoard medication for those symptoms.
6 Convey a caring and responsible attitude. R: The patient has to feel that those caring for him can protect him from physical harm and development of delirium tremens.

7 Allow smoking of cigarettes if patient is alert and tremors are controlled. If patient is shaky, he *must not* be permitted to smoke unattended.

Problem High anxiety level increases discomfort and increases apprehension.

Goal (a) Assist patient in coping with and decreasing anxiety and (b) prevent increase in anxiety.

Approaches

1 Convey a nonjudgmental, nonpunitive, caring attitude. R: Refer to Chapter 4 for an in-depth discussion of the importance of this approach.
2 Explain procedures, routines, and expected components of the treatment process. R: Orientation to the unknown or unfamiliar decreases anxiety to a certain extent.
3 Allow the patient to express his apprehensions and provide informational support where necessary
4 Concentrate on the present, the here-and-now. R: Dwelling on past behavior and failures only exacerbates the alcoholic's feelings of guilt and remorse.
5 Offer realistic encouragement based on obtainable goals. R: Statements like "Everything will be all right" are simply unrealistic to the person who has a history of failure and loss of self-control. Emphasize short-term goals.
6 Be there. Spend time with the patient and his family when appropriate. R: The alcoholic will test the nurse's sincerity and consistency. Therefore, frequent short visits can serve to establish trust and permit the nurse to continue the assessment process.
7 Assist with positioning and other physical comfort measures as a means of decreasing physical tension.

Problem After prolonged, chronic alcohol intake, possible fluid and electrolyte imbalance may exist.

Goal Promotion and maintenance of optimal fluid and electrolyte balance.

Approaches

1 Accurately record intake and output for first few days of hospitalization; include emesis, diarrhea, estimated loss from diaphoresis. R: Gives an indication of kidney function and the information serves as one basis for fluid replacement and maintenance program.
2 Do not force fluids until it has been established that the patient is dehydrated. R: The antidiuretic effect of prolonged alcohol intake, when diarrhea and vomiting are not present, produces a state of overhydration.
3 When measuring urine output, test for specific gravity. R: This can be done on the nursing unit and gives an indication of the kidney's concentrating ability.

4 Test first stools for guiac. R: This will indicate whether the patient has gastrointestinal dysfunction with resultant bleeding.

5 Be sure that the patient takes in an estimated minimum of fluid over each twenty-four-hour period. R: The alcoholic may not cooperate easily when he feels ill. He therefore needs frequent reinforcement as to the importance of fluid intake.

6 Offer favored fluids, gelatins, sherbets, etc., as between-meal snacks. Make them easily available to the patient as permitted by diet. R: Patient is accustomed to frequent, unscheduled liquid intake. Also serves as diversion.

Nursing Care for Acute Hallucinosis and Delirium Tremens

The patient who has progressed to the second phase of withdrawal, hallucinosis, is also in the impending delirium tremens phase—DTs can be expected at any time. For this reason, the nursing care format in this section will cover both acute hallucinosis and delirium tremens. Remember: Appropriate medical intervention in the tremulous phase of withdrawal can preclude the progression to delirium tremens.

Problem Perceptual ability greatly decreased from hallucinations and delirium.

Goal Promote orientation to reality by controlling environmental stimuli and decreasing possibility of distortion.

Approaches

1 Provide a quiet environment. It may be necessary to place the patient in a small private room or in a room where occasional noisy behavior will not disturb other patients. R: (a) With hallucinations and delirium, occasional shouting, talking, and noisy behavior are to be expected and (b) quietude promotes rest and relaxation.

2 Keep a light on in the room, especially during twilight hours and at night. R: Nighttime shadows and reflections assume greatly distorted appearances without illumination. The patient's hallucinations can thus become more terrifying.

3 Maintain an attitude of caring concern consistent with the attitude shown prior to appearance of advanced symptoms of withdrawal. R: The alcoholic is highly sensitive to attitudes of others. An attitude that conveys disgust or shock at uncontrolled behavior can trigger overt rejection of the nurse by the patient.

4 Do not subject the patient to unnecessary stimulation such as radio, TV, conversation within earshot, banging of equipment, etc. R: The patient is highly sensitive to noise, touch, and visual stimuli, all of which can increase agitation.

5 Continually reorient the patient to reality, his surroundings, and who is caring for him. Do not support hallucinations. R: By validating the existence of hallucinatory content, the nurse adds to the patient's confusion. Assisting the patient in distinguishing between reality and illusion, however, will enable him to more readily regain self-control.

6 Unless specifically ordered or absolutely mandatory, do not allow family and friends to visit the patient. R: (a) Knowledge that people who are significant saw him at his worst can be upsetting to the patient and (b) visitors may not understand the reasons for the patient's behavior toward them and can be greatly upset. Visits should be resumed following the acute episode.

Problem Inability to protect self from physical injury due to severity of uncontrolled psychomotor hyperactivity.

Goal Prevent injury to body and body system.

Approaches

1 Administer tranquilizing and sedating medications promptly as ordered. R: Chemical restraints, when properly given, decrease the necessity of using physical restraints.

2 Place a padded tongue blade or acceptable oral airway at the bedside. R: A means to maintain a patent airway and prevent aspiration of the tongue during seizure activity is essential. Always be prepared for the advent of seizure activity during this phase.

3 Side rails should be in upright position at all times. R: Uncontrolled physical agitation and hallucinations cause the patient to try to get out of bed when it is not safe for him to do so.

4 Remove all unnecessary objects that could conceivably harm the patient during acute restlessness, for example, balkan bedframe, trapeze, bed controls and call lights with cords, dangling or easily movable bed lamps, etc. R: While experiencing acute restlessness, the patient may hit his head or other body part on such objects and sustain injury.

5 Remove extra blankets, bedspreads, and pillows from the bed. R: With extreme agitation and disorientation, it is easy for the patient to entangle himself with these objects.

6 Apply extremity and body restraints as ordered and with caution. R: Chemical restraints are preferred. However, the patient who does not respond to medication and who must be restrained in order to prevent injury will perceive restraints as threatening.

7 When restraints are necessary, check extremities for pulse, warmth, color, and reactivity every two hours.

8 Pad extremity restraints as needed.

9 Remove restraints as soon as it is feasible to do so.

10 Turn and position the patient every two hours if possible. R: The patient experiencing acute withdrawal is subject to the many hazards of any patient confined to bed. When the patient is sedated, turning and positioning is a must.

Problem Inability to maintain personal hygiene.

Goal Maintain hygiene and thereby promote integrity of skin and general relaxation.

Approaches

1 Bathe patient once a day. It may be necessary to do this while the patient is sedated. R: Promotes skin integrity and serves as a comfort and relaxing measure.

2 With cool, damp cloth wipe head, neck, and upper chest periodically. R: With diaphoresis, this cleanses skin and promotes relaxation. Conveys a caring attitude.

3 Keep bed linen and pajamas dry by replacing and changing them promptly when damp or soiled. R: Decreases possibility of skin breakdown and promotes relaxation.

4 Do not shave the patient or carry out other cosmetic nursing actions during this phase. R: They are a source of unnecessary stimulation and subsequent agitation.

5 Mouth care should be done at least every four hours and as needed. If patient is uncooperative, use swabs with accepted hospital solution (glycerin lemon, hydrogen peroxide and water or saline, water, mouth wash, etc.).

6 With incontinence, promptly cleanse skin and dry thoroughly.

Problem Difficulty in maintaining adequate nutritional intake and hydration.

Goal Ensure that nutritional intake and optimal hydration are achieved.

Approaches Refer back to the problem of maintaining adequate food intake because of psychomotor hyperactivity (p. 59). Those general nursing measures are also applicable to this phase. In addition, consider the following actions.

1 Estimate fluid loss from diaphoresis and incontinence.

2 For incontinence, discuss with physicians the use of condom catheter for male patient and indwelling catheter for female patient. Caution: The chronic alcoholic has decreased resistance to infection. Therefore, sterile technique in introducing catheter must be flawless.

3 With intravenous fluid therapy, maintain patency and ordered rate of infusion. R: Disoriented and confused patients will attempt to dislodge infusion by jerking it out or knocking over IV fluid container.

4 When tube feedings are necessary, protect placement of tube. Remember: The tube may be inserted via the mouth when nasal passages cannot be utilized.

5 Lubricate dry, cracked lips with water-soluble lubricant.

Problem Possibly the patient may develop complications that are a result of, or related to, acute withdrawal.

Goal Identify symptoms of evolving complications by continuous assessment.

Approaches

1 Monitor blood pressure, pulse, and respiration every one to two hours and temperature every four hours and as necessary. R: Changes in vital signs can be indicative of circulatory, respiratory, or other complications.

2 Conduct neurological checks at the time of vital sign monitoring, i.e., pupil response to light, response to tactile stimuli, strength of hand grasps, etc. R: Behavior that mimics delirium can be from other causes such as subdural or epidural hematoma or cerebrovascular hemorrhage. These can be identified by the physician when accurate assessment data have been obtained.

3 Inspect skin each shift for signs of breakdown or traumatic injury. R: The delirious patient is usually not aware of specific sites of injury or trauma and so cannot communicate their presence to the nurse. Areas where damage has occurred can become rapidly irritated and infected when the patient is severely agitated.

4 Stimulate patient to cough and deep-breathe at least every two hours while awake. It may be necessary to suction the patient to stimulate the cough reflex. (Note: This is one time when stimulation is appropriate.) R: Pneumonia is a major complication in the alcoholic who has lowered resistance. Prevention of stasis of secretions is vital.

5 Carefully evaluate bladder and bowel function. If unable to void, catherization may be necessary. Again, flawless sterile technique is mandatory. Bowel dysfunction should be identified rapidly and reported to the physician.

As the nurse carries out the nursing measures for the patient experiencing withdrawal, she will continually obtain data on the stability of the patient and the development of complicating conditions. Therefore, the assessment process must be carried out on a continuous basis.

NURSING CARE FOLLOWING WITHDRAWAL

Many of the nursing care measures initiated during the withdrawal phase will be continued and, in some cases, amplified afterward. The patient who does not have a complicating illness in addition to alcoholism usually will not remain in the general hospital for an extended period of time after the acute episode has passed.

Immediately following withdrawal or during the last phases of it, the patient is highly susceptible to nursing intervention on the psychological level. He can remember the fears and discomfort of withdrawal and realizes he doesn't want to repeat the experience. It is during this crucial time that nursing intervention aimed at motivating insight and a desire to maintain abstinence can be most effective. To achieve these aims, the nurse works with other health team members, both lay and professional.

Trusting Nurse-Patient Relationships

The trust established between the nurse and patient from the first day of admission and assessment through withdrawal treatment can now be strengthened. Interaction should center on the patient's feelings and reactions to the treatment process and his plans for continued care. The nurse should plan to spend uninterrupted time with the patient during which plans for the future can be examined and analyzed.

Information regarding outpatient clinics, community resources, and lay organizations can be provided during this time. Ideally, first contacts with chosen agencies or groups should be made while the patient is still in the general hospital. In this way, continuity of care is maintained and the patient establishes new lines of communication and support.

Confronting the Problem

It is often necessary to stimulate the alcoholic to admit to himself the impact excessive drinking behavior has on his life. This becomes essential with the alcoholic who believes he really doesn't have a serious drinking problem because he is successfully abstaining while in the hospital, feels good, and has no craving for alcohol. In this case, the nurse must assist the patient in looking at the results of his drinking behavior, emphasizing the visible effects as well as the emotional disruption: "What impact is drinking having on your job, family, social life, and health?" "How would you categorize your drinking—a problem or not?"

Once the alcoholic has admitted to himself (not the nurse) that his drinking behavior is a severe problem, it is then necessary to identify different methods for solving the problem: "If you didn't have alcohol, how *would* you solve your problems?" This approach emphasizes (1) introspection on the part of the patient, and (2) concentration on the present and future, not the past.

It should be clearly stated at this point that the nurse's role does not include forced confrontation of the problem. If denial and resistance are high, the nurse can communicate realistic information to the alcoholic on the impact problem drinking can have and offer support. Preaching and scare tactics are virtually ineffective.

Nutritional Counseling

As the alcoholic is supported in planning for an alcohol-free future, he should be exposed to nutritional counseling and teaching. Information on healthful nutritional patterns is absolutely mandatory. The focus should not be on negating the patient's entire lifestyle but rather on concrete, realistic ways to alter harmful habits and substitute beneficial ones. The hospital dietician should be consulted and asked to discuss nutritional alternatives with the patient. Emphasis should be placed on the nonnutritive characteristics of beverage alcohol and the necessity of maintaining a high-protein, caloric, and vitamin diet.

The patient who is malnourished from chronic alcoholism will require long-term diet therapy. Family members and concerned friends of the single patient should be brought into the teaching sessions. Often they can reinforce the importance of diet and ensure that the patient adheres to his diet.

Coordination of Continuing Care

In many instances it is part of the nurse's role to coordinate continuing care for the alcoholic. This involves discussions with the patient, his family or close friends, and the physician about the most beneficial and appropriate method for follow-up and continuing care: for example, halfway house, residential treatment program, outpatient clinic, public health nurse visits to the home, etc.

The goal of this aspect of nursing care is to ensure that the patient is aware of available facilities and to coordinate contacts with the chosen facilities or groups as needed. The skills and services of the social worker can be utilized when such professionals are a part of the health care team. In such cases, consultation between the patient and social worker regarding continuing care services often is highly successful.

CARE OF THE ALCOHOLIC WITH ASSOCIATED MEDICAL CONDITIONS

The chronic alcoholic is subject to numerous medical or surgical complications which in one way or another are a result of long-term, excessive alcohol intake. When he is admitted for treatment of these complications, he may already be undergoing withdrawal. If he is not exhibiting withdrawal symptoms, they are to be expected during his hospitalization and treatment. Because the stress of withdrawal will be added to the stress originating from the complication(s), nursing care must focus on decreasing and preventing unnecessary stress on a system that is overburdened.

The nursing care measures presented for withdrawal are applicable to the patient with complications who is also experiencing withdrawal. Astute observation and assessment skills must be employed with special attention to behavior or symptoms that indicate change in the medical or surgical condition. For a review of accepted standard nursing care procedures for patients with the medical conditions discussed below, please refer to medical-surgical nursing texts.

Gastrointestinal Disorders

There is some question about the cause-and-effect relationship between alcoholism and gastrointestinal dysfunctions, which vary in severity from simple gastritis to hemorrhaging gastric ulcers. In any event, the nurse will be caring for the alcoholic who has gastrointestinal dysfunction whether due to the stress of his lifestyle, dietary problems, or the action of alcohol on the gastric mucosa.

Patients with gastrointestinal disorders require prompt administration of appropriate tranquilizing medication so that stress and anxiety will not contribute to the damage that has occurred. In addition to standard procedures intense monitoring of vital signs, maintenance of dietary restrictions, and special feedings are extremely important. During recovery, nutritional counseling that concentrates on necessary diet restrictions is vital.

Pneumonia

Contraction of pneumonia represents a major medical complication because the alcoholic has decreased resistance to infection. Intensive pulmonary care aims at decreasing pulmonary stasis and congestion via nursing actions such as frequent coughing, deep breathing, positioning, and administration of ordered antibiotics. These patients are truly a challenge to the nurse who realizes that sedation and rest are necessary during withdrawal but the sedentary conditions promote pulmonary stasis and congestion. In these cases, it is usually advisable to give sedation for withdrawal symptoms, allow it to take effect, and then carry out pulmonary toilet measures. This sequence allows for tranquilization but not sedation.

Liver and Pancreatic Disorders

Liver and pancreatic disorders are frequently seen in the chronic alcoholic. Many nurses have cared for the alcoholic who has cirrhosis or fatty infiltration of the liver, or hepatic failure. The goals of nursing care include making the patient comfortable, preventing the hazards of immobility, and implementing discharge planning.

Often these patients repeatedly are readmitted to the hospital when the disease process cannot be halted. At the same time, many are unable to cease alcoholic behavior even when there is undeniable evidence of its progressive and ultimately fatal influence on the body. It is sometimes extremely difficult for the nurse to give compassionate care to patients who appear to be knowingly and willingly bringing about their own illness and eventual destruction. Perhaps it would be helpful if the nurse viewed these patients in the same light as she does any terminally ill patient, always remembering that alcoholism *is* an illness.

The alcoholic carries a heavy burden indeed when he realizes that chronic alcoholism has damaged vital body systems beyond repair. Intense feelings of guilt and loss are not unusual under these circumstances. This alcoholic is subject to all the feelings associated with grieving—for himself. He may express anger, denial, frustration, and, most of all, fear. The nurse caring for this patient must realize and understand his need to express these feelings and allow him to do so without conveying disapproval or judgment.

Central Nervous System Disorders

Temporary central nervous system (CNS) disorders associated with alcoholism (peripheral polyneuritis, paralysis, etc.) usually respond to vitamin replacement, physical therapy, and comprehensive nursing care aimed at preventing muscle wasting, atrophy, contractures, and skin breakdown. The alcoholic with a chronic CNS disorder resulting in permanent brain damage is usually hospitalized as a result of his inability to properly care for himself, as evidenced by malnutrition, traumatic injuries, or infection. While the patient is under care it is crucial that continuing care plans be made to ensure follow-up and, when appropriate, custodial care.

While in the hospital, the patient must be protected from self-harm due to confusion and disorientation. Feeding the patient is often necessary because of loss of coordination and sometimes lack of interest in eating. Assessment of neurological stability should be integrated into general nursing care measures since the patient may not be aware of the presence of traumatic injury.

Traumatic Injuries

A multitude of traumatic injuries are a byproduct of alcoholism and can be categorized as complications of alcoholism. Alcoholic victims of automobile accidents (approximately 50 percent of all auto accidents involve a drunken driver or pedestrian) suffer a variety of internal, orthopedic, and neurological injuries. Also, the chronic alcoholic who falls is a prime candidate for repeated orthopedic injuries. The alcoholic who is careless with cigarettes is apt to burn himself in varying degrees of extent and severity.

The nurse caring for the alcoholic with traumatic injury should be acutely aware of the need for thorough and continuous assessment. Ensuring that prescribed treatment measures specific to the injury are carried out is frequently made difficult when the patient begins withdrawal. Restlessness and anxiety must be countered with proper amounts of prescribed tranquilizing medication in order not to disrupt established traction, positioning, or attached monitoring equipment. When chemical restraints are not effective, physical restraints can be applied with utmost care to ensure that the goals of treatment and nursing care are maintained. (Always secure a written physician's order before applying physical restraints.) In some instances, especially when restlessness and agitation will prove detrimental to recovery and restraints (chemical or physical) are not appropriate, there can be no substitute for continuous nursing observation.

SUMMARY COMMENT

The nursing care measures outlined in this chapter represent information and approaches that are applicable to the alcoholic patient in the general hospital. Many of the suggested approaches can be implemented in other treatment sites with the determining factor being the patient's need. At all times the nurse should seek new and innovative approaches. As with other sick persons, the care designed for the alcoholic should be individualized and appropriate to his special needs.

REFERENCES

Bates, Richard C.: "An Alcoholic Treatment Unit in a General Hospital," *Hospital Progress*, 30–36, June 1970.
Block, Marvin A.: "The Alcoholic Needs Hospital Care," *Hospitals*, 42:48–51, May 1, 1968.
Bradley, Nelson J.: "Nurses' Role in the Treatment of Alcoholics," *Chart*, 67:236–237, October 1970.
Burkhalter, Pamela K.: "The Alcoholic in a General Hospital," *Supervisor Nurse*, 3:25–33, April 1972.
"Coverage Made Mandatory," *Alcohol & Health Notes*, 1:3, January 1973.
Devenyi, Paul: "The Treatment of Acute Alcohol Intoxication and Withdrawal," *Current Psychiatric Therapies*, 10:130–134, 1970.
Gelperin, Abraham, and Eve Arlin Gelperin: "The Inebriate in the Emergency Room," *American Journal of Nursing*, 70:1494–1497, July 1970.
Hurley, Clarence W., Jr.: "The Alcoholism Counselor in a General Hospital," *Maryland State Medical Journal*, 19:100, August 1970.
Little, Dolores E., and Doris L. Carnevali: *Nursing Care Planning*, J. B. Lippincott Company, Philadelphia, 1969.
Marsh, Virgil W.: "Insurance for Alcoholism Treatment," *Hospitals*, 45:44–46, July 1, 1971.
Nichols, M. M.: "Acute Alcohol Withdrawal Syndrome in a Newborn," *American Journal of Diseases of Children*, 113:714–715, June 1967.

Ryan, Betty Jane: "Nursing Care Plans: A Systems Approach to Developing Criteria for Planning and Evaluation," *The Journal of Nursing Administration,* **III**:50–58, May–June 1973.

"Statement of the Admission to the General Hospital of Patients with Alcohol and Other Drug Problems," American Hospital Association, Chicago, revised November 19–20, 1969.

"The Truth About Alcohol Dependence," *Journal of the American Medical Association,* **211**:114–115, January 5, 1970.

Who Cares About an Alcoholism Program in the General Hospital?, American Hospital Association, Chicago, 1972.

Chapter 6

The Detoxification Unit

In recent years many general hospitals and certain community based health care facilities have instituted detoxification units for the treatment and care of alcoholic and drug abuse patients. These specialty units vary greatly in the approach and extent of services available.

DEFINING DETOXIFICATION UNIT

Since not all detoxification units subscribe to the same philosophy and treatment program, it is not possible to define such a unit in limited terms. Therefore, a general definition that describes the overall philosophy of this approach is offered.

The detoxification unit is a specialty unit designed for the acute treatment and care of the alcoholic or drug abuser undergoing withdrawal or detoxification from a dependence-producing substance.

Most detoxification units are set up as a separate unit. They may or may not be associated with a home unit, that is, a nursing unit to which the detoxified patient will be transferred after withdrawal is completed. Placement of the detoxification unit in a general hospital allows for comprehensive evaluation of the patient's physical and psychological condition. Also, facilities for emergency and intensive care can be utilized in this setting when the need arises.

Some communities have established detoxification units in community based health care facilities such as nursing homes or private organizations. Alcoholics who enter these units receive treatment and care during the withdrawal process and, if suitable, can participate in the continuing care and rehabilitation programs offered by the facility. A potential disadvantage of the detoxification unit in such a setting arises when the patient progresses to severe delirium tremens or experiences severe, life-threatening complications. In these cases, the facility may not have the necessary equipment and medical staff to treat the acutely ill patient and must then transfer the patient to a general hospital. To plan for such eventualities, these community facilities usually make specific arrangements with nearby general hospitals to accept and treat the transferred alcoholic patient.

PHILOSOPHY AND GOALS OF DETOXIFICATION UNITS

The philosophy that guides the operation of detoxification units is based in part on the following beliefs:

Alcoholism is an illness and as such is subject to treatment.

Alcoholic behavior can be interrupted and arrested.

Repeated admissions for detoxification may be necessary before long-lasting sobriety can be achieved.

Withdrawal from alcohol or other drugs can be controlled in a specially designed unit.

The severely intoxicated person is not a criminal and should be allowed to sober up and undergo detoxification in a controlled, equipped environment.

Rapid patient turnover characteristic of treatment for withdrawal is compatible with an area designed for this purpose.

Repeated treatment for detoxification and alcoholism in a beneficial setting may prevent exacerbation of physical conditions associated with alcoholism.

The nurse working in the detoxification unit must believe and internalize this philosophy if she is to be effective with her patients and receive satisfaction from her chosen area of specialization.

The goals of the detoxification unit apply to the person who is acutely intoxicated as well as the alcoholic in withdrawal. General goals of detoxification units can be summarized as follows:

To control and prevent progression in severity of signs and symptoms associated with withdrawal from alcohol

To provide skilled care and treatment for the intoxicated patient and the patient undergoing withdrawal

To initiate continuing care and follow-up measures for the alcoholic who has been detoxified

To prevent the appearance of or exacerbation of conditions associated with alcoholism

To decrease the incidence of alcoholism by interrupting and treating it in a professional manner

To accomplish these goals, the detoxification unit must utilize the knowledge and skills of the nurse, the physician, the social workers, and the alcoholism counselor, to name a few.

LIMITATIONS OF THE DETOXIFICATION UNIT

Detoxification units characteristically establish limitations or boundaries regarding the services they are equipped to provide. These limitations are necessary elements of the policies which govern unit operations and are common to most specialty units.

Admission Policies

Policies that establish admission criteria for detoxification units vary. Generally there are three approaches to admission:

All alcoholics who are intoxicated or are experiencing withdrawal symptoms are admitted regardless of the number of prior admissions.

Alcoholics who have been repeatedly detoxified for a specified number of times will not be readmitted. The rationale for this policy is the belief that the necessary sincerity and motivation to sustain sobriety are not present when the alcoholic repeatedly must be detoxified.

Only alcoholics and problem drinkers are admitted. Those with other drug abuse problems are not admitted.

Changing public drunkenness laws have had definite impact on the admission policies (and possibly the creation) of detoxification units. In those states where incarceration for public drunkenness is no longer supported by law, detoxification units accept all intoxicated and withdrawing alcoholics or problem drinkers. In states that have not enacted such legislation, detoxification unit admission policies may be established by each facility.

Length of Stay

The alcoholic's response to treatment for withdrawal determines the length of stay. Generally withdrawal can be completed within three to five days. In some cases, the alcoholic will be discharged from the unit in two days or as long as ten days following admission.

A second determining factor is the presence of multiple addiction. Many alcoholics become dependent on sedatives, barbiturates, or analgesics and may ingest these with alcohol to produce potentially disastrous results. The patient who is to be detoxified from more than one habituating substance may remain in the unit beyond the normal time allotment.

The individual detoxification unit may establish a minimum length of stay which all patients must agree to in order to be admitted. Programs with a requirement of this nature often include services and treatment beyond detoxification.

The desire and ability of the patient to remain in the detoxification unit is another determinant of length of stay. After sobering up, some alcoholics may reject further detoxification treatment or elope from the unit. Since most units are not locked and are frequently very busy, patient departure may go unnoticed. Depending on the resources and policies of the individual unit, efforts may be made to persuade the patient to return for completion or continuing treatment, or the patient will be officially discharged following a specified period of unauthorized absence.

Extent of Services

Upon admittance to the detoxification unit and depending on the patient's condition, a routine physical evaluation will be conducted. The alcoholic may receive tranquilizing medication before or after this evaluation is completed. He may receive a cursory examination to rule out acute injury and be put to bed. When he awakens, a more thorough physical examination will take place. Routine blood studies and urinalysis are included in the physical evaluation. In those cases where traumatic injury or an accompanying medical condition is identified, further evaluation is initiated. With this information, the physician can formulate a treatment program that will meet the patient's individual needs.

Services available to the alcoholic, in addition to actual detoxification, include initial education about alcoholism, referrals for existing medical conditions, counseling, and plans for continuing care. It must be emphasized that these services are made *available* to the alcoholic but are not mandatory. Because of the patient's physical condition and decreased mental acuity as he experiences withdrawal, in-depth counseling and therapy are not feasible during the short time period in the detoxification unit and should be delayed.

Planning for continuing care involves the social worker, nurse, physician, patient, and family when appropriate. Whether or not this aspect of treatment is included in the services offered by a particular detoxification unit is determined by the unit's goals and philosophy.

NURSING IN THE DETOXIFICATION UNIT

The nurse is the key figure in the detoxification unit. Her astute observations and decisions determine, in large part, the success of the treatment regimen.

Establishing Priorities

The goals of the detoxification unit are also the goals of nursing care, but establishing priorities also assumes vital importance.

The first priority is to provide physical care for the intoxicated patient or the patient undergoing withdrawal. To accomplish this goal, those nursing measures applicable to the nursing assessment, with particular attention to the physical and psychological components, should be implemented. As the nursing assessment is carried out, the nurse initiates appropriate measures aimed at meeting the physical and immediate psychological needs of the patient. (Refer to Chapter 5 for an in-depth discussion of the nursing assessment and nursing care measures applicable to nursing in the detoxification unit.)

The second priority is discussion of the drinking problem with the alcoholic. The physical discomfort of the patient, his disorientation, and the effects of medication may prevent the nurse from talking with him until detoxification is largely completed. Once communication is possible the nurse should determine whether the patient is sincere enough and motivated enough to participate in further treatment. Information about available treatment programs, including an introduction to Alcoholics Anonymous is included.

Nursing Skills and Background

The nurse who chooses to work in the detoxification unit should have experience in medical and/or psychiatric nursing. The assessment and care of the alcoholic requires an ability to identify potential medical complications as well as existing conditions not known to the physician. Experience in caring for patients with illnesses of varying degrees of severity is invaluable and easily transferable to the alcoholic in the detoxification unit.

Educational preparation and experience in psychiatric nursing is extremely valuable in dealing with the alcoholic who tends to be skilled in the manipulation of others. This is not to say, however, that the medical nurse cannot acquire similar skills in dealing with the manipulative alcoholic. (This also holds true for the psychiatrically prepared nurse who wishes to acquire medical nursing expertise.)

Nurses working in the detoxification unit have considerable responsibility in determining when the patient should be sedated and the amount of prescribed medication that should be given. Some physicians write sedative and tranquilizer medication orders strictly on a p.r.n. basis and rely on the nurse to judge when and how often the patient will receive the prescribed drug. In order to carry out this responsibility, the nurse must be thoroughly familiar with the actions of the drugs and the status of the patient.

The bedside nursing care measures presented in Chapter 5 under Nursing Care Planning for the Patient Experiencing Withdrawal from Alcohol are directly applicable to the detoxification unit. A differentiating characteristic of the detoxification unit, as opposed to the general hospital setting, is the intense effort made to prevent progression to delirium tremens. In most cases, the alcoholic who is admitted to the unit is not in delirium tremens and thus immediate intervention can prevent the advent of severe withdrawal.

THE INTOXICATED PATIENT

A major advantage of detoxification units is their policy of admitting persons who are intoxicated. When the intoxicated patient is admitted, nursing care measures emphasize the following:

1 Protection of the patient from self-induced injury
2 Provision of a quiet, safe environment to sleep the alcohol off
3 Periodic monitoring of the patient's condition to ensure system stability
4 Physical assessment to identify possible traumatic injury
5 Implementation of medical orders

The intoxicated patient often will be talkative. He may swear off drinking forever and sound like he means it. The nurse should listen to the patient but not necessarily believe everything he says. Too often the promises of sobriety and pledges to seek long-term treatment made while inebriated prove false when the patient is sober. The nurse should remember that this behavior is characteristic of the alcoholic and not condemn him when he is unable to follow through.

Often the intoxicated patient is subject to overreaction to the strange environment and people in the detoxification unit. The nurse can alleviate such anxiety and fears by constantly reorienting him and reassuring him of his safety. Once again, a sincere and genuine approach by the nurse can be very successful in calming the excited, inebriated patient.

Treatment in certain detoxification units may include induction of a rapid decrease in blood alcohol level by the intravenous administration of fructose in saline solutions. This measure increases the rate of alcohol metabolism and thereby decreases the intoxicating effects of alcohol.

AFTER DETOXIFICATION

After detoxification from alcohol is completed, the patient may be discharged, referred to long-term treatment programs, or transferred to a residential treatment center. It is at this crucial time that the nurse can exert influence on the very susceptible alcoholic and urge further treatment. Frequently such efforts prove to be most successful when the nurse volunteers in a very positive manner to make the necessary arrangements for referral to other facilities or programs. Coordination of transportation to community facilities is also very useful.

THE REWARDS

The nurse who wants to work in the detoxification unit can anticipate a professional challenge, a rapidly changing patient population, a high degree of responsibility and opportunity to exercise nursing judgment, and satisfaction in the knowledge that sick people are being cared for, not incarcerated. The most rewarding experience of all, however, occurs when the nurse learns that her patient *did* seek continuing care, was able to maintain sobriety, and is now enjoying life once again.

REFERENCES

Canning, Mary G.: "Care of Alcoholic Patients," *American Journal of Nursing*, **65**:113–114, November 1965.

Kunian, Louis, James Wasco, and Lawrence Hulefeld: "Sweets for the Alcoholic," *Emergency Medicine*, **5**:44–46, January 1973.

Matkom, Anthony J.: "An Alcoholic Treatment Center in a General Hospital," *Quarterly Journal of Studies on Alcohol*, **32**:453–456, June 1969.

"The Manhattan Bowery Project. Detoxification: A New Concept of Care," *The Journal of Practical Nursing*, 22–27, December 1968.

Whyte, Henry J., and Charles G. Tildon: "Treating Acute Alcoholics," *Hospitals*, **44**:58–62, May 16, 1970.

Chapter 7

Psychiatric Nursing
and the Alcoholic

After the alcoholic has undergone withdrawal, he may choose to continue treatment in a psychiatric setting that provides long-term therapy, care, and rehabilitation. A major advantage of many of these facilities is their institutional nature, i.e., a safe, secure, and controlled environment. As one approach, among many, to the treatment of alcoholism, psychiatric therapy has met with limited success. Approximately one-third of those treated are able to maintain sobriety for an extended period of time.

CHARACTERISTICS OF THE LONG-TERM
PSYCHIATRIC SETTING

Years ago the facilities available for comprehensive, long-term treatment of alcoholics consisted largely of state mental institutions. Fortunately this is no longer the case. Today there are numerous outlets for long-term therapy and rehabilitation.

General Hospital

Certain large general hospitals have created long-term programs located adjacent to their acute psychiatric units. Although these programs are not commonplace, placement of the alcoholic in such locations allows for extensive utilization of not only psychiatric facilities but also necessary medical services.

Day clinics sponsored by the general hospital are an important source of continued treatment for the alcoholic living in the community. In many instances the clinics are used as the meeting place for group therapy sessions, or they may serve as the dispensation site for medications used in various treatment programs.

Day Hospital

Some private and publicly financed psychiatric institutions have created day hospital programs specifically for long-term treatment. These programs are designed so that the alcoholic can continue to live in the community while participating in daily group therapy sessions. He may spend eight to ten hours per day, up to seven days a week, in the day hospital, depending on his progress, his home responsibilities, and the limitations of transportation.

The advantages of day hospital programs are numerous:

Daily Activity For the alcoholic who is learning to cope with his desire to drink, daily participation in a structured program provides security and a source of self-respect. It is a meaningful activity outside the home that resembles employment and provides personal satisfaction in learning to live without alcohol.

Self-controlled Abstinence The alcoholic returns home daily, where the temptation to drink is not restricted by treatment boundaries. Each day that he successfully meets this challenge, his strength to maintain sobriety is increased.

Family Cohesiveness As the alcoholic maintains abstinence and gains insight into his behavior, his family and friends can see these changes. They in turn can acquire understanding of the problems he faces. Furthermore, when the alcoholic family member can remain in the home while treatment continues, the cohesiveness of the family can be strengthened and disruption decreased.

Psychiatric Hospitals

Long-term residential treatment of alcoholism and any underlying psychological problems can be accomplished in the public or privately financed psychiatric hospital. Programs located in such institutions offer a controlled environment in which intensive psychotherapy and group therapy can take place. In addition, many of these institutions also care for the chronic alcoholic with organic brain damage who is no longer able to care for himself. Efforts are aimed at custodial care and treatment rather than rehabilitation and resocialization.

Length of Stay

The length of stay in one of the long-term programs varies considerably. Some programs are six weeks long while others extend beyond a year. If the program is highly structured and geared to help as many patients as possible, the length of stay is usually short. Cost to the program and the patient is also a very real consideration in evaluating the length of a treatment program. Since a majority of these programs are voluntary, the alcoholic may refuse to continue participation or leave the program before it is completed, especially if he becomes frustrated and challenged by the treatment.

Admission Criteria

As with length of stay, the criteria for admission to long-term programs vary greatly. Usually detoxification is not included in such programs and thus the applicant must have previously undergone withdrawal before he can be accepted. Some detoxification units and general hospitals make arrangements with psychiatric treatment programs to transfer the stabilized alcoholic directly from the hospital to the treatment center.

Certain programs exclude the skid-row alcoholic on the basis of demonstrated poor treatment response. Other programs have an open admission policy with no restriction on the number of repeat admissions or the type of patient accepted.

Generally it is desirable for the alcoholic to be drug-free when he enters a treatment program, i.e., no longer taking any tranquilizing or sedating medication. Because most of these programs concentrate on helping the alcoholic face his problems and the subsequent desire to find relief in excessive drinking, use of drugs would only supply another chemical escape mechanism. In some cases, however, it is necessary to temporarily employ tranquilizing medications as an adjunct to the treatment regimen. Such medication is carefully controlled and discontinued as soon as possible. As the patient begins to understand his problem and responds to therapy, he may be given the responsibility of monitoring his own medication. He can take it if he thinks he really needs it. If the privilege is abused, this responsibility is reassumed by staff members.

Many long-term programs are organized in such a way that alcoholics who have various psychiatric disorders can receive treatment (disorders include schizophrenia, sociopathy, and neuroticism). In order to provide such a variety of services, the program must be comprehensive enough to accommodate diverse psychiatric approaches (e.g., psychodrama and therapy groups with mixed or homogeneous membership).

Patient Population

Psychiatric treatment facilities for alcoholism provide services for three main patient populations: (1) the alcoholic who has no apparent acute psychiatric illness but who has underlying psychological problems; (2) the alcoholic who has an identifiable acute psychiatric illness—approximately 15 percent of all alcoholics; and (3) the chronic alcoholic who has resultant organic brain damage—many in this group are elderly persons. Alcoholics in the first patient population constitute the majority of the participants in most long-term psychiatric treatment.

PHILOSOPHY AND GOALS OF LONG-TERM PSYCHIATRIC TREATMENT

Long-term psychiatric programs generally share many of the same basic beliefs, which are used to formulate the treatment process. These beliefs serve as the basis for a philosophy that includes the following premises:

1 Alcoholism, or alcoholic behavior, is a symptom of an underlying psychoneurosis or behavior disorder. Just as fever is viewed as a symptom of physiological dysfunction, so alcoholic behavior is viewed as a symptom or a reflection of personality or character dysfunction.
2 In order to achieve long-lasting improvement and abstinence, it is necessary for the patient to gain insight into the motivations for his alcoholic behavior.
3 The alcoholic can be helped to acknowledge and accept the fact that excessive drinking is a reflection of underlying psychological disorder.
4 The alcoholic can be helped to learn new approaches to problem solving that will replace the need to depend on alcohol.
5 Long-term treatment in a controlled environment creates a less stressful atmosphere in which efforts to acquire personal insight can be facilitated.

It is important to remember that individual psychiatric treatment programs develop a more in-depth philosophy to meet the specific needs of the patients served. For this reason, the components presented here represent general areas of consideration only.

An important concept to always keep in mind when considering the formulation of goals is that the health professional can only *help* the alcoholic. No one can force long-lasting improvement or insight on him—only he can do that for himself. Therefore, the goals of the nurse and other health team members become to guide, to motivate, to facilitate, and to encourage abstinence, insight, and new methods of problem solving.

Besides these fundamental goals, another must be stated: to provide an environment in which resocialization can take place. This is extremely important for the person who has lost self-respect, close interpersonal ties, employment, and self-confidence. To be assisted in regaining these precious elements of life is a specific goal of long-term psychiatric treatment.

THE ROLE OF THE NURSE IN RELATION TO THE TREATMENT PROCESS

The essence of the nurse's role in psychiatric treatment of the alcoholic is *support*. Support in this context takes many forms and may be passive or active. It is passive when it (1) aids in providing a relaxed, open milieu in which the patient begins to examine his behavior; (2) is characterized by sympathetic, nonjudgmental interaction with the alcoholic; (3) conveys respect for him as a person of worth, dignity, and individuality; and (4) nurtures his efforts to understand his alcoholism and the problems that contributed to it. Of course, the manner in which these areas of passive support are implemented may include active elements; for example, providing a relaxed milieu may be accomplished by encouraging the alcoholic to participate in ward government activities.

The nurse can provide active support by (1) encouraging participation in group therapy, (2) promoting the patient's independence and responsibility, and (3) reinforcing a consistent approach to the patient.

The psychiatric treatment process for the alcoholic has many components. In this section, each one will be identified, a brief description will be given, and the nursing approaches applicable to the component will be presented. It is important to remember that many of the approaches are appropriate for more than one aspect of the treatment and care process, and are separately delineated only for the sake of clarity of presentation. Also, not all psychiatric treatment programs will use all the components to be discussed here.

Component

Establishment of a therapeutic community or milieu.

Description

In order for the alcoholic to achieve insight into his alcoholism, understand the problems that led to it, and develop more constructive methods to cope with future problems, he must be in an environment that fosters such introspection. To establish such surroundings is the objective of the therapeutic community.

Nursing Approaches

1 When communicating with the alcoholic, convey respect for him as someone who is being treated for an illness. Impart the idea that slips or relapses are mistakes but not an indication of failure. For the alcoholic who has unsuccessfully attempted various methods of achieving sobriety, knowledge that the nurse and other caretakers do not regard such behavior as failure can add greatly to his trust and confidence in the treatment. On the other hand, the nurse should not convey an attitude that relapse is *expected* and therefore does not constitute a problem in the recovery process. Episodes of relapse to drinking behavior impede the recovery process, but do not necessarily block it entirely.

2 Refer to the alcoholic as a resident or participant in the program, not as a psychiatric patient. This approach is especially important in the beginning phase of long-term treatment, when the alcoholic feels rejected and worthless. Labeling him as "mentally ill" only confirms his worst suspicions. As he begins to understand the factors contributing to his illness, he is better able to accept the idea that he had or may have psychiatric problems.

3 Make work assignments for the alcoholic when this is a nursing responsibility. Many programs use work assignments as a means of encouraging responsibility, thus channeling the patient's excess energy, providing meaningful activity, and fostering a sense of self-worth and capability. Residents are also usually responsible for the maintenance of their own living area and person.

4 Encouraging and, in some cases, requiring the resident to participate in patient government activities is another aspect of the nurse's role. In these meetings, the residents may participate in the establishment of ward rules and regulations, discuss and settle grievances, and sometimes contribute to decisions on therapy measures.

5 Encourage and foster informal interaction with the alcoholic as a means of adding to a relaxed, open environment. For many alcoholics the availability of the nurse and other staff members for informal, spontaneous communication is one of the most meaningful aspects of treatment. Often all the person wants is a sympathetic listener to hear his feelings and ideas. Thus, *being there* is an essential component of the nurse's role.

6 Conduct staff conferences. The nurse who encounters problems in working closely with the alcoholic or who wishes to seek advice should feel free to initiate a staff conference as a means of obtaining guidance and direction. In such conferences the problems with the alcoholic can be discussed and a consistent approach to solving them can be developed. In addition to problem-oriented conferences, there are patient-centered conferences which may or may not include the alcoholic. They concentrate on discussion of and plans for the treatment and care of the newly admitted resident. Subsequent staff conferences discuss the progress of the alcoholic and evaluate the need for modification in the approach.

7 At all times the approach to the alcoholic should be *consistent*. The establishment of limits is absolutely mandatory when dealing with people who have achieved great skill in the manipulation of others. These limits should

not only be clear and explicit but also reasonable, rather than arbitrary. When all members of the team use the same approach, manipulative behavior is discouraged. The alcoholic will usually test the consistency of those caring for him. Finding that different members of the nursing staff establish different limits can encourage further manipulation and loss of confidence in the caretakers.

8 The atmosphere of the treatment program must include *hope.* The nurse contributes to this atmosphere by conveying confidence in the alcoholic's ability to maintain sobriety and complete the program. The nurse's feelings must be genuine, however, and communicated in a sincere, honest, and matter-of-fact manner.

Component

Educational programs on alcoholism.

Description

A fundamental of treatment for alcoholism is the provision of educational information on the dynamics and characteristics of the disease. Various means are employed to accomplish this: films, informal talks, seminars, literature, lectures, etc. Hopefully, the alcoholic will apply this knowledge to his own situation.

Nursing Approaches

1 In many instances, the nurse is responsible for coordinating and organizing the educational programs.

2 The nurse participates in some of the programs by giving talks or lectures on various aspects of alcoholism, by acting as a resource person in the seminar discussions, or by specifically ensuring that the alcoholic is provided with pertinent literature.

3 Informal discussions with the alcoholic on the educational programs or the literature given to him to read serve as a method of clarifying content and eliciting questions. Such discussions reinforce the material and help to establish open lines of communication between the patient and the nurse.

Component

Participation by the alcoholic in group therapy.

Description

Group therapy, in this context, consists of periodic or scheduled group meetings of alcoholics. A trained therapist may or may not conduct the sessions. The patient in the long-term treatment situation takes part in many groups:

activity groups, groups that emphasize the symptom of drinking, or psycho-dynamically oriented groups. Group therapy places the alcoholic in contact with other alcoholics. The benefits of such contact include the mutual giving of support, honesty in examining alcoholism, and shared guidance in learning how to solve problems without resorting to alcohol.

Nursing Approaches

1 The nurse may function as the group leader in orientation groups for newly admitted alcoholics. In these cases, the nurse provides information and answers questions about various aspects of the treatment program.

2 As a group member, the nurse encourages independent problem solving and helps the alcoholic to develop ability in this area. By not solving his problems for him but turning the question or problem back to the group for suggestions, the nurse can stimulate group involvement in the problem-solving process.

3 The nurse's role as a group leader in the informal group is much the same as her group member role. However, impromptu group sessions may simply be geared to blowing off steam and expressing frustrations and anxieties. In these cases, the nurse attempts to foster an atmosphere in which the alcoholic can feel free to express his feelings. For example, the nurse may notice that a particular resident is very irritable and short-tempered with fellow residents and the staff. If one-to-one communication is not successful in reducing feelings, perhaps an open-ended question in the informal group may serve to stimulate the person to discuss what's bothering him. In this situation, other residents can contribute their observations and even share their similar experiences.

4 As a cotherapist for the group that is psychodynamically oriented, the nurse tries to stimulate confrontation of problem drinking or alcoholism by the group member. If the patient has acknowledged his problem, he then moves toward identifying the underlying motivation for excessive drinking. The nurse works closely with the trained therapist (usually a psychiatrist) in determining the most appropriate method of motivating the alcoholic to gain this kind of insight.

At this stage the nurse reinforces the well part of his personality. If he demonstrates ability in certain activities, he is encouraged to assume more responsibility in these areas. In this way, he is gradually stimulated to increase his independence in areas where he is succeeding—this behavior can then form the foundation for initial reacquisition of self-confidence and self-satisfaction.

Component

Maintenance of physical well-being.

Description

Before the person is admitted or as the first step in the program, the alcoholic is given a thorough physical examination. At this time, any medical problems he may have are identified and evaluated and treatment is initiated. As he progresses through the program, these physiological problems must also be attended to and frequently evaluated.

Nursing Approaches

1 Administration of ordered medication and treatments for medical conditions is a responsibility of the nurse. Some areas of this responsibility can often be delegated to other nursing personnel. As a means of engendering self-confidence and responsibility, the nurse may teach the patient how to administer his treatments, at first under supervision and later on his own. (Such delegation, of course, depends on the complexity of the treatment procedure and the patient's capabilities.)

2 Because the nurse is in frequent contact with the alcoholic, she has ample opportunity to evaluate his general physical well-being. For example, she may notice changes in his skin condition, rapid tiring, or loss of appetite. This information should be reported to the physician along with any additional data the nurse collects.

3 Nutritional counseling may not always be a part of the nurse's role in all long-term treatment programs. However, when it is, it can serve as one means of encouraging family participation in the program. The nurse provides nutritional information for the alcoholic and encourages the family to participate in the teaching sessions. Emphasis is placed on high-calorie, high-protein, and high-vitamin foods for the underweight or malnourished patient. Any underlying medical condition must be taken into account when nutritional counseling is done.

Component

Follow-up care after the alcoholic is discharged.

Description

Most long-term programs include follow-up care. The objectives for such follow-up care are to (1) ensure that the alcoholic is maintaining sobriety, (2) determine if he is following prescribed continuing treatment regimens, (3) prevent precipitation of crises by identifying evolving problem areas, and (4) gather statistical data that can be used as a basis for research and program modification.

Nursing Approaches

1 The nurse may determine the alcoholic's status by coordinating home visits through the public health nurse. In some cases, the nurse who cared for the patient in the treatment program may make home visits for a specified period of time following discharge.

2 Telephone communication by the nurse to the alcoholic is an accepted

method of maintaining contact and assisting in achieving the objectives of follow-up care.

3 Certain treatment programs encourage the discharged alcoholic to continue to participate in group therapy until he feels comfortable without such involvement. Under these circumstances, the nurse has another opportunity to evaluate his progress.

SUMMARY COMMENT

The role of the nurse in the long-term treatment of alcoholics is a vital one. The nursing approaches presented represent current, accepted nursing practice. As new and innovative programs for the treatment of alcoholism are created, the role of the nurse will expand and be modified accordingly.

One area deserving mention as an example of the expanding role of the nurse is nursing therapy. In certain alcoholism programs it has been found that the nurse with advanced preparation in psychiatric nursing, usually at the master's level, is quite successful in contributing to long-term treatment. Nurse practitioners in this specialty conduct group therapy sessions with alcoholics and work in a counseling capacity with their families. As this role is more clearly defined and described by those who are involved in its creation, more opportunities for such highly skilled nursing practice will undoubtedly arise.

REFERENCES

Andruzzi, Ellen A.: "Nursing Care for the Alcoholic," *Maryland State Medical Journal,* **19**:93–94, February 1970.

Blane, Howard T.: *The Personality of the Alcoholic,* Harper & Row, New York, 1968.

Blum, Eva Maria, and Richard H. Blum: *Alcoholism: Modern Psychological Approaches to Treatment,* Jossey-Bass Inc., San Francisco, 1967.

Fox, Vernelle, and George D. Lowe: "Day-Hospital Treatment of the Alcoholic Patient," *Quarterly Journal of Studies on Alcohol,* **29**:634–641, September 1968.

Harris, E. Faye: "Early Treatment for Motivated Alcoholics," *Hospital & Community Psychiatry,* **22**:176–178, June 1971.

Hartman, Clarence H.: "A Structured Treatment Program for Alcoholics," *Hospital & Community Psychiatry,* **22**:179–182, June 1971.

Moore, Marcia: "An Account of a Nurse's Role and Functions in an Alcoholic Treatment Program," *Journal of Psychiatric Nursing and Mental Health Services,* **8**:21–27, May–June 1970.

Scott, Edward M.: *Struggles in an Alcoholic Family,* Charles C Thomas, Springfield, Ill., 1970.

Simon, Alexander, Leon J. Epstein, and Lynn Reynolds: "Alcoholism in the Geriatric Mentally Ill," *Geriatrics,* 125–131, October 1968.

Chapter 8

Nursing Care of the Alcoholic in the Community

The nurse working in the community has many opportunities for contact with alcoholics and their families. Community health nursing involves the public health nurse, the industrial or occupational health nurse, the office nurse, the school health nurse, and the nurse working in innovative health care programs. The role of each of these groups varies according to the specific needs of the patient population served. The major challenges faced by the community health nurse in general are: (1) difficulty in identifying the alcoholic in the community and (2) succeeding in motivating him to seek treatment. In spite of these obstacles, however, many nurses working in the community derive professional satisfaction in working with the alcoholic and his family.

ROLE OF THE PUBLIC HEALTH NURSE

The public health nurse (PHN) has a significant contribution to make to the care of the alcoholic and especially to his family. Her role consists of urging the known alcoholic to seek treatment. When such efforts prove unsuccessful, the PHN can shift her focus to the overall care and well-being of his family. In the following sections, components of the PHN's role as it relates to alcoholics will be discussed.

Identification of the Alcoholic

The public health nurse is in a unique position to identify the emerging or existent alcoholic in the community. Because her role includes gaining access to the homes of those in need of health care, she can assess the stability and total health needs of the family as a unit. The sensitive nurse can pick up clues that indicate a drinking problem exists within the family.

In some cases, the client the nurse sees in the home requires nursing care for a medical condition that is related to or a result of alcoholism. The PHN may be made aware of a drinking problem by direct requests for help from family members or from the alcoholic himself. In either instance, the clues the nurse identifies are overt and the problem with alcohol is quite visible. Under these circumstances, the nurse's intervention to help the alcoholic and his family is requested and usually accepted. Unfortunately this is not the case with a large portion of alcoholics who deny their illness, refuse treatment, and are somewhat successful in hiding their problem from those outside the home. What, then, are some of the conditions that would indicate a problem with alcohol exists within the family?

Financial Problems The wife of the alcoholic may express concern about financial difficulties in order to seek public assistance or just as a means of relieving anxiety. As the alcoholic's illness progresses, he is less able to fulfill the responsibilities and requirements of his job and so loss of employment becomes a genuine threat to the family's well-being. If the spouse or other family members express such feelings, the nurse should seek additional information to determine whether the financial problem is related to alcohol abuse and is indeed threatening the family's stability.

Physical Abuse Although this is not a generalized phenomenon, some alcoholics do physically abuse members of their family while intoxicated. Evidence of bruises, noticeable personality changes, and/or unexplained temporary refusal by family members to allow the PHN to enter the home can be indicative of recent abuse. In order to verify suspicions, the nurse must interact with the affected family members to determine if the injury or change in behavior was indeed a result of physical abuse inflicted by the alcoholic. If she cannot make contact with the family, she should consider use of another communication source to get the desired information, e.g., the social worker, chaplain, or physician.

Appearance of the Home   Sometimes the nurse can pick up environmental clues that indicate the existence of alcoholism. Because heavy cigarette smoking frequently is associated with excessive drinking, burns in carpeting or furniture may indicate carelessness while intoxicated. Such burns can come about when ashes are dropped or when the inebriated person falls asleep with a lighted cigarette in his hand. If the problem drinker is a female, or wife, the home may be disordered and messy. Since the PBN normally makes home visits in the daytime, she has an opportunity to evaluate the disarray and may even see empty bottles of liquor or other evidence of day drinking. (If the female alcoholic is still trying to maintain a semblance of normalcy in front of her family, these tangible bits of evidence will usually be removed before the family returns in the evening.)

Increased Sick Leave   As the PHN makes home visits, she may notice that the breadwinner is frequently at home on sick leave. When the spouse continually offers excuses for this behavior but refuses to allow the nurse to offer assistance, the nurse has another clue as to the existence of problem drinking. She also has a valuable clue to the manner in which the spouse is coping with the problem.

Female Alcoholic   If the PHN can gain access to the home of the female alcoholic, she may see very tangible evidence of alcoholism in the physical appearance of the woman. A disheveled, unkempt appearance, bags under the eyes, bloodshot eyes, poor personal hygiene, and dry skin are signs of lack of self-care characteristic of the alcoholic. The alcoholic may attribute her appearance to the illness the PHN is treating, and indeed some of these manifestations may well be a result of the illness. Therefore, the nurse should keep these clues in mind as she observes other behavior patterns that can identify a drinking problem.

Denial of the Problem   Perhaps one of the most potent clues to the existence of a severe drinking problem is excessive denial of *any* problem. When the nurse asks the patient or the spouse if there are any problems with alcohol in the family and receives definite and forceful negative replies, she must reassess the clues she has gathered. One of the alcoholic's most successful barriers to his treatment and recovery is his own denial. If the nurse accepts such denial at face value she may well be overlooking the basic problem. Also, the PHN should always keep in mind that the alcoholic is known to be manipulative. He or she may offer varied excuses for a health problem, may shift responsibility for it to other family members, the PHN, or any number of other persons. Thus, manipulative behavior in itself is another clue to the existence of alcoholism.

Nutritional Clues Home visits for dealing with medical problems of a non-alcoholic family member provide an important opportunity to assess the nutritional status of the family as a whole. When all family members except the suspected alcoholic appear to be well nourished and when there are visible signs of poor nutrition in only the suspected alcoholic, the nurse has a further clue to confirm her diagnosis of alcoholism.

The PHN may find herself acting the part of a detective in seeking confirmation of her diagnosis. Yet, if she is to be an effective advocate of family health and stability, she must assume this role when necessary—and nowhere is this more necessary than in casefinding with alcoholics. Therefore, the areas of consideration presented in this section may serve as useful and initial guidelines for the nurse who suspects that a problem with alcohol exists but feels she needs more evidence before intervening on the patient's or the family's behalf.

Initiation of Treatment for Alcoholism

Many alcoholics attribute part of their motivation to enter a treatment program to the efforts of the public health nurse. The nurse who visits the home of the alcoholic has a chance to build a trusting relationship with the entire family. As a result of her nonjudgmental and accepting attitude, she is in a position to offer suggestions and guidance that can ultimately lead to treatment. On occasion the nurse will receive requests from the alcoholic, his family, or an employer to assist in initiating treatment. When the alcoholic refuses treatment, however, the public nurse can do much to alleviate the anxieties and fears of family members and, at the same time, help the alcoholic toward eventual acceptance of treatment.

Trusting Relationship The trusting relationship the nurse builds as she visits the family can serve as a valued source of support when the family's unity is threatened by chronic alcoholism. Reaffirming the confidential nature of any discussions is usually greatly appreciated by the family not yet able to approach alcoholism openly. The family must feel that they can trust the nurse to help them cope with existing problems and ultimately assist them in urging the alcoholic to seek treatment.

Support Family members of the alcoholic need avenues of expression for the feelings they have toward the alcoholic. The public health nurse can offer considerable support by allowing the family to fulfill this need. As she offers a listening ear and conveys an open, accepting attitude, she can often begin to suggest ways in which the family might be instrumental in getting the alcoholic to seek treatment. Of equal importance are suggestions to the family on how to adjust to the stress and tension resulting from an alcoholism problem.

Confronting the Problem Family members of an alcoholic usually struggle to hide the problem from the outside world. This is especially true during the initial period of alcoholism. The stress that cover-up behavior places on the family is enormous and adds mounting tension to intrafamilial interactions. Also characteristic of most families of alcoholics is initial firm denial that any problem exists. In order to counteract such denial, which can ultimately be destructive to the family's unity, the PHN can assist the family in confronting and acknowledging the problem. She accomplishes this through an honest, nonmoralistic approach. Education about the dynamics and characteristics of alcoholism is invaluable to the family who has believed it is a moral defect to be an alcoholic. Helping the family to face the fact that one of their members, usually a parent, is ill with a chronic, self-destructive disease is a crucial part of the PHN's role.

Once the family understands alcoholism and how it evolves and progresses, they usually realize that hiding alcoholism and thereby creating burdensome stress does not decrease the problem but only prolongs it.

Accepting Limitations When it seems evident that the alcoholic will not seek treatment at a given time, the public health nurse can help the family in accepting the limitations of their efforts to help him. The family's cohesiveness and plans for the future cannot be jeopardized by the alcoholic's refusal to participate in treatment. This concept is often difficult for the nurse and the family to accept, but it is a necessary reality. Convincing the family that although the alcoholic refuses treatment now, they are not deserting him by trying to reorganize themselves without him is a difficult and demanding task.

Of importance to the family is the knowledge that when the alcoholic expresses readiness to undergo treatment, the public health nurse will help him find the appropriate treatment site. Thus, although the family learns over time and with support to refocus their energies away from frustrating efforts to hide the problem and toward more constructive efforts to rebuild family structure, there exists the knowledge that the alcoholic is not deserted and cut off from sources of hope and help.

Knowledge of Community Resources The public health nurse cares for clients of all ages with differing health needs and varied cultural backgrounds. She has a working knowledge of the appropriate community resources for a variety of preventive and interventive aspects of health care. If the PHN is to make referrals for the alcoholic and his family, she must also have a working knowledge of the appropriate treatment, rehabilitation, and supportive services available in her community. With such knowledge, the PHN can make suggestions that fit the specific needs of each alcoholic and his family.

Many communities have found it invaluable to compile alcoholism treatment resource manuals that list all the community facilities for the care, treatment, and rehabilitation of the alcoholic and/or his family. The manuals may include information on the types of treatment programs available, cost, length of program, how contact can be made, who can be contacted for information, and how referrals are made. When the public health agency does not have such a listing, public health nurses may find it helpful to compile an informal listing of their own. Also knowledge that there are facilities designed to care for the alcoholic, as well as offer support to family members, serves to decrease the PHN's feelings of uneasiness when confronted with the unstable family of an alcoholic.

Counseling the Family

Dealing with families is perhaps the core of practice in public health nursing. Knowledge of family dynamics in crisis situations of illness or traumatic injury greatly aids the nurse in helping families adjust and learn beneficial ways of coping with such crises. In one sense, the family of the alcoholic is experiencing a crisis situation. It is usually quite lengthy and demanding, and requires the mobilization of the family's resources in order to prevent total family disintegration.

During the course of active alcoholism, a sequence of adjustments occurs within the family in response to the demands of the illness. The demands evolve from the problems created by the alcoholic's disruptive and disillusioning behavior. Jackson has identified seven stages in this adjustment process.[1] A description of these seven stages is included in the following sections.

Stage I. Efforts to Deny the Problem During the initial period in which bouts of drinking become unpredictable and more frequent, family members avoid discussion of the behavior with one another and with anyone outside the home. The spouse especially worries that inappropriate drinking in social situations will threaten the family's social status and thus the family eventually isolates itself by withdrawing into itself. Suggestions to the drinker that he is having difficulty in controlling his behavior are rejected. Levels of tension and anxiety increase between the husband and wife.

Stage II. Attempts to Eliminate the Increasing Problems The spouse believes that the problems arising from the drinker's behavior should be solved by the family. As a result, the wife covers up and makes excuses for her husband's increasing absences from work. Her efforts to destroy or remove

---

[1] Joan K. Jackson, "The Adjustment of the Family to the Crisis of Alcoholism," *Quarterly Journal of Studies on Alcohol,* 15:(4)568–584, December 1954.

sources of alcohol fail to deter her husband, as do her other attempts to stop his excessive drinking. When the alcoholic is the wife and mother, the spouse may at first make excuses for the behavior by saying that his wife is ill. The husband attempts to convince his wife to stop drinking through direct confrontation, nagging, or argument. If the children question their parent's behavior, the spouse makes excuses for it and shields them from the alcoholic's actions as much as possible. The wife will usually try to bring the children closer to her and alleviate her growing loneliness and feelings of failure. At this stage the children are able to maintain considerable affection for the alcoholic.

Stage III. Disorganization of the Family As the alcoholic husband's drinking behavior continues and shows no evidence of control or decrease, the wife reaches a point of resignation. She accepts the problem and believes it will continue indefinitely. Her feelings of helplessness and failure, loss of self-confidence, insecurity in the ability to make decisions, and fear of the consequences of continued alcoholism all serve to disorganize the family stability. She knows she should be the source of strength in the family but is indecisive about how the problem should be handled. These same feelings may occur with some modification in the husband of a female alcoholic. In that situation, disorganization may occur much earlier because of the wife's central role in the home and responsibility for raising the children.

Stage IV. Efforts to Reorganize the Family In this stage, the wife (or husband) assumes the family roles of the alcoholic and relegates him to a childlike position of dependency within the household. Such action by the spouse is usually precipitated by a crisis in which acknowledgment of the alcoholic's incapacity to perform in his designated role is made unavoidable, e.g., loss of job, physical abuse, criminal behavior. As the husband realizes his loss of status and position within the family, he may try to reenter the family's mainstream of activities only to be rejected by a now skeptical and guarded wife and children. In response to this rejection, the alcoholic begins to express his desire to seek a "cure." If these expressions are followed by tangible action, the family will back the alcoholic but may hesitate to make a permanent emotional reinvestment in him. If he should fail to follow through with treatment, the family's lack of confidence in his honesty and his ability to quit drinking is confirmed.

Stage V. Attempt to Escape the Problems The spouse of the alcoholic, after much deliberation and self-analysis, may decide that the only way to preserve the family's integrity is to leave the alcoholic. Separation may or may not be accompanied by divorce. Arriving at this solution is very difficult for the spouse, who continues to debate the benefits of having a visible, but unsatisfactory father or mother figure for the children against having no parental figure at all. In addition, during the crisis, the spouse may learn that alcoholism is an illness, which would make the decision to leave all the more difficult.

Stage VI. Reorganization of Part of the Family   The spouse and children of the alcoholic establish a new home, and the single parent fulfills the responsibilities and requirements of the family. Often the alcoholic will attempt to make contact with the family in a beseeching or threatening manner.

Stage VII. Reunion of the Family When Recovery Occurs   If the alcoholic is able to recover and maintain sobriety, he may be accepted back into the family on a trial basis. If abstinence is maintained, the recovered alcoholic will want to reassume the roles fulfilled before the advent of alcoholism. Although this is a vital aspect of recovery and rehabilitation, the spouse may find it difficult to relinquish these roles and the status associated with them. Thus, the reunited family still must face the problems of adjustment and must learn new methods for solving its problems.

Not every alcoholic family will experience each of these seven stages of adjustment to alcoholism. Some families will be stuck in one stage and may never reach the point of reorganization. Families that seem to foster and nourish the alcoholic's behavior in a neurotic manner usually will be extremely resistant to suggestions that alcoholism seems to serve a desired purpose. In this type of situation, long-term patient interaction is necessary before the family members can accept and recognize the part their behavior plays in the continuation of alcoholism. This type of insight can best be encouraged by the skilled psychotherapist.

Role of the Spouse in Reinforcing Alcoholism

Within the alcoholic's family, various behaviors evolve which seem to reinforce the alcoholic's drinking pattern. The spouse of the alcoholic, usually unknowingly, contributes to the continuation of the partner's problem in several ways. For example, the alcoholic who projects responsibility onto his wife for continued drinking may do so as a reaction to her nagging or complaining about this drinking. The wife does not intentionally or consciously want to condone and encourage the disruptive activities of the alcoholic. However, in response to the daily stresses, disappointments, and anxieties the wife may continually confront him with his destructive and emotionally damaging behavior. She seeks to convince him to stop drinking but often succeeds only in reinforcing it by offering him justification for continued drinking—escape from harassment.

As the alcoholic's behavior reaches chronic proportions, the spouse finds it necessary to assume the familial responsibilities neglected by the drinker. With the progressive loss of role, the alcoholic becomes dependent on the spouse. The desire to maintain responsibility and control may motivate the alcoholic to attempt to forcefully direct daily activities. In order to avoid conflict that can range from verbal argument to physical violence, the spouse may assume a submissive, overtly passive relationship. In this situation, the spouse and children try to appease the alcoholic by obeying his orders, thereby hoping to avoid confrontation and the emotional turmoil. The result of this behavior can include perpetuation of the alcoholism and the eventual rejection of the alcoholic by family members.

The spouse and children of the alcoholic are repeatedly asked to "give me another chance," that is, treat him as if he had not lost control of his behavior. Each time they comply with his request or demand and he is unable to follow through, the family's trust and belief in his sincerity decreases. Eventually no matter what the alcoholic says, the spouse is unable to truly believe the promises. Yet, in many cases, the spouse gives the alcoholic one more chance, always hoping that "*this* time, he'll quit." The suspicions, distrust, and lack of confidence that build up over the years reinforce the spouse's need to assume the familial responsibilities neglected by the alcoholic. Eventually, it becomes easier and less stressful to the spouse if he or she maintains control within the family. Thus, the alcoholic is not truly held accountable for his behavior, but becomes more dependent on the spouse. The spouse achieves a precarious degree of consistency in daily living by denying the alcoholic's need to be independent while assuming the decision-making responsibilities.

Often the alcoholic uses vicious verbal attack on the spouse to retaliate for the loss of role and self-esteem within the family. For example, the male alcoholic may condemn and harass his wife to the extent that she loses self-confidence and doubts her own abilities. She may become indecisive and insecure in her own ability to hold the family together. The alcoholic often succeeds in giving the spouse a sense of guilt by his projection of responsibility for his drinking. As the wife continually is made to feel responsible for her husband's alcoholism, she may respond by withholding respect, love, and trust. Her actions then reinforce his reasons for drinking— "No one cares."

In summary, the spouse of the alcoholic may reinforce his need to continue drinking, or from the alcoholic's viewpoint, provide justification for the behavior. The spouse then may respond by removing the alcoholic's role responsibilities and assuming decision-making power. These behaviors eventually form a self-reinforcing vicious cycle that can lead to the ultimate disintegration of the family unit.

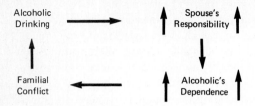

With an understanding of these basic dynamics, the nurse can help the spouse of the alcoholic recognize his or her role. It is a difficult process, but one that must be completed if the family is to successfully reunite after the alcoholic has recovered. In those families where the alcoholic refuses treatment and rehabilitation, the spouse's acquisition of insight into her behavior and its relationship to the alcoholic's can help her regain a degree of self-confidence and self-respect while breaking the cycle of reinforcement that fosters continuation of alcoholism.

Role of the PHN in Family Counseling

Because the family of an alcoholic can be expected to experience varying degrees of emotional turmoil as the illness disrupts regular patterns of interaction, it can greatly benefit from the supportive care of the public health nurse. One of the primary ways the nurse can convey support to the family is through counseling. In order to fulfill this aspect of her role, the PHN should have an understanding of the dynamics of the individual family situation and an open-minded approach to the problems confronting the family. Then, she can identify the response the family is having to the alcoholic either in terms of the seven stages presented here or in relation to another framework of understanding. Thus she will comprehend the reasons for behavior that might be considered confusing under other circumstances, e.g., the wife who berates her husband one minute and then expresses concern about his illness the next.

It is not possible for the PHN to be all things to all her clients. Therefore, it is appropriate and advisable for the nurse to counsel family members of an alcoholic about how to contact and join lay and professional organizations that can lend support and guidance to them. Groups such as Al-Anon and Al-Ateen contribute immensely to the process of gaining insight into the family member's motivations and behavior toward the alcoholic. (Al-Anon groups are composed of the friends and relatives of the alcoholic, and Al-Ateen is composed of teenage children or relatives of the alcoholic.) As each person in the group shares his experiences with alcoholism, the new member learns that many others have trod the same path of misery and self-condemnation. Knowing that others have suffered, have been able to readjust their lives, and are able to lead productive, meaningful existences serves as a source of strength and support to the person who had begun to lose hope.

The nurse's efforts to support the family during home visits adds to their growing awareness that people *do care* about them and want to help them. This caring can seem to the family to be much like the life preserver being thrown to the drowning sailor.

One of the first things the nurse has to convey to the spouse or children is not to hide the problem any longer. In order to do this, however, they must accept the alcoholic's behavior as a manifestation of an illness he cannot control. The nurse can provide the family with literature on alcoholism, express willingness to discuss the illness with them, and/or refer them to community organizations. This may take considerable time and patience on the part of the nurse because it cannot be forced upon the family.

When the spouse of the alcoholic has learned to accept the disease concept, he may then be receptive to information about how his own behavior feeds into or complements the continuation of his spouse's drinking. Discussion of the family's reactions to the progression of alcoholism and responses to the problems arising from it may help the spouse (and the children, when old enough) understand his or her own behavior. Often this process of gaining self-awareness is begun in the group situation outside the home and can be reinforced by the nurse when she makes home visits.

Community resources for financial assistance, in-depth counseling, and other social services can be explained to the spouse. Knowing that such sources of support are available when needed and that the public health nurse will make necessary referrals at the appropriate time can greatly decrease the family's anxiety.

In summary, the public health nurse's contribution to the identification and initiation of treatment for the alcoholic in the community is indeed a significant one. Her ability to interact with families in a trusting and purposeful manner provides a source of caring and hope to the alcoholic and his family. As more knowledge and understanding of the special problems associated with alcoholism are accumulated, expansion of the public health nurse's role in casefinding and family counseling will also be expanded.

ROLE OF THE INDUSTRIAL NURSE

Each year industry loses billions of dollars as a result of problem drinking and alcoholism. Losses are incurred by sporadic absenteeism, decreased quantity of work output, increased accident rates, extended, unauthorized tardiness, faulty judgment, damaged customer relations, and other types of inappropriate behavior. Many alcoholism programs have been devised by industry to counteract these high losses. In most cases, the industrial nurse assumes a key role in the creation, organization, and maintenance of the program. The role of the industrial nurse in relation to employee alcoholism is multifold.

Education

Usually the nurse must overcome the common stereotyped beliefs about alcoholism before a program can be truly effective. Line and supervisory personnel need information about the disease nature of alcoholism, its characteristics, and most of all, the fact that it can be treated and the victim recovered. Educational programs can be conducted via workshops, seminars, audiovisual material, informal discussion, poster campaigns, and so on.

Besides dissemination of information there are two other educational areas of much importance to industrial personnel. The first area concerns educating supervisory personnel on the behavioral signs of alcoholism. These behaviors are only clues but may be the stimulus needed by the supervisor to confront his subordinate. It must be kept in mind that these clues apply to *all* levels of the company or business hierarchy.

Unexplained Absences from Assigned Work Location The alcoholic must drink at work and does so while on extended coffee and lunch breaks. He offers various excuses for his lateness, eventually offering very bizarre or no excuses at all.

Noticeable Mood Changes An obvious change in mood and outlook from sullen, quiet behavior to cheerful, outgoing behavior is another indicator of drinking on the job. When these mood swings occur following breaks and lunch periods, there is increased probability that drinking is responsible. Over time, the alcoholic also separates himself from friends at work. He can then hide his drinking more easily.

Decreased Work Performance As the alcoholic begins to realize that his drinking may jeopardize his job, he tries very hard for a time to carry out his work assignment correctly. In order to do this, he works carefully and slowly, thus decreasing his efficiency and productivity. He also does this to avoid accidents, which would strongly indicate his lessened capabilities.

Increased Absenteeism Frequent absences on Mondays and a greater incidence of leaving work early may indicate that the employee is unable to function after weekend binge drinking. The excuses offered are vague and the evidence of seeking medical attention sparse.

Increased Incidence of Physical Complaints The employee who consistently complains of headache, colds, the flu, or gastrointestinal upsets may be experiencing the results of long-term drinking. He should be referred to the company physician or private physician for treatment as well as for ruling out alcoholism.

Disheveled Physical Appearance During the initial phases of alcoholism, the person will try to maintain a neat, clean appearance. To cover up the alcohol odor on his breath, he will use strong breath mints and chewing gum. As his illness progresses, his physical appearance deteriorates along with his work performance. A disheveled, ungroomed appearance that has evolved over time can be another clue to alcoholism. Also of importance is the identification of an increasing frequency of bloodshot eyes, fine tremors of the hands, unsteady gait, or general signs of hangovers.

The second area that the nurse concentrates on when providing information to supervisory personnel relates directly to their response to the evidence they have gathered. Many supervisors feel that *they* should be able to solve the problem and so it is not referred to the company health department. In actuality, the alcoholic is hurt by this approach, not helped. For this reason, the nurse should emphasize the importance of the supervisor's referring either a suspected or clear-cut problem as soon as it is recognized. At the same time, it should be stressed that it is no reflection on the supervisor's abilities if one of his employees has a drinking problem.

Identification of Patterns of Behavior

By virtue of her job responsibilities, the industrial nurse is in a position to identify patterns of employee behavior that may indicate a problem with alcohol consumption. If the nurse is responsible for recording and maintaining records of absences or health problems, she can identify recurrent trends and note if a pattern is being formed, for example, absences following weekends, holidays, or vacations. Employees who have frequent illnesses such as upper respiratory infections, gastrointestinal flare-ups, or muscular aches and pains may have a problem with alcohol.

In addition to patterns that become evident via written records, the nurse has a personal opportunity to identify suspected alcohol problems as she sees employees in the health department. Frequent visits and requests for headache or tranquilizing medication following weekends, an increase in minor accidents due to tremors of the hands, or frequent hangovers all may indicate an evolving and progressive problem with alcohol.

When patterns do become evident, the nurse has several alternative actions she may follow: (1) She may notify the company physician and request that the employee visit the health department for an examination and discussion of his behavior. (2) She may contact the employee's supervisor to gather more information on work performance and on-the-job behavior. (3) She may discuss the apparent problem with the employee's supervisor and recommend that he discuss the pattern of behavior with the suspected drinker. (4) If part of her responsibilities, she may contact the employee directly and talk with him about his absentee or health problems. Of utmost importance is the fact that the nurse take action. To ignore obvious evidence that *something* is amiss with the employee is to do him a disservice. His problem may turn out to be totally unrelated to alcoholism, or it could be *the* problem. In either instance, the nurse should seek to identify the source of the employee's behavior that is having an adverse effect on work performance.

Counseling the Employee

The position of the industrial nurse within the company structure is usually a neutral one. She has no power to hire and fire and thus is viewed by the employee as a safe, neutral source of help. Therefore, many employees will discuss their concerns about drinking with the nurse following a show of interest on the nurse's part. For the employee who is required to visit the company health department because of increasing performance problems and who is suspected of having an alcohol problem, the nurse must first establish rapport and trust before any counseling can begin. A relaxed, nonpunitive, accepting attitude on the part of the nurse is necessary with the employee who denies he has a problem with alcohol.

The first step in counseling is to provide information on what alcoholism is and how it relates to the job performance problems the employee is having. The second step is to clearly state the threat to his continued employment that alcoholic or problem drinking behavior presents. This can be quite an eye-opener for the employee who thought he was successfully concealing his drinking. Thus for some, realization that their livelihood is threatened is the key to efforts aimed at ceasing such behavior.

The third step consists of informing the employee of the resources available to him for treatment. At the same time, he should be advised about insurance coverage for such treatment, especially when there is a company health plan. Companies that have active alcoholism programs generally do not terminate employees when alcoholism is discovered. This should also be communicated to the employee during counseling by the nurse. In fact this information is most crucial to many employees who may have hidden their problem because they fear that discovery would automatically result in termination.

Making referrals is the fourth step in the nurse's counseling of the alcoholic employee. She makes his appointments with the company physician and provides him with specific community resource information. At this point, the alcoholic is usually told that continued employment is contingent on his seeking treatment.

The alcoholic employee must come to realize that help is available, his job can be saved, and the company will support his efforts within the boundaries of its program. Beyond this, the employee must assume responsibility for participating in a treatment program.

Supervising Medication Regimen

Alcoholic employees who are being assisted to maintain abstinence via Disulfiram therapy are often able to continue employment following initial detoxification. In these cases, the industrial nurse may be responsible for periodically monitoring the person's status and response to the medication. The nurse may be responsible for dispensing the drug each day when the employee arrives at work. Such practices reinforce consistent adherence to the therapy as well as emphasize the employer's interest in and involvement in treatment and rehabilitation.

Follow-up

The industrial nurse is usually responsible for follow-up on the employee's progress. She may accomplish this through visits to the treatment center in which she talks with the employee and assures him that his job will be waiting for him when he recovers. Such reinforcement is very meaningful to the alcoholic who is learning to control his desire to drink. Telephone communication to the nurse at the treatment center can also provide information on the employee's progress and projected date of discharge and/or return to work.

When it is determined that the employee has left treatment or failed to enter a program, the nurse may be responsible for contacting the employee to readvise him of the consequences of his behavior. If she is unsuccessful, the nurse can refer the problem to the employee's supervisor or the company physician.

After the employee has completed an inpatient treatment program, he may be discharged to the home for outpatient treatment. The industrial nurse can contact the public health nurse and request follow-up through her home visits. In some companies, the home visits are the responsibility of the industrial nurse.

In summary, as more companies and businesses devise alcoholism programs for their employees, the role of the industrial nurse will be expanded. For those companies that do not have programs, the industrial nurse should strive to create a recognition of the need for such programs. Knowing that approximately 3 to 6 percent of a company's work force has developed alcoholism or is in the process of doing so[2] should serve as a stimulus to both the nurse and the company to find ways of combating this costly illness.

OTHER COMMUNITY NURSING ROLES

The school health nurse has an opportunity to offer support and guidance to the child of an alcoholic parent. She can educate teachers about behavior in

---

[2] Mary Millsap, "Occupational Health Nursing in an Alcohol Addiction Program," *Nursing Clinics of North America,* 7:123, March 1972.

their students that indicate problems within the home. A child with bruises or one who seems to withdraw from other children may be living with an alcoholic parent. When the nurse suspects or is told by the child that his mother or father is "drunk all the time," (1) she may contact the nonalcoholic parent to communicate the observed effect on the child, (2) she may contact the public health nurse to determine if a home visit could be made, (3) she can learn of community resources in order to advise the nonalcoholic parent who wants guidance, and (4) she may advise the teenage child about the Al-Ateen organization.

The children of alcoholic parents can be adversely affected in one way or another by their parent's behavior. Other children ridicule and embarrass them about their parent's drunken behavior. Over time the child may isolate himself from his peers and cease to participate in the normal activities of growing up. Some children learn to cope with alcoholism by admitting they have a drunk for a father or mother—not knowing that it is an illness. In either situation, the school health nurse can support the child emotionally and teach him that alcoholism is a disease.

The office nurse has many opportunities to interact with the diagnosed and undiagnosed alcoholic. The patient who establishes a pattern of office visits for minor, frequent complaints of headache, nervousness, muscle aches and weakness, loss of weight, or colds may be experiencing the results of excessive drinking. While taking biographical information, the nurse has an opportunity to inquire into the person's drinking habits. When her attitude is matter-of-fact, open, and accepting, the patient is more likely to discuss his drinking problems.

For the patient who is being treated for alcoholism in the office, the attitude of the nurse can be a determining factor in keeping appointments. The nurse who conveys disdain or disgust can create a barrier the patient does not wish to contend with—and so appointments may be skipped. It is necessary, then, that the alcoholic receive the same courtesy, professional approach, and acceptance the office nurse affords to any patient being seen by the physician.

Certain nurses have evolved roles in innovative community programs. In some cases, the nurse participates as a team member in a mobile alcoholism clinic that visits various areas of a large community. The nurse assists with physical care and dispensation of medication, and she may act as cotherapist in group session.

SUMMARY COMMENT

Nurses working in various capacities within the community make significant and vital contributions to the care of the alcoholic and his family. Often their intervention can mean the difference between recovery and eventual self-destruction. Community nursing offers an opportunity to educate the public about the illness of alcoholism. Thus, the nurse must acquire and communicate understanding of this enormous community health problem in those she cares for.

REFERENCES

Bowles, Cheryl: "Children of Alcoholic Parents," *American Journal of Nursing,* 68:1062–1064, May 1968.
Chafetz, Morris E., Howard T. Blane, and Marjorie J. Hill (eds.): *Frontiers of Alcoholism,* Science House, New York, 1970.
Eaton, Merrill T.: "Alcohol, Drugs and Personnel Practices," *Personnel Journal,* 754–758, October 1971.
Ginn, Leona: "The Nurse's Role in the Care of Alcoholics," *Pelican News,* 26: 18–19, Summer 1970.
Jackson, Joan K.: "The Adjustment of the Family to the Crisis of Alcoholism," *Quarterly Journal of Studies on Alcohol,* 15:562–586, December 1954.
Kelly, Sister Dorothy (pseudonym): "Alcoholism and the Family," *Maryland State Medical Journal,* 22:25–30, January 1973.
Maters, Wendy: "The Quarter-Way House: An Innovative Alcoholism Treatment Program," *Maryland State Medical Journal,* 21:40–43, February 1972.
Meeks, Donald E., and Colleen Kelly: "Family Therapy with the Families of Recovering Alcoholics," *Quarterly Journal of Studies on Alcohol,* 31: 399–413, June 1970.
Millsap, Mary: "Occupational Health Nursing in an Alcohol Addiction Program," *Nursing Clinics of North America,* 7:121–132, March 1972.
Oge, Vedad: "Aftercare for Alcoholics Discharged to Distant Communities," *Hospital & Community Psychiatry,* 22:174–175, June 1971.
Scanlon, Mary E.: "An Industrial Visiting Nurse," *Nursing Clinics of North America,* 7:143–152, March 1972.
Scott, Edward M.: *Struggles in an Alcoholic Family,* Charles C Thomas, Springfield, Ill., 1970.
Singewald, Martin L. et al.: "Treatment of the Alcoholic and the Family," *Maryland State Medical Journal,* 21:67–82, January 1972.
Trice, Harrison M., and James Belasco: "Identifying and Confronting the Alcoholic Employee: Role of the Industrial Nurse," *American Association of Industrial Nurses Journal,* 13:7–10, October 1965.
UpdeGraff, Josephine: "Industrial Alcoholism. The Role of the Industrial Nurse," *American Association of Industrial Nurses Journal,* 14:7–9, May 1966.

Part Two

Drug Abuse: Background, Treatment, and Nursing Care

Drug abuse is not a term denoting a new series of health problems. The health and health maintenance problems associated with drug abuse *do,* however, represent newly *recognized* areas of serious concern to the health professions. Nurses frequently care for persons with drug-dependency problems and are, therefore, one group of professionals who not only must recognize the extent of potential or existing drug abuse–related health instability but also seek to evolve effective approaches designed to meet the needs of new care situations. In preparation for assuming the responsibilities for nursing care of the drug abuser in a variety of settings, nurses need to familiarize themselves with basic background information on the topic.

As a means to providing such background information, the first five chapters in Part Two have been designed to include descriptive as well as definitive content. The many drugs or chemicals associated with drug abuse are described individually. Exact drug dosages have not been included since there is wide variation based in large part on the geographic location and abuse patterns of the people using a particular chemical.

Generally, the term *drug abuse* is applied to the designated drugs of abuse as discussed in Chapter 11. Thus, narcotic abuse is included within the broad heading of drug abuse. When narcotic dependence becomes the central topic of discussion, terms such as *heroin addiction* and *heroin addict* are used alternately with *heroin dependence* and *heroin abuse.* All these terms denote the same form of drug dependence. However, the more commonly used stereotyped phrases of heroin addict and drug addict are deemphasized.

The nursing approaches and suggested interventions presented in Part Two are meant to serve as guidelines. Because drug abuse nursing is in the evolutionary phase of development, the nursing actions advocated in Chapters 14 through 16 may be subject to future revision and expansion. Ideally, the dynamic nature of nursing practice should promote modification and evaluation of the interventions discussed and add to the body of knowledge related to drug abuse nursing.

Because the detoxification unit is covered in Chapter 6, Part One, in relation to the nursing care of the alcoholic, a repetitious chapter on the same topic was not included in Part Two. Where necessary reference is made to previous chapters that cover information relevant to the care of drug abusers.

Students of nursing and nurse practitioners are becoming increasingly aware of the personal and professional requirements associated with delivering nursing care to persons with drug-dependency problems. Without a doubt, there are no easy answers to the challenges, frustrations, and questions stimulated by nurses' efforts to administer quality care to drug abusers. The key word, however, is *challenge.* Problems tend to be frustrating, but challenges tend to be professionally rewarding. If a practitioner believes that drug abuse nursing is a challenge and not a problem, the care administered to and received by the patient will be enhanced and the nurse will derive heightened personal and professional satisfaction.

Chapter 9

Defining Drug Abuse

Within the past few decades, and particularly during the 1960s, the American public has been bombarded with the problems surrounding drug abuse. Seldom does a day go by when a person is not confronted with some aspect of this enormous and burgeoning public health problem. Words such as "addiction," "habituation," "dependence," and "drug abuse" appear frequently in the news media and are often a source of confusion and fear not only to the layman but also to the health professional who has direct interaction with the drug user. In order to clear up this confusion, the following definitions are presented and will be used in the remainder of Part Two.

DRUG ABUSE DEFINED

Drug abuse can be described simply as the nonmedical use of chemical substances in the form of drugs. It includes the use of chemicals in excess of normally prescribed dosages and frequency, and routes that intensify or speed up drug reaction. Defined in this way, drug abuse becomes an umbrella term that encompasses the general misuse of drugs—alcohol, narcotics, amphetamines, sedatives, inhalants, etc.

Definition of Drug Abuser

With this definition in mind, it is possible to define the term *drug abuser*. The drug abuser is a person who engages in the nonmedical or nonprescribed use of chemical substances in the form of drugs. The drug abuser's source of supply can be legal—physician prescriptions—or illegal. Therefore, the term includes not only the heroin user in the low-income ghetto but also the business executive who is dependent on prescribed amphetamines.

Habituation and Addiction versus Drug Dependence

Confusion of meaning is easily generated by the terms *habituation* and *addiction*. What distinguishes one from the other? If these words are placed at opposite ends of the drug abuse continuum, at one end would be habituation, the constant use of or desire for a drug, which includes psychological dependence. At the other end would be addiction, the compulsive use of a drug with accompanying craving, tolerance, psychological dependence, and withdrawal syndrome when the drug is decreased or stopped.

DRUG ABUSE CONTINUUM

Habituation   Addiction

Figure 9-1

Between habituation and addiction lie varying degrees of drug abuse, with habituation usually leading to addiction, not vice versa. The next question is: Where does physical dependence fit into this continuum? A good question, for it is possible to have addiction to a drug without physical dependence, but physical dependence *can be* a part of addiction. It's easy to see that the use of so many different terms, each with different meanings, by different people has led to confusion. For this reason, the World Health Organization's term of *drug dependence* has been adopted by most health professionals in place of the terms habituation and addiction.

Drug dependence is described as a state of being in which there is psychological and/or physical dependence on a drug that is taken periodically or on a scheduled basis. To distinguish between the varieties of drug dependence, the term *dependence* is followed by the drug involved, for example, drug dependence of the hallucinogen type or drug dependence of the narcotic type, to name a few. Therefore, drug dependence includes both narcotic and nonnarcotic substances, the common denominators being the fact that the drug is abused and that this abuse has its own particular characteristics. (These characteristics are discussed in Chapter 11.)

Is Drug Abuse an Illness?

Many health professionals consider drug dependence an illness while others believe it is a symptom of an underlying psychological disorder or unresolved psychological problems. Still others categorize the various types of drug dependence as illnesses or symptoms, depending on the substance abused.

For the purpose of clarifying the remainder of Part Two, drug dependence will be considered an illness caused by the psychological and/or physical harm to the user that it induces. Therefore, drug dependence on any drug can be included within these parameters. (The proposed origins and characteristics of this illness are discussed in Chapter 12.)

SCOPE OF DRUG ABUSE

The abuse of drugs occurs throughout American society. For this reason, it is extremely difficult to accurately estimate the number of people affected. Data are available, however, for drug dependence of the narcotic type (principally heroin) because the many users who resort to income-producing crime to maintain their habits are apprehended by various law enforcement agencies. Conservative estimates of the number of heroin-dependent persons in the United States ranges from 100,000 to 600,000.[1,2,3,4] Approximately half this number are under thirty years of age, including children and adolescents. Of some encouragement is the fact that the rate of increase in the number of heroin abusers seems to be decreasing.[5]

The second type of dependence for which there are some statistical data on extent of use is that associated with barbiturates. Unfortunately, many barbiturate abusers acquire and maintain dependence through valid physician prescriptions and thus their numbers remain unknown. It is known that there are a minimum of 3,000 deaths per year in the United States directly attributable to barbiturates.[6] Also, of the estimated five billion legally manufactured barbiturate

[1] K. D. Charalampous, "Drug Culture in the Seventies," *American Journal of Public Health,* 61:1226, June 1971.

[2] Gannet News Service, "Youth Drug Abuse in Isles up Eightfold Since 1966," *Honolulu Star-Bulletin,* p. A-19, December 5, 1972.

[3] Associated Press, "Nation's Heroin Addiction Soars," *Honolulu Star-Bulletin,* p. F-10, December 15, 1972.

[4] "Narcotics: Some Questions and Answers," National Clearinghouse for Drug Abuse Information, Public Health Service Publication No. 1827, Washington, June 1971, p. 3.

[5] Jerome H. Jaffe, "Director's Report," *Drug Abuse Prevention Report,* 1:5, May 1973.

[6] Stanley F. Yolles, "The Drug Scene," *Nursing Outlook,* 18:26, July 1970.

doses per year, possibly half eventually are sold illegally.[7,8,9] When the estimated quantity of clandestine barbiturate production is added to this figure, the amount of this drug being consumed and subsequently abused becomes staggering.

Dependence on amphetamines has steadily increased over the past decade. It is impossible to estimate the number of people abusing amphetamines because many obtain the drug through physician prescriptions or from the black market. A significant number of adolescent amphetamine abusers acquire the drug through parental supplies. Of the legally manufactured amphetamines, it is conservatively estimated that one-half the quantity is diverted into illegal channels for nonprescribed use.[10] The amphetamines are the second most frequently abused drug when compared with the major drugs of abuse (excluding alcohol and tobacco).[11, 12]

The extent of dependence on hallucinogens is also difficult to quantify. During the late 1960s, the hallucinogen LSD (Lysergic acid diethylamide) was extremely popular as a drug of experimentation and for many as a drug of abuse. The use of this drug has declined among the teenage and young adult population since that time.[13] Unfortunately, it is fairly easy for the amateur chemist to manufacture LSD and thus exact data of extent of use are not available.

The second hallucinogen of vital concern to the American public is cannabis, specifically marijuana. To date, estimates of the number of people who have used marijuana range from eight to twenty-four million. Approximately 8.3 million people are currently using it.[14, 15] Of this number, a million might be considered chronic abusers.

Frequently, abuse of LSD follows abuse of marijuana. One study found that of those persons who consistently used marijuana, 77 percent had also tried LSD.[16] Marijuana is generally considered the most popular abused drug, with the exception of alcohol and tobacco. Its popularity is due in large part to its relative low cost and accessibility.

[7] Gannet News Service, loc. cit.

[8] "Sedatives: Some Questions and Answers," National Clearinghouse for Drug Abuse Information, Public Health Service Publication No. 2098, Washington, June 1971, p. 3.

[9] Wolfram Keup (ed.), *Drug Abuse*, Charles C Thomas, Springfield, Ill., 1972, p. 39.

[10] "Stimulants: Some Questions and Answers," National Clearinghouse for Drug Abuse Information, Public Health Service Publication No. 2097, Washington, June 1971, p. 2.

[11] Robert T. Harris, William M. McIsaac, and Charles R. Schuster, Jr. (eds.), *Drug Dependence*, The University of Texas Press, Austin, 1970, p. 272.

[12] Paul H. Blachly (ed.), *Drug Abuse. Data and Debate*, Charles C Thomas, Springfield, Ill., 1970, p. 159.

[13] Stanley F. Yolles, "Recent Research on LSD, Marijuana, and Other Dangerous Drugs," Richard E. Horman and Allan M. Fox (eds.), *Drug Awareness*, Avon Books, New York, 1970, p. 67.

[14] A. J. Vogl, "Drug Abuse: Is the Tide Turning?" *Medical Economics*, p. 82, May 28, 1973.

[15] "Marijuana: Some Questions and Answers," National Clearinghouse for Drug Abuse Information, Public Health Service Publication No. 1829, Washington, June 1971, p. 2.

[16] Edward R. Bloomquist, *Marijuana. The Second Trip*, Glencoe Press, Beverly Hills, Calif., 1971, p. 48.

Dependence on volatile solvents occurs primarily among elementary and junior high school age children. (Solvents include glue, paint thinner, gasoline, carbon tetrachloride, and others.) Determination of the magnitude of this problem is difficult; however, "in the large cities, a few thousand cases come to the attention of the school or enforcement authorities each year."[17]

From the statistics presented here, it can be seen that drug abuse in the form of drug dependence on various substances is widespread. It must be kept in mind that many of these drugs are abused in combination or in sequence, so that it is nearly impossible to obtain data on the full extent of their use.

SUMMARY COMMENT

The definitions of drug abuse and drug dependence presented in this chapter will be adhered to throughout the remainder of Part Two. Because the term drug addict is still generally accepted as indicating the narcotic-dependent person, this term will be used in some chapters of Part Two. However, the terms drug habituation and drug addiction will not be used to indicate the drug-dependent state.

Exact statistical data on the number of drug abusers in the United States are difficult to pin down. The statistics that are available, however, point to the existence of a fluctuating, pervasive public health problem that is of vital concern to all health professions.

REFERENCES

A Federal Source Book: Answers to the Most Frequently Asked Questions About Drug Abuse, U.S. Government Printing Office, Washington, 1971.

Barber, Bernard: *Drugs and Society,* Russell Sage Foundation, New York, 1967.

Blachly, Paul H. (ed.): *Drug Abuse. Data and Debate,* Charles C Thomas, Springfield, Ill., 1970.

Bloomquist, Edward R.: *Marijuana. The Second Trip,* Glencoe Press, Beverly Hills, Calif., 1971.

Charalampous, K. D.: "Drug Culture in the Seventies," *American Journal of Public Health,* **61**:1225–1228, June 1971.

Committee on Alcoholism and Drug Dependence: "Alcohol and Society," *Journal of the American Medical Association,* **216**:1011–1013, May 10, 1970.

Harris, Robert T., William M. McIsaac, and Charles R. Schuster, Jr. (eds.): *Drug Dependence,* The University of Texas Press, Austin 1970.

Horman, Richard E., and Allan M. Fox (eds.): *Drug Awareness,* Avon Books, New York, 1970.

[17]"Volatile Substances: Some Questions and Answers," National Clearinghouse for Drug Abuse Information, Public Health Service Publication No. 2150, Washington, 1971, p. 1.

Milbauer, Barbara: *Drug Abuse and Addiction,* The New American Library, Inc., New York, 1972.

Vogl, A. J.: "Drug Abuse: Is the Tide Turning?", *Medical Economics,* 82–85, May 28, 1973.

Willis, J. H.: *Drug Dependence,* Faber and Faber, London, 1969.

Yolles, Stanley F.: "The Drug Scene," *Nursing Outlook,* 18:24–26, July 1970.

Chapter 10

Sociocultural Aspects
of Drug Abuse

The use and abuse of drugs is extensive throughout American society. Each day people are exposed to the advertising media expounding the virtues of headache remedies, pain relievers, tension reducers, bowel looseners, and body relaxers. Even small children have become accustomed to the promotions for candy-coated medicines suitable for childhood aches and pains. It's no wonder, then, that this pill-oriented, medicated society has developed a gigantic problem with both legal and illegal drugs.

CONTRADICTIONS IN VALUES

Adults question today's youth as to why some abuse drugs. Perhaps one basic answer can be found in the role model many parents establish for their children. A child may see his parents using up to six or more drugs per day—caffeine in their coffee, nicotine in their cigarettes, diet pills to lose weight, tranquilizers to calm down, a few drinks before or after dinner, or both, and sedatives to sleep at night. Such a pattern of drug use is not generally recognized as harmful by the user and indeed in many cases it does not prove harmful when these drugs are used strictly as prescribed. However, such patterns *can* and *do* lead to abuse when medication is not used as intended.

The contradictions surrounding drug abuse are further complicated by the inconsistent approach to the regulation of potentially harmful drugs. As was discussed in Part One, the attitudes toward alcohol use are characterized by inconsistency and confusion. Although the known and potential harm of alcohol and nicotine are well established and supported by extensive research, abuse of these chemicals not only continues but increases. A greater contradiction is the fact that their sale is largely unrestricted (with the exception of age limitations, which are not consistently enforced).

With easy availability of dependence-producing drugs such as tranquilizers and mood elevators, many people turn to these chemicals in search of relief when life's problems become too demanding. Consequently, problems are avoided, solutions are not found, and the cycle of repeated drug use can develop into major drug abuse. When adolescents either see these patterns in their elders or resort to drugs on an experimental problem-solving basis, they are less able to develop meaningful methods to approach their future life problems. The end result of this pattern is the elimination of nondrug alternatives and possibilities as dependence on drugs increases. Avoidance of problems is outwardly condemned by society as indicating weakness and indecision yet is inwardly adhered to by the hidden drug abusers.

These are only a few of the more obvious examples of the contradiction in values regarding drug use and abuse found in American society (many other modern nations face these same problems). The presence of these and other inconsistencies illustrates the most challenging aspect of solving the problems: Before drug abuse can be controlled, eliminated, and/or prevented, society must come to terms with its contradictory approach to drug use among *all* its citizens.

WHO ARE THE DRUG ABUSERS?

Drug abuse can be found in varying degrees in all socioeconomic groups and in almost all age groups. Statistics on the incidence of various types of drug abuse are almost impossible to obtain because abusers often must get their drug through illegal, unmonitored channels.

Drug Dependence at Birth

In recent years there has been a growing awareness that the victims of drug abuse are not always the users. The major example is the baby delivered from a drug-dependent mother. The passive drug dependence experienced by the neonate usually is in relation to the mother's opiate or barbiturate dependence, which is transferred to the fetus via the placenta. Shortly after birth, the neonate experiences withdrawal symptoms and must receive prompt, knowledgeable treatment if he is to survive. (The treatment of the drug-dependent neonate is covered in Chapter 13.)

Data on the number of drug-dependent infants are sparse since most female abusers try to avoid pregnancy. In addition, a significant percentage of the female opiate-dependent population of childbearing age become infertile or experience abnormal menstrual cycles, which interferes with conception.[1]

Childhood Drug Abuse

Over the past few years there have been alarming accounts in the news media and in respected research studies of the spread and identification of drug abuse in grade school children. Many children experiment with cigarette smoking, glue sniffing, aerosol containers of solvents, and other volatile substances. For most, experimentation once or twice is sufficient to satisfy curiosity, and consequently drug abuse ends at this time. Unfortunately, an increasing number of these children seek new experiences with other drugs and thus become familiar with hallucinogens, barbiturates, and amphetamines. Progression to the use of opiates can and does occur with children, but the earliest abusers are usually in early adolescence. Socioeconomic background also plays a key role. The child who lives in the large, urban, low-income neighborhood that has existing drug-dependence problems is highly vulnerable to acquisition of drug abuse behavior. Of course, not all children living under these circumstances will inevitably become involved. It is, however, a significant factor for many in the evolution of adolescent drug dependence.

Adolescent and Adult Drug Abuse

Drug dependence on narcotics, especially heroin, is most prevalent in the major urban centers. It is estimated that approximately one-half of the heroin abusers live in New York City. For the fifteen to thirty-five age group in this city, drug abuse is the leading cause of death.[2,3] The stereotype of the heroin addict portrayed as a member of a minority race, living in a ghetto, and coming from a deprived background is no longer (if it ever was) true. It is now recognized that the typical narcotic abuser is more likely to have a caucasian, middle-class, white- or blue-collar background.[4] He or she may be gainfully employed, a prominent citizen, a student, or a professional.

[1] Sheldon S. Stoffer, "A Gynecologic Study of Drug Addicts," *American Journal of Obstetrics and Gynecology*, 101:780–781, July 15, 1968.

[2] K. D. Charalampous, "Drug Culture in the Seventies," *American Journal of Public Health*, 61:1226, June 1971.

[3] Barry Stimmel, "The Socioeconomics of Heroin Dependency," *The New England Journal of Medicine*, 287:1275, December 21, 1972.

[4] George R. Gay, David E. Smith, and Charles W. Sheppard, "The New Junkie," *Emergency Medicine*, 3:117–118, April 1971.

Abuse of cannabis, particularly marijuana, has become widespread on high school, college, and university campuses. Next to alcohol, it is the major drug of abuse among American youth.[5] Its use has also spread to the subteenage population as well as to the adult, upper-middle class population, where it is usually used sproadically.

Abuse of the hallucinogen LSD occurs among several groups. Narcotic users will occasionally use LSD when supplies of heroin are scarce, or simply out of curiosity. Some abusers use hallucinogens almost exclusively, alternating or combining marijuana, LSD, or other drugs in this category. (See Chapter 11 for a discussion of the major hallucinogens.) These people can be broken down into two subgroups: (1) those who wish to find meaning in life and to understand their fellow man and (2) those who hope to gain personal insight to become enlightened.[6, 7]

Amphetamine and barbiturate dependence can be found in the low-income neighborhood, throughout middle-income areas, and frequently in the upper-middle and upper-income sections of society. These drugs are illegally sold on many school campuses, ranging from the elementary to the university level. Abusers of these drugs can be children or elderly persons. Overdose or continued heavy use of either drug can lead to death (barbiturate-related deaths are estimated to be at least 3,000 per year.)[8]

The amphetamines are abused by housewives, businessmen, college students, truck drivers, and athletes for varying reasons and in varying patterns. Barbiturates are abused by the same groups of people. It is not uncommon to find some people combining these drugs—amphetamines for energy and barbiturates to relax. Within this group lie hidden abusers. These are the people who succeed in hiding their drug dependence from their family, their friends, and society. They get their drugs through valid prescriptions and thus can maintain secrecy. The fact that this type of pattern is hidden may prevent such abusers from recognizing their dependence and subsequently seeking treatment for it. There is no way of knowing how many hidden abusers there are in the United States—the number probably ranges in the millions.

The Older Drug Abuser

There is a growing awareness of the special problems among the older population. Many older citizens become dependent on cathartics, antacids, or sleeping medications. Generally, these are taken as prescribed and are not associated with

[5]Edward R. Bloomquist, *Marijuana. The Second Trip*, Glencoe Press, Beverly Hills, Calif., 1971, p. 39.
[6]Robert Kaplan, *Drug Abuse: Perspectives on Drugs*, Wm. C. Brown Company, Dubuque, Iowa, 1970, p. 24.
[7]Richard E. Horman, and Allan M. Fox (eds.), *Drug Awareness*, Avon Books, New York, 1970, p. 246.
[8]Stanley F. Yolles, "The Drug Scene," *Nursing Outlook*, 18:26, July 1970.

harmful physical or psychological effects on the user. However, as the person becomes less able to precisely monitor medication intake, because of increasing age or physical limitations, it is not unusual for doses to be doubled, repeated, or eliminated entirely. On the other hand, as worries about financial status, health problems, or growing social isolation emerge, many elderly people become dependent on sedatives, or tranquilizing medication.

A second group of older drug-dependent people deserves specific mention: the aging opiate-dependent person. A majority of heroin users, for one reason or another, stop using the drug by age thirty-five, and by forty-five or so, only a fraction continue heroin abuse.[9] Consequently, those who continue beyond forty-five years of age have succeeded in adapting their drug dependence so that it is compatible with their lifestyle. Many of these people began using and became dependent upon opiates when their use was not restricted. Because many of these persons have maintained dependence for thirty, forty, or even fifty years, the treatment applicable to them will necessarily differ from that designed for the younger person who has abused opiates for a shorter period of time.

ATTITUDES TOWARD DRUG ABUSE

Attitudes toward the drug-dependent person have usually centered on the narcotic user. Typically the heroin addict is depicted as a dope fiend, a sex maniac, a violent and dangerous subhuman character living on the fringes of society. Many of these fear-producing characterizations have evolved as a result of the heroin user's criminal practices. He steals and is capable of committing violent crimes in order to get money to finance his habit. Heroin abusers are not sex maniacs or fiends; sexual drives are depressed or eliminated when under the influence of the drug. When the person is in the process of obtaining the drug, that is his *single* objective.

Because possession of heroin is prohibited by law, it must be procured through illegal channels of supply. The heroin-dependent person must have a substantial income each day to maintain his level of drug dependency. A quick way to accomplish this goal is by various forms of criminal activity: theft, burglary, prostitution, or dealing in narcotics, to name a few. Since this type of criminal behavior often leads to arrest and prison, the narcotic abuser acquires the label of ex-con and criminal along with the other stereotypes. Except for delinquents and those who showed criminal tendencies prior to dependence, most heroin addicts become criminals as a result of their need for the drug, not because they voluntarily seek a life outside the mainstream of society.

During the past decade public attitudes toward the abuse of hallucinogens reached almost frenzied heights and then began to subside to their present levels.

---

[9] Andrew A. Sorensen (ed.), *Confronting Drug Abuse,* A Pilgrim Press Book, Philadelphia, 1972, p. 100.

People feared and mistrusted experimentation with the mind-expanding drugs and the "hippie" lifestyle associated with LSD and marijuana. Attitudes became polarized around the younger generation's desire to have unrestricted access to marijuana and the older generation's determination to prevent it. The emotionalism created by these attitudes is recognized today as one symbol of the generation gap and heralds a more liberal approach to the use of drugs. Many of the fears regarding marijuana abuse have been replaced by extensive research projects aimed at determining exactly what the long-term effects of this drug are. Thus, emotionalism in many cases has turned to logical investigation of the controversial chemicals.

Apprehension continues to exist regarding abuse of hallucinogens. However, the current focus is on barbiturates, amphetamines, and continuation of heroin dependence. With the recognition that drug dependence can occur in all segments of society, there has been increasing awareness of the illness concept of this problem. As the belief that the various types of drug dependence are manifestations of sickness is accepted, public attitudes toward the abuser have gradually begun to change.

Many of the negative attitudes held by the public have evolved from the contradictory beliefs about drug use in general. A significant portion of American society believes that it is morally wrong to take a drug for pleasure. One is supposed to be reality-oriented and able to face problems squarely. Because of this moralistic attitude, drugs are categorized as either good or bad, and these values are then promoted via educational programs, law enforcement, or methods of treatment.

Attitudes are also determined by society's generally held belief that drugs are to be taken only for justified illness, and even then one should try to withstand a "little" discomfort or stress before resorting to drugs. Yet, this belief is contradicted by the frequent use of chemicals to promote relaxation (alcohol, tranquilizers), stimulate energy (caffeine, amphetamines), or increase awareness (marijuana)—all practices that can lead to drug dependence.

In summary, attitudes toward drug abuse have begun to change. Instead of considering the drug-dependent person a fiendish character, the trend is to consider his dependency as an illness—one that hopefully can be treated. Concurrent with this positive change in attitude has come the realization that drug abuse is not restricted to the inner city, low-income areas but can be found throughout society. Therefore, stereotyping all abusers as social outcasts would neither be practical to society nor beneficial to the drug-dependent person.

Attitudes of Nurses toward Drug Abuse

The attitudes of nurses toward drug dependency are influenced by their education, the patients they care for, the predominant attitudes of the society, and their experience with drug abusers personally or professionally.

Nursing Education Nursing education places considerable emphasis on ensuring that patients do not abuse prescribed medication. In the course of caring for the sick, nurses daily administer prescribed narcotics, often using professional judgment about the frequency and route when these alternatives are covered by the physician's orders. The nurse is well aware of the potential dangers of dependence on narcotics and sedatives if used over long periods of time and takes steps to protect her patients from such harm.

Some Proposed Reasons for Attitudes Many nurses hold somewhat stereotyped attitudes toward the drug abuser, especially the heroin addict. These beliefs are based on personal encounters with heroin abusers in the course of their work as well as culturally acquired attitudes. Many nurses are very suspicious and mistrusting of the narcotic user—they often fear he will steal syringes, needles, or medication. Frequently, this is a justified feeling, for the heroin addict will attempt to take these materials when the opportunity presents itself. Nurses tend to disbelieve what the narcotic abuser says. Unfortunately for the sincere abuser who truly wants treatment for his illness, many other drug users are great con artists and will say anything to achieve their goal—a second injection for pain, a repeat sedative at night, a replacement for a tranquilizer that supposedly was dropped on the floor. As the nurse learns to identify the many types of manipulative behavior of abusers, she becomes generally skeptical of their motives and sincerity. Undoubtedly this skepticism is conveyed in the nurse's attitude toward the narcotic abuser.

Nurses' attitudes are also colored by their personal experience. Many nurses as members of society as a whole have experimented with drugs on a sporadic basis and most have experienced no ill effects. Some have younger siblings who experiment with or have become dependent on various drugs. Furthermore, nurses themselves are susceptible due to the relative accessibility of drugs. Exact statistics on the incidence of drug dependence among nurses are unknown. However, it is known that those nurses who do become drug dependent tend to abuse meperidine, a synthetic narcotic usually stocked in most nursing stations and morphine preparations.[10]

Suggested Considerations With the increasing acceptance of drug dependence as an illness, nurses can expect to have increased contact with drug abusers as the number of treatment facilities multiply. Therefore, the nurse must thoroughly examine her attitudes toward drug dependence and the person who is dependent on drugs.

If the nurse expresses moralistic, judgmental, and condemning attitudes (either verbally or nonverbally), she will not be successful in communicating

[10] Edward R. Bloomquist, and Burnell H. Blanchard, "Drug Abuse in the Nursing Profession," *GP,* 34:133, November 1966.

with her patient or in identifying his need for help. The nurse who believes that drugs "ruin the mind," that they "drive you insane," that "alcohol is safer than drugs," or that "pot smoking leads to narcotic use" has many stereotypes to overcome before she can be an effective care giver to the drug abuser. Such prejudicial views have not been proven by scientific research but have evolved as a kind of antidrug folklore. It becomes imperative under these circumstances that the nurse acquire substantiated knowledge about the various aspects of drug abuse. With such a background, she can then form opinions and approaches that are supported by rational study and research. This does not imply, however, that nurses should advocate the illegal use or abuse of drugs. It does imply that before a nurse, or anyone, condemns another, she should learn as much about the dynamics of the particular situation as possible.

In developing the ability to feel confident and comfortable with the drug abuser, the nurse can consider the following areas.

1   Seeking insight into her personal attitudes and value system is a demanding yet vital undertaking for the nurse. Only when she feels at ease with who she is can she cope with the challenges to her beliefs that the drug abuser may pose. The nurse who is unsure of herself may not be able to handle the persuasive and manipulative abuser who has created a drug-oriented value system and is able to defend it.

2   As the nurse acquires personal insight, she also needs to determine how she can best maintain a consistently professional manner yet convey a caring and concerned attitude. The person who seeks help for his drug problem or for a related health problem does not want to be preached at or cajoled into admitting the error of his ways. On the other hand, an overly sympathetic, condescending attitude may elicit false compliance on the part of the patient. It is evident, then, that each nurse must evolve an approach that is personally comfortable and effective with the patients she cares for.

3   Sensitivity to the feelings and reactions of others is something nurses generally try to develop. With the drug-dependent person, however, the nurse's skills in detecting mood changes, attitudes, and subtle responses must be highly developed. The lifestyle of the person dependent on drugs may include deceit, criminal activity, and skillful manipulation of others. Because these behaviors can impede treatment and care efforts, the nurse must increase her ability to perceive and identify such behavior patterns. A straightforward, honest approach based on her identification of such behavior can, over time, engender the patient's trust in the nurse.

These suggested areas for consideration are only a few of the many the nurse will identify as she begins to deal purposefully and meaningfully with the drug abuser. As she begins to understand these areas, some of her attitudes may be changed entirely while others may be altered in one way or another. In either case, it is hoped that the practice of introspection will continue to assist the nurse in comprehending the often complex problems associated with the drug abuser.

THE LAW AND DRUG ABUSE

Laws that govern the possession, use, and sale of drugs of abuse have traditionally been controversial, severe, and in many instances inconsistent and overly punitive. Since the enactment of the first narcotic control act in 1914, numerous laws and court decisions have led to the creation of the present climate of fear, mistrust, and lack of confidence in the legal system as it is applied to this problem. A brief summary and comment on many of the most significant legal efforts toward drug abuse control and treatment is contained in the following sections.

The Harrison Narcotics Act

The Harrison Narcotics Act of 1914 was the first attempt by the federal government to control narcotics (opium, coca leaves, and other opiate derivatives) use within the United States. Labeled as a tax revenue measure, the act really was an antinarcotic law aimed at regulating the legal narcotic supply available to those dependent on these drugs.

At the time of its enactment, the Harrison Act was considered highly beneficial. It required that (1) special forms be completed when drugs were transferred and (2) those businesses or persons handling drugs register and pay fees. However, subsequent court cases in which registered physicians were prosecuted and convicted for prescribing narcotics for known users succeeded in ultimately eliminating the narcotic drug user's legal source of supply. The courts determined that a physician could not legally prescribe a narcotic for a person "to keep him comfortable by maintaining his customary use."[11] He could, on the other hand, prescribe them for legitimate medical reasons—drug abuse not among them. As a result of these court interpretations, people dependent on narcotics were forced to seek illegal sources. Thus, the beginning of illegal drug trafficking had begun.

Linder v. the United States

The results of a 1925 court case involving a Dr. Linder had the potential of removing the criminal aura surrounding the narcotic abuser and replacing it with the proper label of illness. Dr. Linder was found guilty of prescribing a narcotic for a known addict. On appeal to the U.S. Supreme Court, the decision was

[11] Alfred R. Lindesmith, *The Addict and the Law,* Indiana University Press, Bloomington, 1966, p. 6.

overturned and for the first time, narcotic abuse was described as an illness that should legally be treated by physicians.[12] Unfortunately, this precedent-setting decision was virtually ignored, largely due to its isolation and lack of support from prominent federal narcotic control agencies.

1937: The Uniform Narcotics Law

The Uniform Narcotics Law, adopted by most states, concentrated on creating a consistent method of record keeping at the federal and state levels, thereby promoting greater cooperation between the two levels of government enforcement. Of major significance was the fact that determination of penalties for use, possession, and/or sale of narcotics was left up to the individual states. Consequently, the severity of penalties and requirements of the law varied widely from state to state.

Marijuana Legislation

The Marijuana Tax Act of 1937 required all persons "who import, manufacture, and otherwise are involved with marijuana to register and pay a graduated tax"[13] (one dollar per ounce or less to a registered purchaser, and one hundred dollars per ounce or less to unapproved purchasers). Failure to comply with the law resulted in stiff penalties that were increased in 1951 and 1956 with enaction of the Federal Narcotic Control Act. This law greatly increased the penalties for narcotic and marijuana violations, so that a first offense for possession was subject to a prison sentence ranging from two to ten years with probation and parole permitted. Maximum sentences ranged from ten to forty years depending on the offense.[14]

1962: Robinson v. California

The 1962 case of Robinson v. California provided the U.S. Supreme Court with an opportunity to reaffirm its earlier ruling (the Linder case) concerning the belief that a person dependent on narcotics is not a criminal by virtue of his dependence but a sick person in need of appropriate treatment. The court held that Robinson could not be convicted or punished as a criminal for the sole reason that he was a narcotic abuser and, therefore, the California statute which made it a crime to be dependent on narcotics was overruled. This reaffirmation of the legal viewpoint of drug dependence as an illness had considerable bearing on subsequent state and federal legislation.

---

[12] Ibid., pp. 8–11.
[13] Paul H. Blachly (ed.), *Drug Abuse: Data and Debate,* Charles C Thomas, Springfield, Ill., 1970, p. 128.
[14] Bloomquist, op. cit., p. 253.

1965: The Harris-Dodd Act

Under the Harris-Dodd Act, the Food and Drug Administration was given strict control over the transfer and inventory from manufacturer to consumer of barbiturates, amphetamines, hallucinogens, and drugs having an abuse potential. Possession of these drugs without a legal prescription was made illegal. The end result of this act was the placement of existing or potential drugs of abuse that were not covered by previous legislation under federal control and restriction.

1966: The Narcotic Addict Rehabilitation Act (NARA)

In 1966 Congress established a national policy for the treatment of the narcotic abuser. If a known abuser was either charged with or found guilty of violating federal criminal law, he might be sentenced to prison or remanded to a narcotic treatment center for detoxification and rehabilitation. Before confinement to a treatment center in lieu of a prison sentence, it had to be determined that the person could benefit and respond to rehabilitation efforts. The act contained detailed provisions for the determination of the abuser's potential for treatment. The mandatory length of stay in a treatment program (federal or local) was six months, followed by periodic follow-up in the community for thirty-six months.[15, 16]

Although NARA decriminalized narcotic abuse to a large extent, there is a major flaw in its design: it screens out the narcotic abuser who is judged to be a potential failure. During the thirty-day examination phase provided by the act, as many as 49 percent of the narcotic users remanded for treatment have been found to be unsuitable.[17] This extremely high rate of rejection illustrates the need for (1) revision in the selection process and/or (2) radical modification in the treatment program, which should take into account the contrasting needs of different narcotic abusers.

The Comprehensive Drug Abuse Control and Prevention Act of 1970

The most recent and enlightened piece of legislation in many decades is the Comprehensive Drug Abuse Control and Prevention Act. Drugs of abuse are dealt with in individual schedules and are no longer categorized as "hard" or "soft." The penalties for criminal violations are coordinated with the known danger and intended use of each drug. Thus, a first offense for the possession of heroin, LSD, amphetamines, or marijuana is subject to a maximum sentence of one year in jail. Although this is not satisfactory to many people, it is a large

[15] Jasbir M. Singh, Lyle Miller, and Harbans Lal, *Drug Addiction: Clinical and Socio-Legal Aspects,* Futura Publishing Company, Inc., Mount Kisco, N.Y., 1972, p. 155.
[16] Blachly, op. cit., pp. 144–146.
[17] Ibid., p. 147.

step in the right direction. A major benefit of this law includes the provision for alternative penalties as deemed applicable by the presiding judge; for example, if the judge deems it more appropriate for the first offender to do volunteer work for one year of weekends, he can impose such a sentence in lieu of prison confinement or a fine. When these conditions are met, the offender's violation can be expunged—erased from the criminal record.

This law undoubtedly has flaws, one being the placement of marijuana and heroin in the same category. However, it repeals the old Harrison Act, the Marijuana Tax Act, and all other acts that applied to drugs to date. Within the next few years, the benefits or detriments of this legislation will become evident. It is hoped that this more realistic legislation will serve as the first step toward greater understanding and acceptance of the drug abuser as a human being with an illness.

Legislative Reform at the State Level

State penalties for drug abuse violations have characteristically been severe, inordinately lengthy, and extremely punitive. In an effort to bring state drug offense penalties in line with the federal law (Comprehensive Drug Abuse Control and Prevention Act of 1970), the 1970 Uniform State Act was drawn up. Several states have already adopted this act, which specifies that the penalty for a first offense for possession can be no higher than for a misdemeanor.[18]

Many of those states that have not as yet adopted the Uniform State Act have instead begun revision of their state drug abuse laws. Individual cities are also following suit and greatly decreasing the penalties for simple drug possession. For example, one city has reduced the nature and penalty for use or possession of marijuana from a felony to a misdemeanor. The penalty was reduced to a $5 fine.[19] It must be remembered, however, that many states continue to legislate harsh penalties as the predominant method of coping with the problems associated with illegal drug use. For example, New York State recently (September 1, 1973) implemented a stringent anti-drug program aimed at prosecuting the pusher of illicit drugs. The prison sentences contained in the law are designed to act as a major deterrent to the seller of drugs. It will take some time to thoroughly evaluate the success of this legislation.

SUMMARY COMMENT

Drug legislation in recent years has begun to be more humane, acknowledging the drug abuser as a sick person. With continued and intensified collaboration

[18]Clinton C. Brown, and Charles Savage (eds.), *The Drug Abuse Controversy,* National Educational Consultants, Inc., Baltimore, 1971, p. 13.
[19]Robert G. Faber, "Marijuana," *Journal of the American Medical Association,* 222: 1424, December 1, 1972.

between the law-making bodies at the federal and state levels, medical experts, and law enforcement agencies, this trend may eventually lead to a decrease in drug abuse while furthering public confidence in the American system of justice.

REFERENCES

"Babies on Barbs," *Emergency Medicine,* **4**:53, July 1972.

Blachly, Paul H. (ed.): *Drug Abuse: Data and Debate,* Charles C Thomas, Springfield, Ill., 1970.

Blachly, Paul H. (ed.): *Progress in Drug Abuse,* Charles C Thomas, Springfield, Ill., 1972.

Bleyer, Werner A., and Richard E. Marshall: "Barbiturate Withdrawal Syndrome in a Passively Addicted Infant," *Journal of the American Medical Association,* **221**:185–186, July 10, 1972.

Bloomquist, Edward R., and Burnell H. Blanchard: "Drug Abuse in the Nursing Profession," *GP,* **34**:133–139, November 1966.

Brown, Clinton C., and Charles Savage: *The Drug Abuse Controversy,* National Educational Consultants, Inc., Baltimore, 1971.

Capel, William C. et al.: "The Aging Narcotic Addict: An Increasing Problem for the Next Decade," *Journal of Gerontology,* **27**:102–196, January 1972.

Carroll, Mary Helen: "Preventing Newborn Deaths from Drug Withdrawal," *RN,* **34**:34–35, December 1971.

Charalampous, K. D.: "Drug Culture in the Seventies," *American Journal of Public Health,* **61**:1225–1228, June 1971.

Cortina, Frank M.: *Stroke a Slain Warrior,* Columbia University Press, New York, 1970.

"Drugs Disturb Foetal Babes," *New Zealand Nursing Journal,* **6**, January 1971.

Farnsworth, Dana L.: "Drugs—Do They Produce Open or Closed Minds? Part II," *Medical Insight,* **2**:34–44, July 1970.

Farnsworth, Dana L.: ' Drugs—Do They Produce Open or Closed Minds? Part II," *Medical Insight,* **2**:22–31, August 1970.

Gay, George R., David E. Smith, and Charles W. Sheppard: "The New Junkie," *Emergency Medicine,* **3**:117–133, April 1971.

Horman, Richard E., and Allan M. Fox (eds.): *Drug Awareness,* Avon Books, New York, 1970.

Kaplan, Robert: *Drug Abuse: Perspectives on Drugs,* Wm. C. Brown Company, Dubuque, Iowa, 1970.

Louria, Donald B.: *Overcoming Drugs,* McGraw-Hill Book Company, New York, 1971.

"Marijuana and Health: A Report to the Congress," *American Journal of Psychiatry,* **128**:189–193, August 1971.

Maurer, David W., and Victor H. Vogel: *Narcotics and Narcotic Addiction,* Charles C Thomas, Springfield, Ill., 1967.

Morgan, Arthur J., and Judith W. Moreno: "Attitudes Toward Addiction," *American Journal of Nursing,* **73**:497–501, March 1973.

Rohde, Ildaura M.: "Panic in the Street," *Nursing Outlook,* 13:45–47, November 1965.

Sorensen, Andrew A. (ed.): *Confronting Drug Abuse,* A Pilgrim Press Book, Philadelphia, 1972.

Stimmel, Barry: "The Socioeconomics of Heroin Dependency," *The New England Journal of Medicine,* 287:1275–1280, December 21, 1972.

Stoffer, Sheldon S.: "A Gynecologic Study of Drug Addicts," *American Journal of Obstetrics and Gynecology,* 101:779–783, July 15, 1968.

"The Tough Approach," *The Honolulu Star-Bulletin,* p. A-22, December 27, 1973.

Wadler, Gary I., John E. Imhof, and Dennis F. Buckley (eds.): *The Federal Challenge to the Community: A Health and Education Program for the Prevention and Treatment of Drug Abuse and Addiction,* Hofstra University, Long Island, N.Y., 1971.

Wilner, Daniel M., and Gene G. Kassebaum (eds.): *Narcotics,* McGraw-Hill Book Company, New York, 1965.

Chapter 11

Drugs Associated with Drug Abuse

Any drug, when taken for a nonmedical reason or for a reason other than its intended purpose, can be a drug of abuse. Thus, to describe and discuss all such chemicals would not be feasible. Those presented in this chapter are the major ones covered by law: stimulants, sedatives, hallucinogens, narcotics, inhalants. Various drugs that are acquiring the drug abuse label are also discussed. Emphasis is on the *abuse* of the chemical, not normal, prescribed use.

STIMULANTS

The major abused stimulants are (1) amphetamines, (2) cocaine, and (3) several nonamphetamine stimulant drugs.

Amphetamines

The slang names for these drugs are uppers, pep pills, and wakeups. Those most abused include the following:

Benzedrine (amphetamine sulfate): bennies, greenies, footballs, cartwheels, hearts, peaches, roses.

Methedrine (methamphetamine): speed, crystal, meth.

Dexedrine (dextroamphetamine sulfate): dexies, Christmas trees, hearts, oranges.

Action　Amphetamines are synthetic chemicals that stimulate the central nervous system (CNS), producing effects similar to those caused by the activation of the sympathetic nervous system. These drugs activate the release of norepinephrine at nerve endings, thereby inducing increases in metabolic processes and general body responses, e.g., fast pulse, dilation of pupils, restlessness, and dry mouth.

By the oral route, the amphetamines produce increased alertness, wakefulness, feelings of well-being, a decrease in feelings of fatigue or boredom, temporary suppression of appetite, and generally increased sensory perception. Users often describe a pleasant feeling of euphoria, or a "high."

When the drug is injected intravenously (specifically Methedrine or "speed"), the user experiences a "flash" or a "rush"—a rapid, intense, euphoric feeling. While taking the drug, the user feels boundless energy, becomes hyperactive, and doesn't eat or sleep. He may "shoot up" (inject the drug) one to ten times a day. The "speed freak" often uses the drug in binges or jags that can last for several days up to a week. During this time, the drug is repeatedly injected to maintain a high level of hyperexcitation. The experience ends with physical exhaustion, adverse effects of the experience, or a lack of the drug.

Characteristics of Amphetamine Dependence　Amphetamine abusers characteristically have a strong desire or need to continue taking the drug. Although physical dependence and subsequent craving do not occur, a psychological dependence does evolve in which a strong emotional dependence on the effects of the drug is developed. Tolerance, or the need for increasingly large doses of the drug, is characteristic of amphetamine abuse. However, there is no physical withdrawal syndrome associated with discontinuance.

Adverse Effects　*Amphetamine psychosis* is a major adverse effect of chronic oral intake and can also be induced in a short period of time when the drug is injected intravenously. It consists primarily of paranoia, which can trigger uncharacteristic aggression and violent behavior. Delusions of persecution occur and can complicate treatment efforts if the user misinterprets the help he is receiving. Visual and auditory hallucinations add to the patient's fear of others and can contribute to his defensive reactions.

Rebound depression appears when the person stops taking amphetamines or ends a binge. This period of mental depression is also known as the "crash" and generally follows prolonged use and/or high doses. There may be thoughts of and attempts at suicide along with confusion, apprehension, and dizziness.

Exhaustion follows a speed binge. The person sleeps for one or two days straight and awakens with a tremendous appetite. He also experiences a deep depression that can stimulate another binge.

Combining amphetamines with sedatives such as barbiturates and alcohol is common among amphetamine abusers. Many take sedatives to even out the high and prevent the crash associated with cessation of stimulant intake. Combination practices are potentially disastrous for the acutely ill person seeking medical attention. Prescribing physicians must exercise extreme caution in treating the patient to avoid exacerbating or potentiating the action of drugs ingested.

Physical reactions may include acute abdominal cramps, cardiac arrhythmias, occasional hypertensive episodes, and malnutrition with associated weakness.

Cocaine

Slang names are snow, dust, coke, happy dust, C, stardust, majo, bernies, flake, gold dust.

Action Cocaine is a short-acting, white crystalline powder that acts as a strong stimulant to the central nervous system. It is generally taken by being sniffed up the nose, where it is quickly absorbed via the nasal mucous membranes. The abuser feels a euphoric excitement and elation with magnified feelings of confidence and the capability to undertake physically demanding tasks. Cocaine is often used in combination with heroin or morphine—a "speed-ball"—either sniffed or injected intravenously with the narcotic. Because cocaine is short-acting, some heavy abusers inject it as frequently as ten-minute intervals. Such instantaneous, intense stimulation is sometimes anxiety-producing to the user and, therefore, he will combine intravenous cocaine with the narcotic to avoid the flash.

Characteristics of Cocaine Dependence Cocaine abusers have a strong desire and need to continue using the drug either by the oral or the intravenous route. There is no physical dependence or development of tolerance to the dose or effects of the drug. Consequently, there is no withdrawal syndrome when use is discontinued. Strong psychological dependence is developed in the chronic abuser and serves as the major motivating factor to continued use in spite of adverse effects.

Cocaine is generally not as popular as the amphetamines with regular drug abusers. However, it recently has enjoyed an increase in popularity as middle-class drug abusers discovered its rapid high and short action when sniffed.

Adverse Effects   Because tolerance to cocaine is not developed with continued, chronic abuse there is considerable danger of overdosage or acute toxic
reactions, especially when the drug is self-administered intravenously at frequent
intervals.

Characteristically the person dependent on cocaine experiences intense anxiety or fear, paranoia, depression, excitement and/or hallucinations (auditory,
visual, or tactile) when the immediate effects wear off. The paranoid feelings and
delusions associated with the "letdown" following cocaine euphoria are often
responsible for the violent, aggressive behavior of the user. In actuality, he is
defending himself from imaginary enemies and attacks. Defense may take the
form of overt attacks on innocent bystanders who are thought to be hostile.
Cocaine abusers also may physically harm others while trying to obtain money
to buy drugs. These types of drug-associated violent behaviors have been instrumental in characterizing the drug abuser as a "dope fiend."

Nonamphetamine Stimulant Drugs

There are several nonamphetamine stimulant drugs which generally act in the
same way as amphetamines on the central nervous system. Included in this group
are methylphenidate (Ritalin), diethylpropion (Tenuate®, Apisate), and pheno-
metrazine (Preludin®), to name a few.[1] Many of these drugs are secured by
prescription from physicians but subsequently are abused. Psychological dependence on the "high," euphoric feelings, or feelings of well-being occur with
abuse of these drugs.

SEDATIVES

The primary action of sedative drugs is relaxation and/or depression of the
central nervous system. The barbiturates are the major sedatives of abuse and
considered to be dangerous, dependence-producing chemicals. There are several
nonbarbiturate sedatives (chloral hydrate, paraldehyde, bromides) and tranquilizers (Doriden, glutethimide, and meprobamate—Equanil and Miltown) that
mimic the depressant action of sedatives. However, the emphasis in this section
will be on the barbiturates. (Keep in mind that the actions of such nonbarbiturate drugs closely resemble those of the barbiturates.)

Barbiturates

Slang names are downers, barbs, sleepers, candy, cap. The most abused barbiturates include the following:

---

[1] Jared Tinklenberg, "A Current View of the Amphetamines," Paul H. Blachly (ed.),
Progress in Drug Abuse, Charles C Thomas, Springfield, Ill., 1972, p. 249.

Sodium amytal: blue heaven, blue devils, blue angels, blue birds.
Tuinal (amobarbital sodium or secobarbital sodium): Christmas trees, tooies, rainbows, double trouble.
Nembutal (pentobarbital sodium): yellow jackets, dolls, goof balls, nimbie.
Seconal (secobarbital sodium): seggy, red devils, red birds, seccy, reds.
Luminal (phenobarbital): phennies, pink lady.

Action The person dependent on barbiturates can take large doses. Resultant behavior is characterized by staggering, slurred speech, decreased emotional control, confusion, loss of balance, quarrelsome disposition, and dizziness, i.e., the general appearance of someone who is quite drunk. In prescribed doses, the barbiturates induce relaxation and sleep. In the high doses of the abuser, however, they may produce agitation, excitement, restlessness, and possibly delirium.

Barbiturates are frequently used in combination with alcohol, opiates, cocaine, or amphetamines. The chronic alcoholic may substitute large doses of barbiturates for alcohol or may take them with alcohol. When so taken, the barbiturate potentiates the action of alcohol. The heroin addict may use high doses of barbiturates to potentiate the action of poor-quality heroin, to achieve heavy sedation during withdrawal from heroin, or to reduce self-awareness of unacceptable behavior (prostitution, stealing). Barbiturates are also often combined with cocaine to reduce the anxiety and depression associated with the abuse of cocaine alone.

The "upper-downer" syndrome appears frequently with chronic amphetamine and barbiturate abuse. The amphetamine user will take the sedative to bring him down when hyperexcitability needs to be decreased, and the barbiturate abuser will take the stimulants to lessen the central nervous system depression associated with sedative use. This syndrome can quickly become a vicious cycle as the user takes larger and larger quantities of both drugs, which can ultimately lead to overdose and death.

Characteristics of Barbiturate Abuse People dependent on barbiturates develop a strong desire and need to continue using the drug. Increased doses are required because an incomplete and inconsistent tolerance evolves with continued use of the drug, i.e., there can be mental confusion and dulling with larger doses, rather than a maintenance of the desired effect for which the barbiturate is taken. Psychological dependence also develops from the user's need to decrease the tensions and anxiety attributed to (1) the reasons for originally taking the drug and (2) the unpleasant effects resulting from decrease or discontinuance of the drug.

Physical dependence is characteristic of barbiturate abuse. Therefore, the user must maintain a constant and increasing intake in order to ensure that a level of equilibrium remains constant. When this level is not maintained, a self-limited withdrawal syndrome is developed that can be reversed with resumption of the drug. (The components of this potentially fatal withdrawal syndrome are discussed in Chapter 13).

Adverse Effects There are three major adverse effects associated with barbiturate abuse. The first is the ever-present danger of *overdose*. Overdose can happen when the dependent person takes large doses, experiences an intoxicated, depressed feeling, and then unknowingly proceeds to take more of the drug. In many cases, the result is death due to total depression of the respiratory mechanism. It is hypothesized that many persons who appear to have committed suicide with sedatives did not do so intentionally, but unknowingly continued to ingest barbiturates while in a groggy, disoriented state. Overdose can also be precipitated by the "upper-downer" syndrome previously mentioned. As the abuser takes more of the barbiturate to counteract or moderate the effects of larger doses of amphetamines, he can inadvertently ingest such a large cumulative amount that overdose occurs.

The second major adverse effect of barbiturate abuse is the *withdrawal syndrome* that evolves when intake of the drug is decreased or stopped. This syndrome is as potentially harmful as the delirium tremens associated with alcohol withdrawal. (The details of this adverse effect are presented in Chapter 13.)

Impairment of physical and mental capabilities is the third adverse effect of barbiturate abuse. These drugs can bring about lessened emotional control, greatly reduced perceptual ability, an increase in distortion of surroundings, and confusion. The dependent person may continue to attempt activities that require a degree of alertness and concentration that he cannot attain. Consequently, automobile accidents, self-injury from falls, and acute anxiety reactions may follow. These responses to chronic abuse are also responsible for the social withdrawal and isolation many barbiturate-dependent persons experience. As loss of control over his behavior increases, the abuser begins to withdraw from those situations which require responsible and alert reactions.

Methaqualone: A Nonbarbiturate Sedative

Slang names are sopors, luding, Quaalude, soapers, "the love drug," "heroin for lovers," mandrakes.

Action Methaqualone is a nonbarbiturate sedative marketed under various names: Parest, Quaalude, Optimil, Sopor, Somnafac. It is available by prescription only and is not yet covered by the Controlled Substance Act of 1970. Methaqualone taken orally is readily absorbed via the gastrointestinal tract and induces normal sleep and sedation. Studies to date have demonstrated no significant changes in respiration, heart rate, or blood pressure when the drug is administered as a preanesthetic sedative. Claims by abusers of this nonbarbiturate sedative of enhanced sexual pleasure or performance have not been supported by research. Thus, although methaqualone is not an aphrodisiac, it does increase sexual desire and promotes a relaxed, at ease feeling characterized by fewer inhibitions.

Characteristics of Methaqualone Abuse   Because abuse of methaqualone has only recently been recognized as a serious drug problem, in-depth research has not been completed regarding its real or potential dependence characteristics. At present, tolerance, psychic dependence, and a strong desire to continue taking the drug have been initially demonstrated. Evidence of physical dependence relies heavily on select and limited incidence of a delirium tremens-like withdrawal syndrome precipitated by cessation of methaqualone intake. Preliminary proof of cross tolerance with barbiturates has also been shown with some abusers of methaqualone.

Adverse Effects   The sedative action of methaqualone is potentiated and intensified when the drug is taken with other central nervous system depressants such as alcohol barbiturates, and antianxiety drugs. The chances of overdosing with such drug combinations are consequently increased. When overdose occurs with accompanying coma, the gag reflex remains intact.

High doses of methaqualone result in abolition of the person's arousal response to painful and auditory stimuli. The user is thus unaware of injury and the warning signal of pain associated with it. Besides an increased pain threshold, some users experience feelings of indestructibility. Methaqualone also potentiates the pain-relieving action of codeine.

Physiological adverse effects include headache and dizziness, menstrual disturbances, dryness and cracking of mouth corners, hangover, nosebleeds, skin eruptions and rashes, diarrhea, nausea and vomiting, anorexia, depersonalization, and pain in the extremities.

HALLUCINOGENS

The hallucinogens (commonly known as the mind-expanding drugs) have been of national concern for the past several years. Some of the drugs in this group have been in use for hundreds of years while others have been synthesized within the last few decades. The hallucinogens discussed in this section represent the major ones of abuse in the United States today. The responses produced by these drugs vary from drug to drug and are heavily dependent upon (1) the user's attitude toward the drug experience and (2) the overall tone or atmosphere of the surroundings. Therefore, the actions of each major drug are separately discussed.

Marijuana (Cannabis, Marihuana, Marajuana)

Slang names are Mary Jane, J, hay, joints, reefers, pot, grass, hash, stuff, dope, tea, hemp, love weed, roach, weed, and many others.

Action THC (tetrahydrocannabinol) is the active ingredient in marijuana that produces the effects, which are noticed within minutes. If it is orally ingested, it may take an hour or longer for the drug to take effect. The exact mechanism of action is not clear at this time. However, it is known that after inhalation, the smoke rapidly enters the circulatory system and produces various effects.

Cannabis affects the eyes by producing irritation in the form of bloodshot eyes or injected conjunctiva. Some users' eyes become photosensitive and consequently these people may habitually wear sunglasses as eye protectors. As with cigarettes, marijuana smoke also irritates the respiratory tract. The mouth becomes dry and the throat feels scratchy. The lungs react to the irritating smoke by increasing secretions. Thus, the frequent marijuana smoker coughs up copious respiratory secretions.

Changes in blood pressure vary from person to person. An increase in the pulse rate is common. A water diuresis may be stimulated for those who orally ingest the drug, and recent studies have found a significant incidence of liver dysfunction in chronic marijuana abusers. Other general physical reactions are dizziness, nausea, and hunger.

Although subjective effects vary with the amount and quality of the drug used, typical responses include change in time sense such that the user overestimates the passage of time; alteration in space perception; a pleasant, relaxed, euphoric feeling, or "high"; changes in mental awareness—dulling of attention, confusion, short-term memory loss, altered sense of identity; increased sensitivity to auditory and visual stimuli; decreased inhibitions such that conversation is facilitated, laughter is exaggerated. Usually the smoker maintains self-control and seeks to attain only the high.

As the dose is increased, subjective actions of the drug are magnified and may cause illusions, visual distortions, dissociation from one's body or body part, or paranoia. The effects may last anywhere from three to twelve hours but vary considerably. The incidence of a hangover phenomenon is low, but it can occur.

Characteristics of Marijuana Dependence A basic characteristic of marijuana abuse is the *variability of response.* The variation is partly due to the personality of the user, his expectations of the experience, the strength of the drug, and the quantity used. Physical dependence on marijuana has not been demonstrated and, therefore, the withdrawal phenomenon does not appear when the drug is discontinued.

Psychological dependence does occur with frequent marijuana abuse. The abuser may experience anxiety and irritation when the drug is not available. Psychological dependence on the high or relaxed feeling induced by the drug maintains the user's desire to continue use. Some marijuana-dependent persons demonstrate their psychological need for the drug by rapidly returning to its use when temporarily deprived of it.

A *reverse tolerance* seems to develop whereby a smaller dosage is required to produce the desired effects after the abuser has become accustomed to the drug. Reverse tolerance may be attributed to the cumulative effect of the drug in the body since there is a prolonged excretion rate associated with frequent marijuana use.

Adverse Effects Although the full extent of the adverse effects associated with marijuana dependence is not known, several significant reactions have been identified to date. Some relate to the drug experience while others relate to the behavior changes concurrent with long-term use.

Personality Changes Long-term use of marijuana has been closely correlated with certain personality changes, which have been noted by nonuser observers as well as frequent cannabis users. These changes include (1) reduced ability to concentrate for long periods, to master new concepts, or to complete tasks; (2) apathy characterized by loss of interest in social problems, lethargy, and less desire to achieve (especially when such a desire existed prior to cannabis abuse); (3) impaired communication skills such as decreased verbal, writing, and speaking ability.

Closely related to these described personality changes is the concept of the *amotivational syndrome.* It has been hypothesized that the heavy, chronic abuser of marijuana has a tendency to evolve a lethergic, amotivated attitude that consists of loss of conventional motivation, increasing inability to tolerate frustration, heightened inability to cope with reality, and loss of capacity to establish and accomplish realistic goals. It has not been possible to prove or disprove the existence of such a syndrome because it is extremely difficult to determine whether or not the affected person would have "dropped out" even if he had never abused marijuana. Research into this question continues and it is hoped that an answer to the question, "Does marijuana abuse cause the amotivational syndrome?" will be found.

The Bad Trip For some, the mind-altering properties of marijuana produce a negative, unpleasant, and often frightening experience known as a "bad trip." If the unpleasant sensations are transitory and the abuser can control the experience, the trip becomes a "bummer." The bad trip experience varies significantly from person to person and consequently it is difficult to make generalizations about this phenomenon. However, for some people, a bad trip might contain elements of anxiety, paranoia, fear, headache, illusions, hallucinations, feelings of dismemberment or separation of the mind from the body, and/or confusion of past, present, and future.

Panic Reactions For some people, marijuana produces an acute reaction of panic. Commonly the person experiences anxiety, agitation, and fears of impending insanity or death. These feelings are generated by the misinterpretation of the physiological and psychological effects of the drug. The experience is self-limiting and may occur more often in the person who cannot accept or cope with the alternations in time and perception induced by marijuana.

Flashbacks The flashback consists of a replay, or repeat, of an experience that happened while under the influence of the drug. It comes on when the person is drug-free. Depending on the content of the flashback, it may be viewed as a good trip or a bad trip. This experience can initiate a panic reaction in the person who is unfamiliar with the experience or when the content of the flashback is like that of a bad trip. The flashback may be triggered by a stimulus similar to that which was present during the person's past episode of marijuana use, for example, hard rock music or a specific environment. Also, some drug abusers experience a flashback of a past LSD experience that seems to be triggered by marijuana smoking. The mechanism of the flashback phenomenon has not been identified, but it continues to be an adverse effect of marijuana abused.

LSD (Lysergic Acid Diethylamide Tartrate, LSD-25)

Slang names include acid, blue acid, the Hawk, royal blue, sugar cubes, pearly gates, heavenly blue, 25, instant Zen, trip, and others.

Action LSD is a clear, tasteless, odorless, synthetic chemical with potent hallucinogenic properties. It is found in capsule or powder form and is rapidly absorbed into the circulatory system through the intestinal tract. The effects last for about eight to twelve hours. The drug may also be found in any substance or object impregnated with it, e.g., sugar cubes, cookies, liquids, or a smooth surface that can be licked. It can be injected intravenously.

The exact mechanism of LSD action has not yet been identified. It has been hypothesized that the drug's effects result from changes in brain chemical levels that may block the normal sensory filtering process. The drug mimics sympathetic or autonomic nervous system stimulation. Physical responses may include increased blood sugar, tachycardia (rapid heart rate), widely dilated pupils, lowered body temperature with attendant shivering, fluctuation in blood pressure, nausea, dizziness, headache, and fine tremors of the hands and fingers. LSD intensifies and magnifies visual nerve impulse transmission via the optic nerve to the brain. Thus colors seen by the LSD abuser, or "acid head," acquire startling vividness and intensity. Interpretation of sights and sounds can become dependent on each other so that the user "hears" color, "feels" visual images, and/or "sees" music.

LSD gained popularity as a result of its mind-altering actions, that is, its ability to sharpen perception, release the mind from its customary inhibitions, and remove boundaries to thinking and intellectual experience. The LSD effects vary from person to person. It does, however, possess some general psychological changes common to most users of the drug.

Alteration in Perception   The LSD experience is characterized by perceptual distortion of the immediate environment. Surrounding objects or persons can be perceived as moving, tilted, or distorted in configuration. Illusions and hallucinations appear as a major visual effect of the drug. The interpretation of environmental qualities also becomes distorted so that the sky is perceived as intense, vivid blueness, not simply as the sky. Qualities of plants and other natural materials become magnified. In general, the person's sensual perceptions are much more acute.

Time perception is also altered. The person may think time is standing still or moving slowly. Because of these perceptions, the present assumes major importance.

Distortion of Body Image   Extreme alteration and distortion of body image is virtually unique to the LSD experience and can serve as the stimulus to acute anxiety and panic reactions in the user. Body image distortions and hallucinations may include losing contact with parts of the body; seeing a dismembered limb floating in space; separation of mind and body; feeling that supernatural acts such as flying are possible; seeing images of the body in a dismembered state or in death; experiencing a loss of boundaries between the body and space; and many others.

Expansion of Intellectual or Spiritual Awareness   Many LSD abusers claim to have achieved awe-inspiring, life-changing insight from the drug experience. Some have described a sensation in which the self views the self bringing about significant insight into personal philosophies, goals, and future plans. Feelings of having attained spiritual oneness with a supreme being are also attributed to the LSD experience. Many LSD users express belief in having achieved in-depth self-awareness and religious insight which subsequently transforms their life and its meaning.

In a sense, LSD users who experience such self-awareness have gone on a trip —they have been somewhere in their mind, have returned, and are somehow different because of the experience. It is this intellectual and accompanying emotional experience that has led to the creation of the term *LSD trip.*

Fluctuations in Emotions   A significant aspect of the LSD experience is the intense change or fluctuation in the emotions. Mood changes may be rapid with a general intensification of emotions—laughing, crying, anger, fear, anxiety, Opposing emotions can be felt simultaneously and can produce confusion and anxiety. For example, depression and elation, happiness and sadness, or tension and relaxation can be felt at the same time. Most of the emotions experienced are related to the perceptual distortions and hallucinations of the trip.

Characteristics of LSD Dependence   There is no demonstrated physical dependence associated with LSD abuse. Consequently, withdrawal symptoms do not appear when intake is halted. Those who continually abuse LSD develop a psychological dependence on the pleasurable, mind-expanding, or awareness-stimulating effects of the drug. Tolerance also develops quickly and the user must ingest larger amounts of the drug or inject it intravenously to achieve the desired effect. Tolerance is short-lived, however, if the person stops taking the drug. Within three days of abstinence he becomes susceptible once again to its effects. If a person has developed tolerance to LSD, he will also have a cross tolerance to other hallucinogens such as psilocybin or mescaline.

Adverse Effects   There are several adverse effects of LSD abuse, some having been widely publicized. The major ill effects associated with the LSD trip can be divided into two categories: (1) those occurring during the drug experience and (2) those occurring after the trip is over.

Acute Anxiety and Panic during the Experience   The perceptual distortions, body image changes, and especially the fear that the LSD trip can't be stopped after it has begun can produce acute anxiety in some people. This anxiety can reach panic proportions in which the person becomes terrified of what's happening to him. The onset of anxiety, fear, terror, or panic turns the drug experience into a bad trip. Anyone who has such an experience is said to have "freaked out." In an attempt to physically escape from the fearful drug experience, the user may inadvertently injure or possibly kill himself.

Feelings of Superhuman Powers during the Experience   The fact that LSD can in some way stimulate the person to believe he has superhuman powers does not necessarily have to be an adverse effect. However, it does become harmful if the user acts on such beliefs to his own detriment. For example, the person who feels he is invincible or invulnerable may try fatal ventures such as flying, floating on air, or stopping an oncoming automobile. Although these instances of seriously impaired judgment are infrequent, they do represent a major adverse effect to the LSD abuser.

Adverse Effects Occurring after the Drug Experience Four significant adverse effects may appear after the acute drug experience.

1 *Flashbacks.* As long as twenty months or more after an LSD experience, a person may undergo a repeat of the trip. This flashback phenomenon occurs spontaneously, without warning, and can induce feelings of panic or fear of losing one's mind.

2 *Potential chromosome damage.* To date there has been no definite demonstration of a link between LSD abuse and chromosome damage. Certain studies have identified chromosome breaks, while others have described birth defects in infants born of mothers who said they had taken LSD. As a result of inconclusive research findings, the risk of producing chromosome damage from LSD abuse remains a potent possible adverse effect.

3 *Paranoia.* The LSD abuser can become paranoid during the drug experience, and the paranoia can continue for up to three or four days. The person may become violent toward others he imagines are a threat to him. Reactions can include extremely poor judgment and suicide attempts that seem to be related to the body-mind dissociation induced by LSD abuse.

4 *Withdrawal from society.* When the LSD-dependent person begins to come off his trip, he may experience depression. This response may be caused by the incongruence of the mind-expanding insights achieved with the drug and the reality the person returns to. The user often finds that the insights attained via LSD are not compatible with reality-oriented living. As a result of these discoveries, the person may retreat more and more into his own drug-oriented world. Such withdrawal, or dropping out, happens more frequently with the adolescent user who has not yet been able to achieve a comfortable sense of identity.

Other adverse effects can be short- or long-term. Many have not been clearly defined and supported by research findings. Among the areas under intense investigation and study are the aspects of LSD-induced brain damage, psychosis, and birth defects.

Other Hallucinogens

Several other hallucinogens found in nature or chemically synthesized have become popular abused substances. In general, the hallucinogenic effects of these drugs are similar to LSD. For this reason, the descriptions of these hallucinogens will concentrate on those effects and patterns of abuse that distinguish them from LSD.

Psilocybin   Also called magic mushroom and sacred mushroom, psilocybin is a natural hallucinogen found in certain mushrooms. It is less potent than LSD and is available in crystalline, liquid, or powdered form as well as in whole mushrooms.

The hallucinogenic experience with psilocybin is generally shorter than that with LSD—approximately three to five hours. Physical responses to the drug appear within thirty minutes of oral ingestion and include giddiness, muscle twitching and aching, abdominal discomfort, restlessness, anxiety, and numbness of the tongue or mouth. The pupils dilate and a slight increase in pulse, blood pressure, and temperature is a common experience. Visual distortions and startling vividness of colors occur with the eyes closed. Acuity of hearing is increased but verbal communication becomes slurred. Depth perception and time perception are impaired as the person experiences a self-introspective euphoria.

Tolerance to psilocybin is developed but not as quickly as with LSD. The person who has a tolerance to psilocybin can also have a cross tolerance to LSD. No physical dependence has been correlated with psilocybin abuse.

A major adverse effect associated with psilocybin abuse is intense anxiety or panic during the drug experience. As with the LSD trip, these reactions are related to the interpretation of subjective perceptual distortion induced by the drug. Following the immediate episode, there may be mood changes, paranoid or depressive reactions, or the inability to differentiate between fantasy and reality.

Dimethoxamphetamine   Also known as STP (Serenity-Tranquility-Peace) and syndicate acid, DOM is a synthetic amphetamine with hallucinogenic properties believed to be one-tenth as potent as LSD and approximately a hundred times more potent than mescaline. The length of the drug experience ranges from sixteen to twenty-four hours or longer. Physical response closely parallels that of LSD and psilocybin. Also, there may be drowsiness that apparently has no direct effect on the central nervous system. As with LSD, the user experiences perceptual distortion and acuity with an emphasis on introspective, emotional thinking and bombardment of perceptual apparatus of visual, auditory, and tactile stimuli.

DOM abuse is characterized by rapid development of tolerance, but no physical dependence. The drug has lost much of its popularity due in large part to the length of the trip and its atropinelike side effects (dryness of mouth, tachycardia, photophobia, blurred vision). These two factors are also thought to be responsible for the panic reactions that can occur with DOM. Those who are unprepared psychologically for such a long drug experience may respond by panicking when the effects continue beyond desired limits or expectations.

Mescaline—Peyote   Sometimes referred to as mesc, Big Chief, cactus, the button tops, half moon, a moon, P, tops, mescal beans, the bad seed, mescal button, and other names, mescaline is legally used only by members of the Native American Church of North America in religious rites. It is found in the peyote cactus, but it also has been chemically synthesized in the laboratory. The drug is generally taken by mouth but can be dissolved and injected subcutaneously or intramuscularly.

Mescaline is chemically related to epinephrine and norepinephrine and, therefore, its primary physiological effects are attributed to this chemical similarity, i.e., pupil dilation, increased blood pressure, pulse and body temperature, sweating, flushing of face, tremors, and nausea. Effects of the drug last from around five to twelve or fourteen hours.

The subjective effects of mescaline closely resemble those of LSD and include distortions of the visual field, body image alterations, emotional lability, and brilliant visual hallucinations. An additional specific effect of mescaline is found in the visual field—objects may seem to come to life, move, and take on vivid colors and unusual shapes.

In general, it takes approximately three to six days for tolerance to mescaline to evolve. As with the other hallucinogens, cross tolerance to LSD and psilocybin accompanies tolerance to mescaline. Although there is no physical dependence or the subsequent withdrawal syndrome, psychological dependence can develop with frequent mescaline abuse.

The two major adverse effects are the nausea and vomiting that often start during the first hour or so following ingestion, and the bad trip experience. For some users, the physical discomfort associated with the drug is a deterrent to further use. Many people take mescaline in hopes of attaining significant emotional or intellectual insight—suggested attributes evolving from Indian use of the drug in tribal rituals. As with the other hallucinogens, however, the experience can turn into a nightmare that seems endless—a bad trip.

Dimethyltryptamine   Also called businessman's special or forty-five-minute psychosis, DMT is a short-acting hallucinogen derived from powdered seeds of a Caribbean plant. The largest portion of the illegal supply of DMT comes from the synthetic manufacture of the drug. Like LSD, DMT produces a hallucinogenic trip with perceptual distortion, body image change, and emotional lability. Unique to the DMT experience is its rapid (often described as rough or harsh) onset and short duration—forty-five minutes to two hours. The drug can be injected but usually is smoked alone or in combination with marijuana, parsley leaves, or tobacco. To date, physical dependence has not been associated with DMT abuse. However, psychological dependence on the effects of the drug may occur. Since tolerance develops, larger doses are required to achieve the desired effect. Adverse effects are usually focused on the rough onset of the trip and, for some, the short duration of the experience. Bad trips can occur with DMT but may be less of a deterrent because of the rapidity with which the drug effects dissipate.

Phencyclidine Sometimes referred to as peace pill, angel dust, hog, or synthetic marijuana, PCP is an animal tranquilizer that has been diverted to illegal, street use by some drug abusers. It produces actions similar to hallucinogens and stimulants to the central nervous system. This powdered drug can be taken in capsule form, in which it is usually combined with LSD or mescaline. It is also sprinkled on parsley, marijuana, and other smoked substances.

PCP acts as a depressant to the central nervous system, imitating alcohol intoxication with muscular incoordination, numbness of extremities, and, in high doses, convulsions. Diaphoresis, double vision and dizziness, flushing and mild decrease in blood pressure are common. The PCP trip is characterized by progression from body image changes to perceptual distortion (hallucinations are infrequent) to feelings of estrangement and apathy. Drowsiness is common as are depressive thoughts of death, feelings of emptiness, and the sensation of being in a void. Users of PCP also experience an inability to sort out and organize incoming sensory stimuli while under the influence of the drug. In general, PCP is not a drug of choice among abusers. The experience it produces is not euphoric, light, or mind-expanding as compared with that produced by LSD, psilocybin, and mescaline.

NARCOTICS

In this book, the term *narcotic* drugs will be used to refer to the opiates, opiate derivatives, and synthetic opiatelike preparations. The principal narcotic of abuse is the opium derivative heroin. Other major opiates include morphine, hydromorphone, and codeine. Significant synthetic opiates of abuse are meperidine and methadone. In addition to these drugs, there are numerous other narcotics less frequently abused.

Morphine is derived from opium. Heroin, codeine, and hydromorphone are derived from morphine, with heroin being the most potent of the derivatives. Although the actions of the opiates are similar, each will be presented with its unique effects. In general, the opiates are considered to selectively depress the central nervous system.

Opium

The poppy plant is the source of the narcotic opium. It may be eaten in capsule or powder form or smoked after initial refinement. Onset of the drug's effects is more rapid when it is inhaled than when it is eaten. Intake of opium results in a euphoric feeling with elimination of aches or pains. It induces a languid, relaxed, pleasurable feeling. Sense of time becomes distorted and the person may feel self-confident with a superior attitude or become talkative and outgoing. As dependence on the pleasurable effects of the drug increases, the user neglects self-care in diet and personal hygiene, and experiences depression when the effects wear off.

Morphine and Heroin

Slang names are as follows: heroin—H, junk, shit, snow, stuff, horse, dope, boy, hard stuff, joypowder, skag, smack, and others; morphine—Miss Emma, morf, morphie, monkey, M, dreamer, white stuff, hocus, unkie, and others.

Action As an analgesic, morphine is a highly valued drug in medical treatment in the United States. It tends to be abused by heroin-dependent persons when supplies of heroin decrease. Both drugs can be taken in a variety of ways: ingested orally, snorted via the nasal passages, subcutaneously injected by skin-popping, or injected intravenously by mainlining. The most common routes used are subcutaneous and intravenous. When taken subcutaneously, morphine and heroin reach their peak effects within thirty minutes to an hour. The duration of both drugs' effects is approximately four to six hours. The intravenous route produces more rapid effects, with heroin acting more quickly than morphine. Duration of the intravenous heroin and morphine experience is also approximately four to six hours. Although morphine and heroin produce similar actions, heroin is abused more frequently than morphine. The following discussion of the action of heroin applies to morphine also.

After or during intravenous injection of heroin, the user experiences an immediate "rush"—a jolt to the central nervous system. The rush is subjectively described as an orgasm in the stomach, an orgasm all over, or an intestinal orgasm. A euphoric high follows the rush in which the person may experience drowsiness, slurred speech, impaired muscular coordination, depressed reflexes, and cessation of pain. Some people can experience anxiety during initial use of heroin. Heart rate slows, respiration is depressed, appetite is depressed, pupils are constricted, and smooth muscle fibers are also constricted. The high described by one person can differ significantly from that of another.

Codeine

Also called junk or schoolboy, codeine is derived from opium or morphine in crystal or powdered form and produces effects similar to morphine. It is about one-sixth as potent as morphine and is not used by addicts as the major drug of abuse. Certain cough syrups contain limited amounts of codeine (elixir of terpin hydrate with codeine) and are abused if taken in large quantities when stronger opiates are not available.

Hydromorphone

As a fine, white crystalline powder, hydromorphone (Lords, Dilaudid, D) is derived from morphine and has shorter actions, but similar analgesic and sedative actions. Because it is not generally prevalent on the streets, it is not a major abused narcotic. Supplies of hydromorphone are illegally diverted from medical, pharmaceutical, or hospital sources.

Meperidine

Synthetically prepared in a white crystalline powder, meperidine (Dolantal, Pethidine, Demerol, Isonipecaine) acts similarly to morphine. It may be taken orally or by injection (intramuscularly, intravenously). Additional actions specific to this narcotic include dilated pupils and decreased gastrointestinal secretions. As with hydromorphone, street supplies of meperidine are illegally diverted from medical, pharmaceutical, or hospital sources.

Methadone

Abuse of the synthetic narcotic methadone (dollies, dolls, dolophine, amidone, adanon, 10-8-20) has greatly increased in recent years. The effects of the drug are similar to morphine but develop more slowly and last longer. If methadone is taken by an opiate-dependent person, it will block or prohibit the action of any opiate taken subsequently. Such blocking lasts while methadone is active in the body. It is this blocking action that provides the rationale for methadone maintenance treatment programs for heroin dependence. (Refer to Chapter 13 for a discussion of methadone maintenance treatment.) Methadone may be taken orally or injected intravenously.

Characteristics of Narcotic Dependence

The rapidity and extent to which characteristics of dependence are induced are related to the specific narcotic, e.g., heroin dependence occurs more rapidly than dependence on codeine.

Tolerance to increasing doses of narcotics develops rapidly with heroin and morphine, and stems mainly from the analgesic and sedative effects of the drugs. Many narcotic-dependent persons can take large single doses without harm. If the same amount were to be taken by a nonuser, death would most likely result.

A strong psychic or emotional dependence on the euphoric, pleasurable effects of narcotics is rapidly created. The user feels an increasing compulsion to continue taking the drug in order to reproduce the desired sensations. Physical dependence also develops rapidly and increases as the dose increases. It is the withdrawal syndrome resulting from decrease or cessation of narcotic intake which is related to physical dependence that reinforces the compulsion to continue taking the drug.

Adverse Effects of Narcotics

Major adverse effects associated with narcotic dependence can be divided into four categories.

Overdose The most dangerous adverse effect of narcotic dependence is undoubtedly overdosage. An overdose is usually reached when the user mainlines a quantity of heroin that is significantly more potent than the customary supply. The person may or may not know that the heroin is more potent. Some addicts believe their body can cope with a stronger dose, others are unaware of the dose difference. Incidences where a user is found dead with the needle still in the vein or the tourniquet in place have been reported and indicate the rapidity with which an overdose can occur. (The specific signs and symptoms of overdose will be discussed in Chapter 13.)

Decreased Self-Care Persons dependent on narcotics often neglect their diet, personal hygiene, and preventive health care. Self-care assumes a low priority when the user is preoccupied with getting a drug supply in order to prevent withdrawal. Malnutrition and undernutrition accompany muscle wasting, loss of fatty tissues, and decreased ability to stave off infection.

Increased Incidence of Constipation Because narcotics reduce intestinal secretions, increase smooth muscle relaxation, and depress appetite, constipation is a common problem found in addicts. Stools tend to be hard and are passed with considerable difficulty.

Disturbances in Reproductive System Menstrual irregularities and decreased ability to conceive or temporary sterility are common in female narcotic addicts. Men experience a lack of interest in sexual activities while under the influence of the drug, but there is no evidence that sterility is a problem.

Physical Problems Associated with Method of Administration Abscesses at injection sites are fairly common and are attributed to unsterile or unclean technique as well as contaminated drugs. Such poor technique also contributes to and is largely responsible for the high incidence of tetanus, hepatitis, endocarditis, septicemia, and lung complications (congestion, abscesses, infection, or clots). Thus, although there is yet no evidence of narcotic-induced damage to various organs, the behavioral patterns associated with drug administration can cause serious physical adverse effects.

VOLATILE SUBSTANCES

Volatile substances consist of those chemical preparations that when inhaled produce altered states of consciousness and varying degrees of inebriation. These inhalants are divided into three groups and are considered central nervous system depressants.

Aerosols

Numerous volatile substances found in aerosol containers have become subject to abuse. Most can be found in the home and are easily purchased by those seeking to inhale them. Abused aerosols include glass chillers that may contain Freon, insecticides, hair sprays, and deodorants.

Commercial Solvents

The commercial solvents are perhaps the most frequently abused volatile inhalants. They are sold in various retail stores and thus control of sales is extremely difficult. These solvents include model airplane glue, paint thinner, lacquer, plastic cements, gasoline with varying amounts of lead, nail polish remover, cleaning fluid, and lighter fluid. Inhalation of glue vapors can be considered the most physically damaging form of drug abuse.[2] These commercial solvents contain varying amounts and combinations of toluene, naphtha, acetone, benzene, carbon tetrachloride, Xylene, and other volatile solvents.

Anesthetics

In recent years there has been a significant increase in the abuse of various anesthetic inhalants. Chief among the abused substances in this category are chloroform (which may be swallowed as well as inhaled), nitrous oxide (laughing gas), and ether. Obtaining supplies of these agents may require more effort than commercial solvents or the aerosols since they tend to be used in specified surgical, dental, or hospital procedures.

Action of Volatile Substances

Generally, the abused volatile substances produce similar effects, with some variation according to how long the substance is inhaled each time, the chemical composition, and the psychological set of the user. Depending on the dose inhaled, the experience may last for minutes or hours.

Initial responses to inhalation of volatile vapors are similar to those found with alcohol intoxication: slurring of speech, loss of coordination, lessening of inhibitions, dizziness, ataxia, diplopia (double vision), tinnitis (ringing in the

---

[2] Richard Ashley, *Heroin: The Myths and the Facts*, St. Martin's Press, New York, 1972, p. 112.

ears). Also, the user may experience hallucinations, hazy euphoria, muscle spasms, marked behavioral and personality changes and/or impaired perception and judgment. As the effects wear off, the person generally feels drowsiness, possibly depression or stupor, sometimes nausea, and in some instances lapses into unconsciousness. With long-term abuse of inhalants, the person can experience significant weight loss.

After the effects of the drug have worn off, the user generally does not remember all the events or sensations that took place during the drug experience.

Characteristics of Dependence on Volatile Substances

Some of the characteristics of dependence do develop with abuse of volatile substances but only over prolonged periods of time. Tolerance to glue, gasoline, hair sprays, and other inhalants does build up and requires an increased dose in order to produce the desired reactions. Over time, psychological dependence on the pleasureful, conscious-altering effects also occurs. The person becomes increasingly dependent and actively tries to maintain availability of the drug as well as to organize activities around the inhalation experience.

To date, physical dependence on volatile substances has not been clearly demonstrated. Consequently, there is no definite evidence of a withdrawal syndrome following cessation of intake.

Adverse Effects of Dependence on Volatile Substances

The severity of the adverse effects associated with abuse of volatile substances is related to the substance used, its strength, the amount inhaled, and the presence of other drugs in the body.

Overdose Reports of overdose with glue and gasoline are more frequent than with other volatile substances. Some overdose victims arrive at the hospital emergency room with the plastic bag used to concentrate the glue vapors still over the head. Overdose can be attributed to (1) miscalculation of tolerance by the user, (2) the use of such accessories as plastic bags over the head that close off air intake when the person becomes unconscious, and (3) the simultaneous intake of other central nervous system depressants, especially alcohol.

Physical Damage Evidence of serious and sometimes permanent damage to certain organ systems and cellular functions has been associated with inhalation of volatile substances. Damage to lung tissue may vary from simple congestion to hemorrhage with prolonged glue sniffing. Bone marrow depression, damage to liver, kidneys, and spleen may also result. Because of these physical hazards, most manufacturers have added an oil of mustard preparation to airplane glues and cements. The preparation prevents abuse by inhalation but does not decrease the effectiveness of the product.

Excessive inhalation of hair sprays can cause extensive respiratory damage such as fibrosis, thickening of lung tissues, and chest pain and tightness. Gasoline abuse may lead to lead poisoning. In both cases, with proper treatment and cessation of inhaling practices, damage will be temporary.

Sudden death from freezing damage to lung tissue, laryngospasm, anoxia, asphyxiation, and frostbite is related to inhalation of Freon preparations. Death may come with a first experience or after numerous experiences. In either instance, death is due to cardiac arrhythmia as oxygen is displaced by Freon and carbon dioxide levels in the alveoli increase sharply.

Preliminary evidence of chromosome breakage and altered chromosomes has been associated with long-term glue sniffing. More research into this aspect of physical damage is necessary before conclusive statements can be made about the implications of such genetic changes.

Severe burn injury may result when volatile substances are inhaled near a source of combustion such as lighters, sparks, or matches. Although this is not a major physical adverse effect of inhalant abuse, it nevertheless is significant in terms of the extent of damage and danger in abusing volatile preparations.

Personality Changes   Persons who chronically abuse inhalants may be subject to significant personality changes. Some people experience mild, transitory changes while others exhibit serious, pathological changes, such as psychosis. Juveniles have been known to engage in petty theft, physical abuse of children, or unusual sexual practices. As with alcohol intoxication, many abusers of volatile substances experience mood changes and bizarre behavioral changes, e.g., the quiet adolescent who attacks a sibling or family pet while under the influence of an inhalant, or the extroverted teenager who becomes depressed and withdrawn after sniffing volatile vapors.

Distorted Perceptions   Abusers of volatile inhalants experience distorted perceptions, visual and auditory. When they undertake activities requiring astuteness and mental alertness, they may not ever harm themselves but can endanger the well-being of innocent bystanders. Also, in those cases where hallucinations and feelings of indestructibility result from the drug experience, the person may attempt to fly, stop oncoming vehicles, or in other ways demonstrate the newly acquired, imaginary powers.

SUMMARY COMMENT

Drug abuse is an ever-expanding, invasive problem in the world today. A great deal is known about the major abused substances presented in this chapter. Unfortunately, the gaps in understanding the "whys" of drug abuse are less clearly comprehended and under continued study. Seldom does a day go by when one does not read about a drug-related problem in newspapers, magazines, or other information media. Reports of exotic and bizarre drug abuse patterns seem astounding yet continue to occur. Drugs not controlled by federal or state legislation become abused as people experiment in the search for new experiences and altered states of consciousness. As an example, it is known that such drugs as propoxyphene hydrochloride (Darvon®) are injected intravenously. The trip is short-lived but pleasant, and the drug is readily obtained through both illegal means and legal prescription sources. The harm done to the body by such experimentation can be severe: renal failure, blood chemistry abnormalities, and intravascular coagulation.

Undoubtedly there are innumerable other legally obtained drugs that are subject to abuse orally, intravenously, or subcutaneously. As health professionals, nurses must expand their individual awareness of drug abuse behaviors beyond the boundaries of this chapter. With such knowledge and perception, potential detrimental drug use patterns can be disrupted before dependence sets in.

REFERENCES

Arndt, Jack R., and William L. Blockstein (eds.): *Problems in Drug Abuse,* The Wisconsin Pharmacy Extension Bulletin, Madison, 1970.

Ashley, Richard: *Heroin: The Myths and the Facts,* St. Martin's Press, New York, 1972.

Blachly, Paul H. (ed.): *Progress in Drug Abuse,* Charles C Thomas, Springfield, Ill., 1972.

Bloomquist, Edward R.: *Marijuana: The Second Trip,* Glencoe Press, Beverly Hills, Calif., 1971.

Byrd, Oliver E. (ed.): *Medical Readings on Drug Abuse,* Addison-Wesley Publishing Company, Reading, Mass., 1970.

Chambers, Carl D., Arthur D. Moffett, and Walter R. Cuskey: "Five Patterns of Darvon Abuse," *The International Journal of the Addictions,* **6**:173–189, March 1971.

Cumberlidge, Malcolm C.: "The Abuse of Barbiturates by Heroin Addicts," *Canadian Medical Association Journal,* **98**:1045–1049, June 1, 1968.

"Dependence on Cannabis (Marijuana)," *Journal of the American Medical Association,* **201**:108–111, August 7, 1967.

Desk Reference on Drug Abuse, American Hospital Association, Chicago, 1971.

Drugs of Abuse, U.S. Government Printing Office, Washington, 1972.

Edison, George R.: "Amphetamines: A Dangerous Illusion," *Annals of Internal Medicine,* **74**:605–610, April 1971.

Fort, Joel: "Comparison Chart of Major Substances Used for Mind Alteration," *American Journal of Nursing,* **71**:1740–1741, September 1971.

Gamage, James R., and E. Lief Zerkin of STASH, "Methaqualone," *Report Series: National Clearinghouse for Drug Abuse Information,* ser. 18, no. 1, October 1973.

Horman, Richard E., and Allan M. Fox (eds.): *Drug Awareness,* Avon Books, New York, 1970.

"IV Trip on an Oral Drug," *Emergency Medicine,* 4:102, July 1972.

Jacobson, Cecil B., and Cheston M. Berlin: "Possible Reproductive Detriment in LSD Users," *Journal of the American Medical Association,* 222:1367–1373, December 11, 1972.

Kaplan, Robert: *Drug Abuse: Perspectives on Drugs,* Wm. C. Brown Company, Dubuque, Iowa, 1970.

Kaufman, Karl L., and O. L. Salerni: "Today's Drugs of Abuse," *Bedside Nurse,* 4:13–19, September 1971.

Kreek, Mary J.: "Medical Safety and Side Effects of Methadone in Tolerant Individuals," *Journal of the American Medical Association,* 223:665–668, February 5, 1973.

Levy, Marvin R. (Director): *Resource Book for Drug Abuse Education,* U.S. Government Printing Office, Washington, 1969.

Lichtenstein, Grace: "Methaqualone, A Love Drug . . . ," *The New York Times* Service, in *Honolulu Star-Bulletin,* p. D-3, June 15, 1973.

Lynn, Edward J: "Amphetamine Abuse: A 'Speed Trap,'" *Psychiatric Quarterly,* 45:92–101, 1971.

"Marijuana and Health: A Report to the Congress," *American Journal of Psychiatry,* 128:189–193, August 1971.

Maurer, David W., and Victor H. Vogel, *Narcotics and Narcotic Addiction,* Charles C Thomas, Springfield, Ill., 1967.

Richards, Louise G., Milton H. Joffe, and George R. Spratto: *LSD-25: A Factual Account,* U.S. Government Printing Office, Washington, 1970.

Schmitt, Richard C., Harold A. Goolishian, and Sally Abston: "Gasoline Sniffing in Children Leading to Severe Burn Injury," *The Journal of Pediatrics,* 80:1021–1023, June 1972.

STASH: "DOM (STP)," *Report Series: National Clearinghouse for Drug Abuse Information,* ser. 17, no. 1, May 1973.

STASH: "Mescaline," *Report Series: National Clearinghouse for Drug Abuse Information,* ser. 15, no. 1, May 1973.

STASH: "Psilocybin," *Report Series: National Clearinghouse for Drug Abuse Information,* ser. 16, no. 1, May 1973.

Swift, Pamela: "Beware of New Drugs!", *Parade,* April 1, 1973.

"Volatile Substances: Some Questions and Answers," National Clearinghouse for Drug Abuse Information, Public Health Service Publication No. 2150, Washington, 1971.

Willis, J. H.: *Drug Dependence,* Faber and Faber, London, 1969.

Winek, Charles L.: "Discouraging Drug Abuse," *The New England Journal of Medicine,* 281:740, September 25, 1969.

Chapter 12

Theories of Causation and Characteristics of Drug Abuse

The characteristics of drug abuse to be discussed in this chapter concern the major psychological, physiological, and social problems that arise as a result of drug abuse patterns. Much of the information presented requires further research and study to substantiate proposed hypotheses.

PROPOSED THEORIES OF CAUSATION

The many proposed causes of drug abuse behavior can be broken down into two broad categories: (1) causes that initiate drug abuse behavior and (2) causes that relate to continued drug dependence. These proposed and hypothetical causes are not meant to be all-inclusive and, therefore, some less prominent theories are not included.

Theories Related to Initiation of Drug Abuse

Drug abuse with pursuant drug dependence can be attributed to one or a combination of several causes. Some of the proposed causes pertain most specifically to adolescents; other causes may also apply to members of the adult, older generation.

Alteration of Consciousness It has been hypothesized that man's basic nature includes the search for altered states of consciousness. Thus, as man seeks suitable and satisfactory methods of achieving this alteration, he may experiment with drugs that foster unusual perceptual distortion and stimulation of a sense of heightened awareness or insight. The development of drug dependence is a negative result of this search, which may be conscious but is more likely unconscious.

Seeking New Experiences The desire to discover new and diverse experiences, to satisfy curiosity about the unknown, and to explore new sensations all contribute to the initiation of drug abuse behavior. The greatly increased economic and material affluence prevalent in American society, coupled with relatively easy availability of illicit drugs, gives many adolescents and young adults the means to experiment with such chemicals.

Adolescents are relatively well informed about the excessively advertised mystical properties of certain drugs. Exaggerated claims of achieving true philosophical or religious enlightenment as a direct result of a drug experience reinforce the adolescent's desire to experience similar awareness. In addition, the uninitiated hear and read about the unparalleled sensual and euphoric effects attainable. When such claims of heightened awareness and physical ecstasy are touted as the general response anyone can enjoy after taking a particular drug, it is no wonder that nonusers consider and actually partake of such chemicals. This desire for new and exciting experiences, then, can serve as the initial stimulus to take illicit drugs.

Parental and Societal Example Many adolescents and young adults are accustomed to their parents' use of various chemicals, such as alcohol, nicotine, caffeine, tranquilizers, and sedatives and thus see nothing wrong in following their example. But the drugs chosen by the youngster may differ considerably from those used by his parents. In many cases, there is a significant correlation between parental drug use and abuse and consequent drug abuse behavior patterns of children of these parents.[1]

As stated earlier, Americans are drug-oriented, often seeking solutions to life's basic problems and trials by resorting to chemical placebos. From early childhood, we are taught to get medicinal cures for everything from minor aches to major trauma. Such practices in themselves are not harmful. It is when resort to drugs becomes the most acceptable path to comfort and carefree living

[1] Wolfram Keup (ed.), *Drug Abuse: Current Concepts and Research,* Charles C Thomas, Springfield, Ill., 1972, pp. 149–152.

that drugs become abused. With such prevalent drug-oriented attitudes permeating society, adolescents and young adults find it difficult to reject exotic drugs as "morally wrong" or "poison to the body and spirit."

As a result of the examples set by those most intimately involved with instilling values in the emerging generation—parents—and the rather extensive and condoned use of drugs in society in general, it should not be surprising that large numbers of young people accept and use illicit drugs.

Escape   The desire to experience changes in perception and sensation can be interpreted as escape or avoidance behavior. The inhabitants of inner-city poverty areas and racial ghettos are often cited as exhibiting escape behavior because of their extremely high drug abuse rates. For many drug abusers who have been reared in economically and often emotionally deprived homes, resorting to pleasant, euphoria-producing chemicals provides a temporary release from continuous confrontation with their surroundings.

Escape to drug abuse may also come from a person's efforts to avoid anxiety related to uncertainty, insecurity, new and frightening demands, certain life crises, or loneliness. These feelings of anxiety produce unpleasant, threatening sensations of varying degrees of intensity. When the person feels or anticipates such anxiety or when existing levels of anxiety increase, he may turn to drugs as a means of escaping the real or imagined threat. "Turning on" and "tuning out" allow the drug user to temporarily escape unpleasantness while granting him a sense of control over his destiny. Also, the perceptual distortion and alteration in mental alertness provides a means of escape from decision-making responsibilities. Such avoidance may be a prominent behavior characteristic with the person who has a low frustration tolerance; that is, in order not to make errors which could lead to frustration, he avoids the decision-making process altogether. In reality, however, the drug user *does* make a decision when he turns to drugs to escape threatening decisions—the decision to reject the situation requiring judgment.

The person who uses drugs as a means of escape may be addressing only the overt problem, e.g., poverty, social deprivation, anxiety, or fear. The basic problems leading to such feelings and external living conditions are not ameliorated by drug abuse—they are usually intensified. Thus, the *visible* causes of escape to drug abuse behavior can be only the symptoms of the real underlying problem.

Rebellion   It has been hypothesized that one of the most effective means of expressing contempt, hatred, or defiance of authority figures is through behavior deemed to be unlawful or undesirable by those same authority figures. For some this need to express rebellion results in the initiation of drug abuse and ultimately the development of drug dependence.

The need to be rebellious can be associated with peer group pressure and the desire to achieve peer status. Adolescents highly value and need the security provided by peer group approval and consensus. When the peer group identifies rebellion against parental and societal values as its goal or badge of acceptance, the group members search for ways to achieve the needed acceptance. The current antiestablishment, antiauthoritarian viewpoints espoused by the youthful generation are a prime example of such rebellion. Use of establishment-defined "harmful" drugs by rebellious adolescents becomes a significant means of expressing dissatisfaction and contempt for the values and goals of the establishment majority.

Being an "in" member of the peer group is of major importance to adolescents and also to many young adults. Thus, if some group members are experimenting with illicit drugs, other members are more likely to do the same in order to conform to accepted group norms.

It has been said of most younger generations that they are alienated from society. One expression of current youthful alienation may be use of drugs. Disenchantment with the status quo can be tolerated when certain chemicals stimulate feelings of philosophical wholeness and maturity. Some drug users show greatly enhanced feelings of inner peace and satisfaction coupled with awareness and significance of life after experimenting with "mind-expanding" drugs.

The abuse of drugs may also reflect deep-seated, unsatisfied emotional needs. Lack of love in the home, emotional insecurity, lack of parental guidance and direction can all contribute to the desire to punish those who are perceived to be the source of neglect. Although the attention and caring received in response to drug abuse behavior is often negative and punitive, it is a form of attention and may be sought in spite of the potentially disastrous consequences.

The drug use attributed to youthful rebellion may also be viewed as only a symptom of underlying, complex problems permeating society: unpopular and protested wars, drastic economic upheavals, political instability. In the search for stability and predictability of life, some people may turn to drugs. The frustration aroused by incomprehensible events can then be masked.

Undoubtedly numerous other theories about why people turn to drugs could be proposed. The theories presented here are the major ones currently being studied and considered. It is hoped that a more specified definite hypothesis will be proposed in the near future.

Theories Related to Continuation of Drug Dependence

After a person begins to abuse drugs, he may or may not continue to do so. If he finds their effects undesirable or if the drugs do not meet his needs, he may discontinue them. If he does receive satisfaction, he is likely to continue the behavior, which then can result in some degree of dependence. Several explanations have been offered on the causes of such continuation of drug abuse patterns, especially when adverse effects appear.

Physical Dependence   One of the most compelling reasons for continued drug abuse is the physiological dependence associated with several of the misused chemicals. With the development of tolerance, physical craving, and physiological dependence on the properties of the drug, the user experiences a withdrawal phenomenon when intake is decreased or halted. Therefore, the body's need for the continued effects that prevent withdrawal can serve as the main stimulus to continued use.

Positive Drug Experience   Most drug-dependent persons say that continued use can be attributed to the positive, gratifying, and satisfying sensations resulting from drug intake. The high, rush, or flash of mental or physical ecstasy is considered to be the major reward. Other pleasurable feelings of calm, avoidance of conflict, and perceived attainment of philosophical insight all positively reinforce continuation.

Avoiding Withdrawal   Continued drug intake patterns may be attributed to negative reinforcement specifically associated with the relief of withdrawal symptoms. Generally, opiate-dependent persons at one time or other experience varying degrees of physical withdrawal when street supplies are depleted or tight. These symptoms can be immediately relieved by more intake. Thus, the negative stimulus (withdrawal symptoms) can be removed by drug administration (heroin) creating a situation in which drug-taking behavior is repeatedly negatively reinforced—the user continues to take the drug to avoid the aversive stimulus of withdrawal.

Personality Characteristics   Efforts to identify a specific series of personality components that would assist in predicting potential drug abusers have thus far proven unsuccessful. Like research into the possible existence of an alcoholic personality, the study of drug abusers' personalities takes place after the fact— after drug dependence has evolved.

Many drug-dependents have been raised in stifling, depressed home environments in which healthy personality growth was smothered. In such cases, resort to and continued dependence on drugs served as an escape but at the same time further narrowed the possibility of developing healthy coping mechanisms and patterns of problem solving. As a person comes to rely more heavily on chemical security and oblivion, his insecurity about reentering the mainstream of society increases. He may develop fear of the "straight" world, lack confidence in his ability to achieve, evolve defensive behaviors to cope with his needs and society's conflicting values, and reject the straight world as a "rip off" or "bummer."

The role of personality in the continuation of drug dependence cannot be denied and at best remains hypothetical. Specific identified characteristics of drug-dependent persons are discussed in a later section of this chapter.

Lifestyle The unique lifestyle of many drug abusers contributes to continued dependence. Abusers rely on the rituals associated with obtaining and administering the drug, the peer group's values and norms, and the living patterns of the drug culture. After perceiving rejection by the dominant society as a result of drug use and associated behaviors, the user retreats further into the security and sense of belonging provided by his adopted lifestyle. Continued association with the drug-oriented peer group reinforces dependence as a means of maintaining group acceptance.

Certain aspects of drug use such as intravenous injection, preparation of the drug for injection, and contact with suppliers also become sources of positive secondary reinforcement. The person begins to associate such experiences with the desired sensations themselves.

Drug abuse is a complex, multivaried health problem. The causes of this behavior are also complex, often unfathomable, and highly challenging. It should be stated clearly that the reasons why one person takes up drug abuse will vary considerably from the reasons another person does the same thing. In addition, it is extremely difficult to investigate the causes by focusing on current users— they tend to be very successful in camouflage or blocking insight into the behaviors that motivated initiation and continuation of the problem. The brief summaries of the current thinking on the causes of drug abuse should, therefore, serve as the stimulus to further, in-depth study of this important aspect of drug abuse nursing.

PERSONALITY CHARACTERISTICS ASSOCIATED WITH DRUG ABUSE

A multitude of terms have been used to describe the personality of drug-dependent persons. Adjectives like psychopathic, weak-willed, emotionally unstable, passive-dependent, rebellious, infantile, neurotic, basically normal, and many more are liberally sprinkled in publications and conversations. Considerable study and research have been undertaken to identify "drug-dependent personality" types, i.e., a relatively consistent series of personality characteristics that exist prior to drug abuse or result from drug abuse.

Attempts to categorize the drug-dependent personality have usually resulted in the inclusion of all the personality types that exist. In large part, this is because normal, socially functioning people abuse illicit drugs at least as frequently as do socially deprived and socially nonfunctioning people. Also, in order to successfully identify a certain drug-dependent-prone personality type, it is necessary to be able to clearly describe the nonprone personality as well. To date, niether of these goals has been met with any degree of success.

It must be stated, however, that many drug abusers have identifiable personality dysfunction that, at least, contributed significantly to the development of dependence. The important thing to remember is that blanket labeling of a drug abuser as one personality type or another without fully investigating and learning about that person as an individual will succeed only in reinforcing negative, inhibiting stereotypes. Only when those in the helping professions overcome such tendencies can frank, straightforward approaches to interaction with drug-dependent persons be achieved.

The "Lame" in All of Us

Perhaps the only fairly safe thing that can be said about the drug-dependent personality and the normal personality as well is that there is something of the "lame" in both. For the person who depends on drugs, this aspect of incompleteness or crippling is momentarily overridden by the effects of the drug. For the normal, well-adjusted person, the "lameness" is coped with through other, more socially acceptable and achievable channels. Thus, the challenge of identifying causation is clouded because many people with severe physical or emotionally crippling problems never turn to drugs while others with similar disabilities do.

Personality and Drug of Abuse

Although no conclusive statements can be made about the relationship of specific personality characteristics and the drug(s) of abuse, it is possible to describe certain recurring idiosyncracies associated with some of the major abused drugs.[2] With the exclusion of alcohol dependence, it has been proposed that heroin dependence is more often associated with passive dependence, low frustration tolerance, and impulsiveness when compared with stimulant, hallucinogen, or sedative dependence. However, abusers of the last three drug categories also experience a certain degree of the same emotions.

Personalities of hallucinogen abusers include degrees of depression, anxiety, boredom, thrill-seeking, and repressed hostility, Stimulant abusers may also experience significant degrees of depression and boredom, which may contribute to initiation and continuation of drug dependence. Degrees of psychopathy and antisocial behavior are hypothesized to be more prevalent in persons dependent on heroin, intravenous stimulants, and certain hallucinogens than in those dependent on sedatives, marijuana, or oral amphetamines. These traits may be

[2] Ibid., p. 255.

influenced by the methods used to secure drug supplies, maintain dependence, and prevent withdrawal symptoms.

When discussing proposed relationships between drug(s) of abuse and personality it becomes evident that the problem of determining the validity of such hypotheses is enormous. First, studies that emphasize the personality structure of drug-dependent persons are working with "after-the-fact" subjects. Second, the bias and attitude of the researcher can easily shadow the response from the interviewee. Thus, one must maintain a reasonably skeptical attitude when reading or studying data that claim to draw solid connections between personality constructs and the abused drug.

Major Personality Traits Identified with Drug Dependence

The demands inherent in obtaining certain illicit drugs necessitate the development of specific personality traits in order to be successful in such endeavors. Securing supplies of amphetamines, barbiturates, and hallucinogens often requires the abuser to establish illegal drug connections and maintain a level of economic resources sufficient to continue purchase of the drugs. In those cases in which the drug is obtained through valid physician prescriptions, it often becomes necessary to invent reasons that justify continuation of the prescription or to seek out other physicians unfamiliar with the person's past treatment who will prescribe new supplies.

The amount of deception, dishonesty, and camouflaging necessary to maintain this type of drug dependence while continuing to participate in family or employment activities greatly increases with the middle-class, "hidden" drug-dependent person. The abuser who has divorced himself from valued interpersonal relationships, however, is less concerned about camouflaging his drug dependence. He is, on the other hand, quite concerned about maintaining his drug dependence and may resort to criminal activity in order to achieve this goal.

It is important to remember that dependence on barbiturates, amphetamines, and hallucinogens is often associated with intermittent use, relatively uncomplicated accessibility, and multiple drug abuse. Therefore, the person usually is not completely disabled by a single drug but combines two or more to attain a level of "normalcy" and ability to sporadically secure employment. Other abusers who are receiving familial economic support usually choose to hide their dependence from those people, often fearing embarrassment and humiliation to themselves or their family. Again, development of skillful deception and camouflage often are essential to achieve this goal.

Some abusers of amphetamines, barbiturates, and hallucinogens turn to drug dependence as a means of punishing other people. The rebellion, proclamation of independence, or aggression expressed by drug dependence may fulfill a deep-seated need to hurt these particular people. Generally, these desires are not at a conscious level and often succeed only in perpetuating the need to blot out awareness of reality.

Those abusers who possess identifiable personality disruption (psychoses, schizophrenia, etc.) usually exacerbate the symptoms associated with the dysfunction. Thus, an abuser with some degree of schizophrenia can become more deeply involved with his illness. Much has been written about the personality of the heroin-dependent person. A brief description of some of the more consistent personality characteristics will be given here. The heroin addict (the dominant term used to identify the heroin-dependent person) has been described as devious, cunning, shifty, deceptive, a copout, perverted, amoral, unfeeling, etc. Indeed because of these traits, heroin addicts are extremely difficult to work with. They usually acquire great skill in "gaming" others—"putting them on," conning them, or generally practicing deception to achieve their ends. This ability to con others often forms one of the most impenetrable barriers in treatment situations. It also forms a solid defense against personal attack or penetration to basic personal conflicts.

Addicts are also successful in "rounding" and "imaging." Rounding is verbal skill in avoiding unpleasant or unproductive subjects. For example, when a person talks about the methods being used to obtain drugs, the addict begins to get very uncomfortable with the probing questions. He may either change the subject or turn the questions back to the interviewer, thereby avoiding the stressful topic. When these methods don't succeed in blocking the conversation, he may simply ignore the questions and comments, or attempt to put the other person on the defensive by challenging his authority, knowledge, or experience. Imaging occurs when the addict projects an image of himself in order to achieve a goal—it may be money, drugs, or avoidance of the law. The image projected may be a personality normally considered desirable or acceptable by the straights that are trying to help him. These interpersonal and sometimes intrapsychic techniques are used to avoid direct confrontation with others or oneself regarding true personal feelings and motivations. They also serve as unique methods of assuming different identities that assist in avoiding harassment and securing drug supplies. As with gaming, rounding and imaging are defensive personality components necessary for basic survival in most cases.

The Criminal Addict Personality

Heroin addiction is associated with crime, generally theft, shoplifting, prostitution, and burglary, but in recent years it has been coupled with an increase in physical violence, e.g., muggings, use of weapons, killings. Not every heroin addict becomes a criminal, but a substantial number do rely on illegal activities in order to get money for drugs. Addicts with expensive heroin habits usually require several hundred dollars a week to satisfy their physical dependence, and the amount of merchandise or personal property that must be stolen is correspondingly great.

Because of the continuous need to steal, practice prostitution, resell stolen material, and purchase illegal supplies of heroin, addicts develop considerable skill in devising ever-varying approaches to the problem of money. This almost continuous need to hustle can be successfully carried out over a long period of time only by people who are quite energetic, fairly creative, and of above-average intelligence.[3] Successful avoidance of arrest for theft, violent activity, prostitution, or drug dependence also demands a degree of skill, acuity, and perseverance.

That many heroin-dependent persons use defined criminal activities to support addiction and are not criminals by preference does not alter the fact that such behavior is destructive to society as a whole. (In some states, drug dependence on heroin is a crime in itself and is punishable by imprisonment.) But to continue to label drug dependence as criminal will not solve the problem—it will merely reinforce more devious and perhaps violent behaviors as the addict strives to maintain his habit. A vicious cycle results in which greater numbers of citizens are harmed and fewer addicts are helped to overcome drugs.

PHYSIOLOGICAL COMPLICATIONS OF DRUG DEPENDENCE

Of the many characteristics of drug dependence, perhaps none are quite so visible as the medical complications associated with long-term drug abuse. Nurses and other health professionals care daily for patients with these often serious health problems. A brief summary of the more frequently occurring complications of drug dependence follows.

Circulatory-Respiratory Complications

Bacterial Endocarditis A relatively frequent complication of intravenous drug dependence is bacterial endocarditis. The infecting organism is usually staphylococcus aureaus, with occasional cases of infection from unusual organisms such as Serratia marescens. The heart valves most commonly involved are the aortic, mitral, and tricuspid. Primarily the left side of the heart is affected. The mortality rate of heroin addicts with bacterial endocarditis ranges from 28 to 75 percent.[4,5]

---

[3] Richard Ashley, *Heroin: The Myths and the Facts,* St. Martin's Press, New York, 1972, p. 73.

[4] Ruth G. Ramsey, Rolf M. Gunnar, and John R. Tobin, "Endocarditis in the Drug Addict," *The American Journal of Cardiology,* 25:618, May 1970.

[5] "Medical Complications of Heroin Addiction," *California Medicine,* 115:48, November 1971.

Intraarterial Injection Whether by accident or by specific intention, intra-arterial injection of oral drugs of abuse produces serious complications. Gangrene of the extremity distal to the arterial injection site is a common sequelae. Eventually the necrosed limb may require amputation. It is hypothesized that chemical damage to the intimal lining of the artery by relatively undiluted oral drugs is the mechanism of damage. Treatment consists of relieving tissue ischemia, edema, and thrombosis of the involved artery.

Vascular Disorders Acute and chronic thrombophlebitis and the sclerosing of veins used for injection are common and often necessitate skillful utilization of inconspicuous sites. Injection of contaminated drugs can also lead to severe extremity lymphedema due to obstruction of veins and lymphatics serving the limb. Gangrene can result. Instances of intracranial hemorrhage related to amphetamine abuse have been reported and correlated with the hypertensive effects of the drug.[6]

Pulmonary Embolism The intravenous route of self-administered drugs carries with it the hazard of introducing foreign particle emboli into the circulatory system. The most common emboli are talc, cornstarch, and cotton wool. Talc and cornstarch are usually used as fillers in commercially prepared oral medications, and cotton wool is used as a filter prior to injection of the diluted drug. As these emboli are carried to the lungs, granulomas or pulmonary fibrosis may result. Diminished diffusion capacity is often the first indication of pulmonary dysfunction.

Respiratory Infections Heroin addicts have a relatively high incidence of respiratory infection due in large part to general lack of health care, poor diet, and poor living conditions. Commonly occurring respiratory infections include pneumonia, bronchopneumonia, pulmonary abscesses, and tuberculosis.

Hepatic Dysfunction

Hepatic dysfunction generally consists of acute and chronic hepatitis usually attributed to communal use of contaminated needles for intravenous injection of drugs—especially the amphetamines and heroin. (The role of alcohol intake along with intravenous drug administration as it relates to hepatitis has not been clearly defined.) Approximately 10 to 15 percent of heroin addicts have biochemical abnormalities consistent with acute hepatitis.[7] Another 60 to 76

---

[6] Stanley J. Goodman, and Donald P. Becker, "Intracranial Hemorrhage Associated with Amphetamine Abuse," *Journal of the American Medical Association,* 212:480, April 20, 1970.

[7] "Medical Complications of Heroin Addiction," loc. cit.

percent have biochemical or biopsy evidence of chronic hepatitis or liver disease.[8,9] In general, hepatitis continues to be one of the most frequently occurring medical complications of drug abuse.

Gastrointestinal Disturbances

Severe, rapid weight loss has been associated with amphetamine abuse. Poor nutritional habits and specific vitamin deficiencies develop with heroin and amphetamine abusers. Long-term abuse of opiate drugs creates severe constipation and hemorrhoid problems. The incidence of other gastrointestinal disorders such as duodenal ulcers and gastritis is minimal.

Skin Complications

Frequently seen complications involving the skin consist of hyperpigmentation over intravenous injection sites, scarring, abscesses, cellulitis, and ulceration. Abscesses at infected injection sites are common as is cellulitis when skin-popping is practiced. With intravenous injection of barbiturates and extravasation of some of the drug into surrounding tissue, the incidence of necrotic ulcerating lesions increases. Infectious skin complications are most often associated with injection (intravenous or subcutaneous skin-popping) and therefore have the potential for initiating system infections.

Muscular Disorders

Heroin addicts often experience a fibrosing myopathy from long-term subcutaneous injection. Over time, veins become blocked and obliterated, resulting in edema. The edema can lead to cellulitis and myositis with continued injections. Chronic muscle damage may be the ultimate result.

Miscellaneous Complications

Tetanus Although tetanus is not a major medical complication of heroin dependence, its incidence is higher with this population than in the general population. The frequency of tetanus is greater in females than males, since women tend to skin-pop more than men, thus providing the clostridium organism with an easy route of infection. The mortality rate is extremely high.

Eye Emboli Besides circulatory-respiratory complications induced by foreign body emboli, retinal hemorrhages with edema and reduced vision have been reported.[10] In most cases the damage is temporary.

[8] Ibid.
[9] J. A. Ratherdale et al., "Hepatitis in Drug Users," *The American Journal of Gastroenterology,* 58:284, September 1972.
[10] William E. Atlee, Jr., "Talc and Cornstarch Emboli in Eyes of Drug Abusers," *Journal of the American Medical Association,* 219:49–51, January 3, 1972.

Traumatic Injury   A small percentage of drug-dependent persons experience traumatic injuries such as burns, fractures, lacerations, and contusions as a result of carelessness with cigarettes, loss of coordination, and decreased judgment when under the influence of the chosen abused drug.

SUMMARY COMMENT

The major psychological, social, and physiological characteristics of drug abuse have been presented in this chapter. The proposed theories of causation represent the current major areas of study and concern. In order for nurses to give thoughtful, planned, and adequate care to patients with drug-dependence problems, a working knowledge and understanding of the information in this chapter is vital. However, it must be emphasized that further, in-depth study into specific areas (such as personality development or individual drug abuse patterns) is to be encouraged.

REFERENCES

Abrams, Arnold, John H. Gagnon, and Joseph J. Levin: "Psychosocial Aspects of Addiction," *American Journal of Public Health*, **58**:2142–2155, November 1968.

Arndt, Jack R., and William L. Blockstein (eds.): *Problems in Drug Abuse*, The University of Wisconsin, Madison, 1970.

Ashley, Richard: *Heroin: The Myths and the Facts*, St. Martin's Press, New York, 1972.

Berger, Herbert: "Localized Gangrene Complicating Drug Abuse," *Journal of the American Medical Association*, **218**:1707, December 13, 1971.

Cortina, Frank Michael: *Face to Face*, Columbia University Press, New York, 1972.

Crowley, Thomas J.: "The Reinforcers for Drug Abuse: Why People Take Drugs," *Comprehensive Psychiatry*, **13**:51–62, January 1972.

Douglas, F. G., K. J. Kafilmout, and N. L. Patt: "Foreign-Particle Embolism in Drug Addicts: Respiratory Pathophysiology," *Annals of Internal Medicine*, **75**:865–872, December 1971.

Glasscote, Raymond M. et al.: *The Treatment of Drug Abuse*, American Psychiatric Association, Washington, 1972.

Guttman, Herta A.: "The First Trip: Life Crisis and the First Experience with Hallucinogenic Drugs," *The Journal of Nervous and Mental Disease*, **154**:453–456, June 1972.

Lindell, Thomas D., John M. Porter, and Claire Langston: "Intra-Arterial Injection of Oral Medications," *The New England Journal of Medicine*, **287**:1132–1133, November 30, 1972.

Litt, Iris F. et al.: "Liver Disease in the Drug-Using Adolescent," *The Journal of Pediatrics*, **81**:238–242, August 1972.

Louria, Donald B.: *Overcoming Drugs,* McGraw-Hill Book Company, New York, 1971.

Morgan, Arthur J.: "Attitudes Toward Addiction," *American Journal of Nursing,* **73**:497–501, March 1973.

Ramsey, Ruth G., Rolf M. Gunnar, and John R. Tobin: "Endocarditis in the Drug Addict," *The American Journal of Cardiology,* **25**:608–618, May 1970.

Reinert, R. E.: "General Observations on Drug Habituation," *Bulletin of the Menninger Clinic,* Topeka, Kans., **34**:195–204, July 1970.

Rho, Yong-Myun: "Infections as Fatal Complications of Narcotism," *New York State Journal of Medicine,* **72**:823–830, April 1, 1972.

Richter, Ralph W.: "Neurological Complications of Addiction to Heroin," *Bulletin of the New York Academy of Medicine,* **49**:3–21, January 1973.

Seevers, Maurice H.: "Psychopharmacological Elements of Drug Dependence," *Journal of the American Medical Association,* **260**:1263–1266, November 4, 1968.

Vollum, Dorothy I.: "Skin Lesions in Drug Addicts," *British Medical Journal,* **2**:647–650, June 13, 1970.

Weidman, Abraham I., and Michael J. Fellner: "Cutaneous Manifestations of Heroin and Other Addictive Drugs," *New York State Journal of Medicine,* **71**:2643–2646, November 15, 1971.

Weil, Andrew: *The Natural Mind,* Houghton Mifflin Company, Boston, 1972.

White, Abraham G.: "Medical Disorders in Drug Addicts," *Journal of the American Medical Association,* **223**:1469–1471, March 26, 1973.

Whitney, Peter J.: "Inadvertent Intra-Arterial Injection in Drug Abuse," *Arizona Medicine,* **29**:784–786, October 1972.

Wurmser, Leon: "Why People Take Drugs," *Maryland State Medical Journal,* **19**:62–64, November 1970.

Chapter 13

Drug Abuse:
How Is It Treated?

To answer the question, How is drug abuse treated? it is necessary to define the meaning of treatment. Treatment of drug abusers is the attempt to alleviate or arrest the symptoms and health dysfunctions caused by the misuse of chemical substances. The type of treatment depends on (1) the primary drug of abuse, (2) the presence or absence of multiple drug abuse, (3) the individual personality and health status of the abuser, (4) the facilities available for treatment, and (5) the abuser's reason(s) for accepting or seeking assistance in altering drug-taking behavior.

DRUG OF ABUSE

The type of treatment required for the drug abuser will depend on the nature of his dependence. Those who are not physically dependent on a drug are not involved with the problems of physical withdrawal when intake ceases. Thus, dependency on amphetamines, hallucinogens, and volatile substances does not require treatment for physical withdrawal. But dependence on barbiturate sedatives or the opiates and opiatelike narcotics does. Overdose on opiates and opiatelike narcotics, barbiturates and other sedatives, and volatile substances is an emergency requiring immediate intervention. Overdose on hallucinogens and amphetamines is possible, but the immediate behavioral and physiological symptoms are not as life-threatening as with narcotics, sedatives, or volatile substances. However, overdose is a serious condition requiring rapid intervention in order to prevent the possibility of death.

The methods used to obtain the drug, to administer it, and the drug experience itself also determine which type of treatment is applicable. For this reason, treatment for the hallucinogen abuser is usually different from that for the narcotic-dependent person. One reason for this difference lies in the fact that obtaining supplies of illegal hallucinogens does not generally require the financial resources necessary to secure illegal narcotics. Thus, the narcotic addict's behavior patterns not only result from the drug experience but also from activities necessary to secure money to purchase drugs and the complex motivations for initiating and maintaining drug dependence.

Effects of the abused drug also influence the type of treatment prescribed. Drug dependence that requires regular intake in increasing amounts to maintain the desired effect will necessitate different treatment from dependence on drugs taken sporadically.

MULTIPLE DRUG ABUSE

Treatment of the person who is dependent on two or more drugs requires careful planning in order to avoid serious complications as well as to ensure optimal physical recovery. The abuser may or may not know that he is dependent on more than one drug. For instance, the heroin addict may also be dependent on barbiturates since some street supplies of the narcotic are cut, or diluted, with barbiturates. As the need for increased heroin occurs, barbiturate intake also increases, ultimately resulting in dual dependency.

Certain treatment programs use methods to make certain that participants do not maintain or acquire multiple drug abuse patterns. Persons dependent on heroin, for example, often try to switch to sedatives when opiates are withheld or blocked in effectiveness. To prevent this, the program can require analysis of urine specimens to detect the presence of abused drugs in the body. Policies for continued treatment include disciplinary action or alteration in approach when evidence of drug intake is found in the urine.

When dual drug dependency is not known by or reported to the treatment personnel, the abuser can experience life-threatening complications, especially when the unknown drug is a barbiturate sedative. The complications are related to the delayed onset of barbiturate withdrawal symptoms and the necessity for rapid intervention to control them. Because of this and other potential problems of multiple drug abuse, many treatment programs will not accept the person who is dependent on or abusing more than one chemical.

PERSONALITY AND HEALTH STATUS

The abuser who has complex health problems as a result of drug dependency will require extensive treatment and intervention. Specific treatment modalities are designed to meet the immediate physiological and psychological needs created by drug-taking behavior. For example, heroin or barbiturate overdose requires both immediate intervention to prevent death and long-term care and rehabilitation.

How and where care is obtained will depend on the care givers' ability to deal with the drug-dependent person. At the same time, because persons dependent on drugs either develop or have preexisting personality dysfunction, many health professionals find it extremely difficult to work with such people. Therefore, the type of treatment available will vary according to the abuser's personality characteristics and overall health status and needs. These two variables also directly influence the degree of continuity of treatment efforts; i.e., treatment for physical problems is often not associated with or coordinated with ongoing therapy aimed at controlling drug abuse behavior.

AVAILABLE TREATMENT FACILITIES

Many health care institutions such as general hospitals, clinics, and rehabilitation facilities will not accept persons for treatment who have a primary diagnosis of drug abuse. The reasons for these admission policies are based in large part on (1) fears of bizarre, threatening, violent, and unpredictable behavior of the drug abusers while being treated, (2) apprehension about community reaction if drug-dependent persons are admitted, (3) a general lack of knowledge about the needs of such patients, and (4) a lack of understanding and misinformation about the drug-abusing patient population. These variables and many other economic rationalizations have frequently justified restrictive admission policies.

Of some encouragement in recent years has been the trend in the large urban centers to establish specific facilities for the care and treatment of drug dependency. In many instances, the local county or publicly financed general hospital has become the center for detoxification, initial rehabilitation efforts, and treatment of medical problems associated with drug abuse. The establishment of community based, residential, or day care programs for long-term care has greatly increased the number of people who can be treated as well as those who will accept or seek treatment. Initiating treatment programs within the neighborhoods where the drug abuser lives has often succeeded in fostering community interest and participation. Perhaps the primary importance of such community programs has been their visibility—addicts and drug abusers can see how the program is run, who is being treated, and the outcome of treatment. This visibility and accessibility offers support and guidance to the drug abuser who wants help. In addition to the publicly and privately supported hospital and community based treatment programs, many areas use psychiatric facilities for acute and long-term therapy. In many cases, admittance of the drug abuser to a psychiatric institution is not because of any psychiatric disorder but because of the lack of other treatment facilities and negative, punitive attitudes toward the abuser. Similar attitudes propagated by hostile and punitive laws aimed at decreasing illicit drug traffic have succeeded in incarcerating many drug-dependent persons—the "treatment" received in these institutions frequently succeeds only in reinforcing drug-taking behavior and the need for criminal activity to support it. This might more appropriately be called the "nontreatment of drug abuse."

Rural areas generally have a lower incidence of drug dependence than urban areas. However, although the percentage of abusers and the types of drugs involved often vary from that in the large urban centers, there is still a need for community based and general hospital treatment facilities in many rural areas.

The person who is dependent on drugs, whether obtained legally or illegally, can usually receive treatment for medical conditions related to drug-taking practices by being admitted to the hospital with a diagnosis other than drug abuse. After the condition or illness is treated, the person is discharged and returns to his old habits. The lack of continuity in treatment when long-term facilities are available is a major impediment to successful rehabilitation. On the other hand, many communities do plan for and implement organized and comprehensive programs. Unfortunately, they are in the minority.

REASONS FOR SEEKING OR ACCEPTING TREATMENT

Treatment means different things to different people and will vary especially in relation to the reason treatment is undergone. If the drug abuser defines treatment differently from the care giver, the drug abuser may not benefit from the treatment and the care giver may experience frustration when failure seems evident.

Some common reasons why the drug abuser seeks or accepts treatment are:

1 *To reduce the drug habit.* Sometimes the need for increased doses and more money to support the habit will motivate a person to find ways of reducing the total amount of drug used. The periodic necessity of reducing total drug intake is seen especially with heroin abuse—possibly the most expensive of the drug dependencies.

When the person desires to reduce his drug habit, he usually presents himself voluntarily to a treatment program and says he wants to "kick"—withdraw from drugs and not return to them. Once he has undergone withdrawal, he may leave the treatment facility either by discharge or simply by leaving—"splitting." He then can resume taking drugs and will have acquired two benefits from the temporary abstinence: (1) the amount of drug necessary to produce the desired experience will be decreased and (2) the intensity of awareness of the drug experience will be temporarily renewed. In a relatively short period of time, tolerance again builds up and the cycle may be repeated.

A major danger of this practice is the increased likelihood of overdose. With a reduced tolerance due to temporary abstinence, the heroin addict may inject a potent quantity of the drug sufficient to cause overdose—the actual dose may be the same as prior doses, but the lowered tolerance has created an increased sensitivity to the effects of the drug.

2 *To kick the drug habit.* Awareness of the need to stop taking harmful and illicit drugs occurs in many drug abusers. For some, this basic insight comes early in the drug abuse career, while others avoid such awareness for many years. When it does happen, however, the person acquires and expresses a sincere desire to kick the habit. This decision is often reached after a threat of impending loss —spouse, other loved ones, freedom, or health. Regardless of the process leading to the decision, the person desiring to kick seeks a treatment center, often on impulse. Once in a hospital or program, however, he may have second thoughts.

Determining the patient's sincerity to cease drug-taking behavior is extremely difficult and often impossible. The drug abuser is usually an expert in manipulative behavior, often to the point of deluding himself about his inner feelings and motivations. Therefore, some programs emphasize performance of the drug abuser over an extended period rather than overt verbal expressions during the initial phases of therapy.

3 *To obey a court order.* In some cases involving prosecution for crimes associated with drug dependence, the presiding judge may remand the person to a treatment program instead of sentencing him for a specified period of incarceration. The person may or may not be given a choice between the two alternatives, i.e., jail or treatment. When the drug-dependent person enters a program under these circumstances, his motivation and desire to successfully participate may be minimal. Thus, if success in treatment is anticipated in such instances, the care givers can be sorely disappointed.

Drug abusers quickly become familiar with the treatment methods used by various programs. When faced with the likelihood of confinement where drug supplies are uncertain, although often obtainable, or entrance into a program offering minimal physical discomfort from withdrawal, the person may appear motivated to enter such a program. Health professionals and care givers operating treatment programs take these common superficial motivations into account when planning the treatment regimen.

4 *To avoid withdrawal.* Sometimes street supplies of drugs are not readily available. These "famines" are referred to as "panic in the streets." Some abusers, particularly and almost exclusively heroin addicts, will accept treatment in order

to avoid withdrawal. After detoxification, the addict can return to the street, await the return of drug supplies, and use other drugs such as alcohol and barbiturates as temporary substitutes.

Abusers frequently believe that they can stop taking drugs and maintain abstinence without the assistance of others. Because of this generally erroneous belief, the abuser may enter a program to detoxify and evade the often exaggerated withdrawal syndrome. Following this experience, he may leave the treatment center thinking or saying that he can make it on his own. With rare exception, he resumes taking drugs within a short period of time.

These four reasons for seeking or accepting treatment illustrate the necessity of understanding what treatment means to the drug abuser. For example, if it means avoiding withdrawal or jail, the treatment approach must reflect a realization of the person's motivation.

GOALS OF TREATMENT

As with alcoholism, the sole goal of treatment of the drug abuser is not an immediate cure of the behavior but varying degrees of recovery. By its very nature, drug-dependence behavior cannot be cured in the traditional meaning of that word. It cannot be cured quickly as can many medical illnesses. It is characterized by relapse, as is alcoholism. Thus, goals must not be so rigid that they establish unrealistic expectations on the part of the patient or the care giver.

Realistic goals for treatment of drug abuse may seem insignificant when compared with the often astounding achievements many patients make in response to severe physical trauma or insult. However, to the drug-dependent person who has led a drug-oriented life for a long period, attainment of simple and limited goals becomes vitally important.

Goals can be viewed as a series of steps, each based on the capabilities of the person, the length of dependence, the particular drug involved, the treatment facilities available, the goal of the abuser, and the presence or absence of physical or psychological complications associated with drug dependence. Different programs will establish different goals. Some emphasize control of drug intake through the use of chemical blocking agents, while others require complete abstinence from all drugs. The following sections summarize some of the major goals of treatment. Each of these proposed goals is not applicable to everyone undergoing treatment. Each program is designed to meet the individual needs of its particular patient population and takes into account the characteristics of the drug of abuse.

Short-term goals pertain to the initial stages of treatment and are therefore limited. Certain short-term goals are most suitable in general hospitals while others may be achieved in outpatient clinics or community based programs. These goals are as follows:

1 To initiate and support uncomplicated withdrawal or detoxification from the drug of dependence
2 To treat the physical complications associated with drug abuse
3 To block the action of dependence-producing drugs via use of chemical agents such as methadone or narcotic antagonists
4 To stop criminal activity caused by drug dependence—with emphasis on helping the person to stop taking drugs and thereby eliminating the need for criminal activity

Intermediate goals focus on the desired outcomes following withdrawal and/or initiation of drug maintenance so that the person will:

1 Remain in and continue participating in the treatment program
2 Begin seeking self-understanding in relation to drug dependency
3 Maintain abstinence from illicit drugs of dependence

Long-term goals are ultimate objectives of long-term treatment. They take into account the concept that some abusers will have attained success by continuing to depend on chemical blocking agents, while others will be successful when total drug abstinence is achieved. These goals are:

1 To continue regular, scheduled participation in an ongoing program and continue taking the prescribed chemical blocking agent
2 To foster the ability to independently maintain abstinence from dependence-producing drugs—with emphasis on abstinence after completing a treatment program
3 To develop self-awareness as it relates to past, present, and future desires for chemical dependence
4 To achieve abstinence from all drugs of dependence—including methadone or other chemical treatment agents
5 To become a socially functioning and contributing member of society, i.e., (a) to return to former employment or to initiate a new employment career and (b) to stabilize and reunite the family unit where appropriate

For most drug abusers, attainment of goals occurs sequentially. That is, withdrawal is followed by continued participation in the program which ultimately aims at assisting the person in reentering society with the capabilities necessary for drug-free living. Each treatment program will establish specific treatment goals based on the program's philosophy.

TREATMENT FOR DEPENDENCE ON STIMULANTS

The treatment modalities for dependence on stimulant drugs to be presented here will center on the amphetamines and cocaine. Treatment for non-amphetamine drug dependence is generally the same. Treatment for associated medical conditions related to the method of drug administration—i.e., hepatitis, abscesses, dermatological conditions, etc.—can be found in nursing textbooks.

Treatment for Amphetamine Dependence

Treatment for amphetamine dependence is based on abrupt or gradual detoxification. Because there is no physiologically life-threatening abstinence syndrome when intake is discontinued, treatment for dependence on amphetamines generally is not physically traumatic. Psychological and physical reactions to cessation of intake do occur and can consist of severe psychic depression, tiredness or exhaustion, hunger, lethargy and general malaise, and suicidal behavior. Patients undergoing withdrawal after a "speed binge" will generally sleep for one or two days after detoxification. Because depression and suicidal behavior are relatively common following amphetamine withdrawal, protective and supportive measures must be taken to prevent self-inflicted injury or suicide for several days up to several weeks after detoxification. Thus hospitalization is a necessity when continued observation cannot be maintained in the home or clinic.

While the person is undergoing withdrawal, he may experience periodic bouts of the jitters or "jumpy nerves" and alternating episodes of lethargy and general disinterest in surrounding activities. The person who wishes to withdraw from amphetamines or who is taken to a treatment facility usually benefits from supportive care and observation. A quiet environment will lessen sensory stimulation, and frequently repeated, clear but softly spoken statements regarding the patient's location, safety, and time orientation will aid the patient in gaining control, and maintaining contact with reality.

Use of sedative-hypnotics such as diazepam is occasionally prescribed when the patient is extremely agitated, debilitated, and unable to tolerate prolonged central nervous system stimulation. These drugs are used with extreme caution, however, because it is often not known if the patient has ingested other drugs in addition to the stimulants, e.g., barbiturates. The possibility of inadvertent over-sedation and resulting respiratory depression must be avoided whenever there is a question about the composition of the drugs ingested or injected. In some instances, gastric lavage with tap water or induction of vomiting may be necessary and effective due to the delayed emptying time of oral amphetamines in the gastrointestinal tract.

With patients who have amphetamine psychosis, interventive therapy is not always necessary since behavioral manifestations of the condition resolve as detoxification is completed—within two to seven days up to several weeks or months. However, some physicians prescribe and use the antipsychotic drugs of the phenothiazine type to decrease patient symptoms and emotional discomfort.[1] The emphasis is on supportive care and plans for long-term therapy to deal with the underlying motivations leading to drug-dependence patterns. If such plans are not made and implemented, the person will often return to drug abuse after discharge.

Treatment for Cocaine Dependence

Withdrawal from cocaine is less severe than amphetamine detoxification because of the shorter period of action and general pattern of abuse. Treatment consists of maintaining abstinence and providing a supportive and protective environment. Sedatives may be used for acute agitation but are usually not necessary. Abrupt cessation of cocaine abuse does not induce a physiological abstinence syndrome but can cause severe depression and continued delusional experiences for several weeks after withdrawal.

TREATMENT FOR BARBITURATE DEPENDENCE

Dependence on barbiturates requires varying degrees of treatment depending on the status of the abuser. For this reason, treatment for barbiturate withdrawal, overdose, and long-term care will be discussed separately.

The Withdrawal Syndrome and Treatment

Because chronic barbiturate abuse includes physical dependence, an abstinence or withdrawal syndrome occurs when intake ceases. The severity of the syndrome is related to the length of time from the last dose and is considered life-threatening when left untreated or when allowed to advance in severity.

Symptoms of Barbiturate Withdrawal Barbiturate withdrawal symptoms usually begin about fifteen hours after the last dose. Some patients do not experience symptoms this soon, but they will manifest some symptoms within the first twenty-four hours after intake has stopped. Withdrawal symptoms from barbiturates are progressive in severity. The initial symptoms may be muscular weakness, with the mildest activity; anxiety; postural faintness; anorexia, which may precipitate nausea and vomiting; and tremors that occur with movement. As the syndrome progresses, the patient may have hallucinations, delusions associated with the onset of acute psychosis, and convulsions. The intensity of

[1] Lloyd H. Smith, Jr., Martin J. Cline, and Hebbard E. Williams, "Changing Drug Patterns in the Haight-Ashbury," in Oliver E. Byrd (ed.), *Medical Readings on Drug Abuse,* Addison-Wesley Publishing Company, Reading, Mass., 1970, p. 150.

the symptoms peaks at thirty to forty hours after onset. In some cases, there is delirium with disorientation, confusion, severe tremors, and hallucinations. Seizures generally do not come on until the second or third day after the last dose, but have been known to appear as late as eight days after. Barbiturate abusers are often able to describe an aura before a convulsion begins. Seizures may consist of grand mal convulsions or repeated convulsions culminating in death.

Treatment for the Withdrawal Syndrome   The overall goals of treating the barbiturate withdrawal syndrome are to (1) prevent seizure activity, (2) gradually detoxify the patient by controlled drug therapy, and (3) prevent the onset of psychiatric sequelae, e.g., psychosis, delirium, or acute panic states. With rare exception, detoxification and withdrawal should be carried out in a hospital because of the possibility of life-endangering seizures. With adequate and consistent follow-up care, however, controlled barbiturate withdrawal can be carried out successfully on an outpatient basis.[2]

Controlled withdrawal from barbiturates is achieved by substituting another barbiturate over a specified period and gradually reducing the dosage. The two barbiturates frequently used in this method of treatment are phenobarbital and pentobarbital.

Phenobarbital Regimen   Phenobarbital (Luminal®) is a long-acting (over six hours) barbiturate. The longer-lasting action results in relatively consistent levels of the drug in the bloodstream and therefore a decreased likelihood of withdrawal symptoms. The use of phenobarbital in substitution therapy also allows for prescription of small doses.

The dosage of phenobarbital is determined by the size of the barbiturate doses the person was accustomed to taking. In general, approximately 30 mg or more of phenobarbital is substituted for each dose of the abused barbiturate.[3,4,5] Say, for example, that a barbiturate-dependent person is accustomed to taking 1500 mg of secobarbital per day, which is equal to fifteen doses. If 30 mg of phenobarbital is determined to be the sedative dosage, then the patient would require 450 mg of phenobarbital per day (15 doses × 30 mg = 450 mg/day). The total amount of substitute drug is usually divided into four doses given every six hours, the evening dose being larger than the others so as to facilitate sleep.

[2] George R. Gay et al., "Outpatient Barbiturate Withdrawal Using Phenobarbital," *The International Journal of the Addictions,* 7:17–26, 1972.
[3] Ibid.
[4] David E. Smith et al., "New Developments in Barbiturate Abuse," *Clinical Toxicology,* 3:62, March 1970.
[5] David E. Smith, and Donald R. Wesson, "Phenobarbital Technique for Treatment of Barbiturate Dependence," *Archives of General Psychiatry,* 24:57, January 1971.

If the patient enters treatment with obvious or advanced withdrawal symptoms, the first dose of medication may consist of a short-acting barbiturate that induces physiological stabilization. Once this is accomplished, the phenobarbital regimen can be initiated. Patients may be maintained on the phenobarbital regimen for two to three days, during which time they usually exhibit some symptoms of mild intoxication or sedation. Gradual, scheduled reduction in the phenobarbital dosage begins at a rate of 30 to 100 mg per day, depending on the total maintenance dosage and the patient's responses to reduced dosage. If abstinence symptoms appear when the dosage is reduced, the physician may temporarily halt the schedule until the patient again stabilizes on the current regimen. Graduated reduction and subsequent detoxification takes about eight days but varies according to the patient's response.

Variations in the phenobarbital regimen include: (1) the administration of an intramuscular or oral "loading dose" in order to verify the patient's tolerance to barbiturates before the drug substitution regimen is begun; (2) a scheduled increase in phenobarbital until the total calculated substitute amount is reached, followed by a graduated reduction, similar to the regimen previously described; and (3) PRN administration of intramuscular phenobarbital doses and a concomitant reduction in the scheduled oral dose when abstinence symptoms appear or become intensified.

Pentobarbital Regimen   Sodium pentobarbital (Nembutal®) is a short-acting (less than three hours) barbiturate that can be used in substitution withdrawal therapy. After the barbiturate-dependent person is admitted to the hospital or clinic, he is given a test, or loading, pentobarbital dose, usually 200 mg by mouth. He is then observed for symptoms of intoxication. If none appear, the next dose is equal to or greater than the test dose. This sequence is repeated until the patient exhibits symptoms of sedation or intoxication—slurred speech, unsteady gait, slowed mental processes, and tremors. The total amount of pentobarbital required to produce intoxication represents the daily equivalent amount of barbiturate the patient is dependent upon. The total amount is divided into equal doses and is given every four to six hours orally or intramuscularly. The schedule is maintained for two or three days, during which time the patient should evidence symptoms of sedation and intoxication.

After the period of stabilization, a gradual schedule of dosage reduction is begun. It is recommended that reduction not exceed 100 mg of pentobarbital per day, or 10 to 20 percent of the total calculated dosage,[6,7,8] thereby decreasing

[6] Abraham Wikler, "Diagnosis and Treatment of Drug Dependence of the Barbiturate Type," *American Journal of Psychiatry,* 125:760, December 1968.

[7] John N. Chappel, "New Hope for the Hopeless," *Chart,* 67:252, October 1970.

[8] *Drug Dependence: A Guide for Physicians,* American Medical Association, Chicago, 1970, p. 109.

the likelihood of stimulating acute withdrawal symptoms. If abstinence symptoms do appear during the reduction schedule, the physician may order a temporary increase in the dosage, or temporarily halt the detoxification process until the symptoms subside. Depending on the total calculated dosage of pentobarbital and the patient's reactions to the withdrawal regimen, detoxification will take approximately two weeks.

The patient who is admitted with abstinence symptoms can be given 200 to 400 mg of pentobarbital orally or intramuscularly. If his symptoms do not subside within an hour or two, the dose can be repeated. Once he is sedated and does not manifest withdrawal symptoms, a gradual planned schedule of reduced doses can be implemented.

It should be remembered that gradual detoxification from barbiturates requires careful evaluation and assessment of individual patient responses and careful calculation of the substitute drug dosage regimen. Some persons may be extremely sensitive to seemingly small doses of pentobarbital and can be oversedated if precautions are not taken. In addition to substitution therapy, patients may benefit from intravenous fluid and electrolyte replacement, dietary management, rest, and treatment of the underlying physical complications of barbiturate dependence and the abstinence syndrome.

Neonatal Withdrawal from Barbiturates Women taking prescribed or illicit barbiturates during pregnancy or only through the last trimester can give birth to infants who will eventually exhibit symptoms of withdrawal. Symptoms in the infant may begin in a few days or a week or more after birth. These symptoms may consist of excessive shrill crying, vasomotor instability, disturbed short sleep periods, restlessness, tremors, voracious appetite, overactivity, and diarrhea. Realization that the infant's unusual behavior is related to his mother's use of barbiturates may not come for several days up to two weeks. The delayed onset is attributable to the functional immaturity of the baby's renal and hepatic systems, the primary channels of barbiturate excretion.[9] Treatment consists of supportive therapy and, when necessary, institution of a controlled drug withdrawal schedule using 3 to 5 mg of paregoric per kilogram of body weight over twenty-four hours in equal or divided doses, or 1 mg of chlorpromazine every four to six hours.[10]

Treatment of Barbiturate Overdose

Barbiturate overdose is the most serious complication of barbiturate dependence and a major cause of accidental and intentional suicide. An overdose may

[9] Murdina M. Desmond et al., "Maternal Barbiturate Utilization and Neonatal Withdrawal Symptomatology," *The Journal of Pediatrics,* 80:192–195, February 1972.
[10] "Babies on Barbs," *Emergency Medicine,* 4:53, July 1972.

consist of (1) repeated large doses over a short period of time, (2) a mixture of substantial quantities of long- and short-acting barbiturates, or (3) unknown but potent quantities of barbiturates that are used as filler or potentiators of other illicit drugs (e.g., heroin).

Signs and Symptoms of Barbiturate Overdose The patient overdosed on barbiturates will be comatose and will also exhibit a variety of signs. Vital sign fluctuations include:

1 Pulse: weak, rapid, or slow weak
2 Respiration: slow, rapid and shallow, or Cheyne-Stokes respirations
3 Blood pressure: low
4 Temperature: may be lowered several degrees

Pale, cyanotic skin is also common. Urine output is usually depressed and may reflect an underlying medical disorder such as circulatory or renal dysfunction. Shock may be present on admission or may develop after treatment is begun.

The coma that is indicative of barbiturate overdose has been described in four stages,[11] which are shown in Table 13-1. It is clear that the treatment plan will be determined by the depth of the coma.

The length of the coma can be influenced by several factors. Underlying medical problems (liver or kidney disease, other drug dependencies—heroin, alcohol) can adversely affect barbiturate excretion rates since the short-acting drugs are degraded by the liver and the long-acting drugs are more slowly excreted by the kidneys.[12] Thus, impaired function of these organ systems can slow excretion and adversely prolong the comatose state. The sedating and central nervous system depressant action of barbiturates can be potentiated by

Table 13-1 Stages of Barbiturate Coma

Stage	Painful Stimuli	Reflex response	Vital Signs
1	Withdraws	Deep tendon reflexes intact	Stable
2	Unresponsive	Deep tendon reflexes intact	Stable
3	Unresponsive	Loss of deep tendon reflexes	Stable
4	Unresponsive	Loss of deep tendon reflexes	Depression of respiratory-circulatory function

[11] C. E. Reed, M. F. Driggs, and C. C. Foote, "Acute Barbiturate Intoxication: A Study of 300 Cases Based on a Physiological System of Classification of the Severity of the Intoxication," *Annals of Internal Medicine,* 37:290–303, August 1952.
[12] Roscoe R. Robinson et al., "Treatment of Acute Barbiturate Intoxication," *Modern Treatment,* 8:565, August 1971.

other depressants, especially alcohol. The action of the particular barbiturate ingested also influences the length of the coma. Overdose of short-acting drugs tends to produce a more rapid onset of coma, while overdose of longer-acting drugs produces a slower onset.

The serum barbiturate level is not generally accepted as a valid indicator of the duration of the coma. It can be a valuable tool, however, in evaluating and guiding therapy. For example, initial plasma concentrations of 3.5 mg/100 mg for short-acting drugs and 8.0 mg/100 mg for long-acting drugs is generally considered fatal.[13]

Specific Interventions for Barbiturate Overdose The immediate goals of treatment depend on the status of the patient upon admission. Thus maintenance of respiratory stability is the primary immediate goal if the patient is having or will have difficulty breathing. Other life-preserving measures must be implemented immediately, and concurrent efforts to promote rapid excretion of the barbiturates are also vitally important.

In the following sections, brief summaries of currently accepted medical interventions for different aspects of overdose are presented. Since specific dosages for drugs and intravenous solutions vary considerably, they will be included only where a consensus of opinion exists.

Maintenance of Respiration Opening and maintaining the patient's airway is of primary importance. It is accomplished by clearing the mouth and pharynx of secretions and other foreign matter and then inserting an oral airway if the patient has not aspirated and is breathing on his own. Further clearing of the pharynx can then be conducted through the airway. When acute respiratory depression is present, intubation with a cuffed endotrachial tube is appropriate. Assisted ventilation on room air can be accomplished through use of positive pressure breathing equipment. If the patient will require assisted ventilation for more than two or three days, a tracheotomy is usually performed. Removal of respiratory secretions is greatly facilitated with the endotrachial tube or tracheotomy.

Correction of Circulatory Depression When evidence of impaired circulatory function such as low vital signs and blood pressure, decreased or absent urinary output, and depressed respirations exists, the condition must be treated immediately. Upon admission, an intravenous infusion is started, which serves as the primary channel of therapy for (1) correction of dehydration, hypovolemia, and electrolyte imbalances (5 to 10 percent dextrose in water, percentages of dextrose in saline in water, percentages of saline in water); (2) administration

[13] Ibid., p. 568.

of plasma expanders (normal human serum albumin, varying percentages of dextran, artificial plasma preparations) to increase plasma volume, which will stimulate increased blood pressure, and (3) administration of vasopressor agents (levarterenol bitartrate, metaraminol bitartrate) to increase systolic blood pressure. A central venous pressure catheter is frequently inserted to allow close monitoring of the progress of intravenous fluid therapy and plasma expansion, thus reducing the possibility of overexpansion of circulatory volume and such complications as congestive heart failure.

Removal of Barbiturate from Body Rapid removal of the barbiturate from the body can be accomplished in several ways.

1 *Emptying gastric contents.* After an endotrachial tube with cuff has been inserted and the cuff inflated, the insertion of a nasogastric tube will allow for aspiration of gastric contents for analysis and prevent further barbiturate absorption. Gastric lavage may be ordered but is more effective when the patient is brought for treatment within hours of the overdose. Emetic-induced vomiting in the comatose or highly intoxicated patient is contraindicated because of the danger of pulmonary aspiration.

2 *Stimulating forced diuresis.* Since the rate of barbiturate excretion in the urine is in direct proportion to the rate of urinary excretion, stimulation of a forced diuresis is often successful in removing barbiturates from the body. To accomplish forced diuresis, chemical diuretic agents are used, e.g., furosemide, ethacrynic acid, thiazides, organomercurials, or mannitol. (The danger of producing some of the side effects of these potent diuretic agents is weighed against their potential life-saving benefits to the acutely ill patient.) Urine output is measured at least hourly so that fluid replacement will be coordinated with excretion rates. Insertion of an indwelling catheter into the bladder is essential in order to accurately record urine output volume.

Since urinary excretion of phenobarbital is enhanced with an alkaline renal filtrate, some physicians administered alkalizing chemical agents to further increase urinary excretion rates. Sodium lactate, THAM buffer, and sodium bicarbonate are three of the most frequently ordered alkalinization-producing agents.

3 *Instituting dialysis.* In order to enhance and increase the removal of barbiturates from the body of the overdosed patient, peritoneal dialysis or hemodialysis may be instituted. Dialyzing procedures are generally not indicated when previously described measures produce desired results. However, peritoneal dialysis can significantly increase the rate of drug removal and therefore is highly beneficial when used in combination with diuresis and other supportive measures. Hemodialysis, if carried out by highly skilled professionals, can greatly increase barbiturate removal rates, especially with the long-acting drugs. It is most appropriate and life-saving when used with critically ill patients, patients with renal or hepatic impairment, patients intoxicated with other dialyzable drugs in addition to barbiturates, and patients who are unresponsive to other treatment methods.

Additional Supportive Measures Care is taken to prevent the hazards of immobility when a comatose patient is admitted. Necessary measures include frequently turning the patient, administering artificial tear solutions, patching or taping his eyes to prevent corneal damage, and general intensive supportive care and treatment. (See Chapter 14 for the details of nursing care.)

Complications of Barbiturate Overdose Perhaps the most common complication of barbiturate overdose is respiratory infection, which is more likely to occur if the patient is comatose for a long time or in poor health. Other respiratory complications include pulmonary edema, atelectasis, and aspiration. Urinary tract infections are also frequent and are caused by the use of an indwelling bladder catheter. Besides serving as a valuable diagnostic clue to barbiturate abuse and overdose, severe bullous (blisters or vesiclelike) lesions of the skin are a further complication of barbiturate overdose.

After the acute episode is over and the person has regained physiological stability, he should continue to receive professional help. Long-term therapy is necessary to help the person in overcoming drug dependence and reduce the possibility of repeated barbiturate overdose and suicide. (Long-term treatment for drug-dependent persons is discussed in later sections of this book.)

TREATMENT FOR DEPENDENCE ON NARCOTICS

The treatment of persons dependent on narcotics can involve the use of emergency and acute care hospital facilities, community based drug abuse programs, long-term residential rehabilitation programs, outpatient clinics and day care centers, and many combinations of these outlets. The goals and purposes of the individual treatment program determine whether care givers will be professionals, lay persons, or recovered drug abusers. Many programs rely exclusively on nonprofessional ex-drug abusers, requesting professional assistance only for conditions requiring skilled medical intervention.

Heroin dependence is the predominant form of illicit narcotic abuse in the United States. For this reason, specific aspects of treatment for narcotic abuse will focus on heroin dependence and therapy for overdose, withdrawal, and associated complications.

Treatment for Heroin Overdose

Overdose represents the major complication of heroin dependence. Success in preventing death relies on rapid, accurate identification of the problem and immediate intervention. Overdose with heroin results when abusers (1) inject an excessively potent amount of the drug, believing that their body can tolerate it; (2) decrease their habit and then inject too potent a dose; or (3) inject an excessive amount for other reasons, e.g., suicide. As with the person overdosed on barbiturates, it may be necessary to institute emergency cardiopulmonary resuscitation for the totally unresponsive patient. The necessity of implementing these efforts should always be foremost in the minds of health professionals caring for heroin addicts.

Symptoms of Heroin Overdose The cardinal symptoms of heroin overdose are pinpoint pupils and respiratory depression, which may include shallow, gasping breathing, irregular respiration with periods of apnea, tachypnea, dyspnea, or orthopnea. The skin will therefore be pale or bluish, depending on the depth of respiratory difficulty. Areflexia, hypotension, and bradycardia are common. The finding of a strong pulse and heartbeat, in the presence of the other diagnostic evidence, can be deceptive in that they may herald the onset of a terminal arrhythmia. Evidence of recent needle tracts on extremities, in the groin area, or under the tongue also confirm the diagnosis.

The symptoms of meperidine overdose are different from those of heroin overdose. The patient may have tremors, muscle twitches, convulsions, dilated pupils, and hyperactive reflexes.[14]

Specific Interventions for Heroin Overdose Although heroin overdose requires immediate, purposeful intervention to prevent death, it does not require such complex treatment as barbiturate overdose. The reason is that drug antagonists are available to treat heroin overdose but not barbiturate overdose.

Establishment of Patent Airway The most urgently needed intervention for heroin overdose is establishment of a patent, unobstructed airway. Depending on the facilities available for treatment, efforts may consist of mouth-to-mouth or mouth-to-nose resuscitation preceded by manual clearing of secretions and foreign matter from the mouth and pharynx. Endotrachial intubation is appropriate if employed immediately. Use of an oral airway facilitates respiratory assistance and can usually be rapidly inserted and subsequently used to suction mucous from the pharynx and trachea. The patient's respiratory status must be closely monitored until he is fully responsive.

Administration of Narcotic Antagonists Intravenous administration of specific narcotic antagonists produces immediate results when the overdose is due to narcotics. Thus, use of one of these drugs definitely confirms heroin overdose. The narcotic antagonists should be used with caution because excessive amounts can result in intensified respiratory depression or can precipitate the onset of rapid, acute withdrawal symptoms. Frequently prescribed drugs and recommended dosages are Nalorphine hydrochloride (Nalline®), 2.5 to 10 mg I.V.

---

[14] Raynaldo G. Sandoval, and Richard I. H. Wang, "Emergency Treatment of Narcotic Overdose," *Wisconsin Medical Journal,* **71**:220, September 1972.

with repeated doses at three- to five-minute intervals and Levallorphan tartrate (Lorfan®), 0.5 to 1.5 mg I.V., which may be repeated at fifteen- to thirty-minute intervals.[15, 16, 17] Repeat doses are appropriate when pupil size and respiratory rate do not improve following the first dose. Naloxone hydrochloride (Narcan®) is also frequently used to reverse respiratory depression from opiate overdose. The first dose is usually 0.4 mg I.V. or I.M. If respiratory depression is not eliminated within two to five minutes, the dose can be repeated two or three more times, or a single second dose of 0.8 mg I.V. or I.M. can be given.[18, 19] The patient will usually respond immediately after the drug is injected, often spitting out the airway and trying to sit up. If he then lapses into coma, he again can be given the antagonist. The patient who does not respond to two injections of the narcotic antagonist should be examined carefully for traumatic injury or metabolically induced coma.

Although the patient may appear alert and oriented after injection of the narcotic antagonist, he should not be left unattended. This is especially true when the nonspecific respiratory stimulant doxapram (Dopram®), 3 to 5 cc I.V., is administered. It is an extremely short-acting drug, about three to five minutes. If such a patient were left alone, he could quickly lapse into a state of acute respiratory depression and die.

The treatment for heroin overdose is relatively uncomplicated and successful when rapidly instituted. Delay in implementing respiratory assistance is the major hazard of overdose therapy.

Complications of Heroin Overdose   Perhaps the major pulmonary complication of heroin overdose is acute pulmonary edema usually associated with the severe respiratory depression characteristic of the patient's condition. In many cases, pulmonary edema will subside substantially after institution of respiratory assistance and the administration of narcotic antagonists, both of which contribute to improved respiratory function.

Respiratory aspiration of gastric contents is another serious complication and can lead to aspiration pneumonia. For this reason, intubation with a cuffed endotrachial tube must be carried out before aspiration of gastric contents or lavage, and to prevent aspiration if vomiting should occur.

There may be cardiac complications, but they are usually transitory and consist of basic heart arrhythmias, which often cease spontaneously without treatment.

[15] "The Shot That Kills," *Emergency Medicine*, 2:31, March 1970.
[16] George R. Gay, David E. Smith, and Charles W. Sheppard, "The New Junkie," *Emergency Medicine*, 3:125, April 1971.
[17] Sandoval, op. cit., p. 222.
[18] Ibid., p. 221.
[19] *Desk Reference on Drug Abuse*, American Hospital Association, Chicago, 1971, p. 9.

Treatment for Withdrawal from Heroin

The current treatment of withdrawal from heroin may focus specifically on the relief of symptoms or depend on methadone (Dolophine) as an agent useful in controlled withdrawal techniques, or as a drug for long-term maintenance therapy. These two approaches are discussed in the following sections. Familiarity with different programs and approaches is of vital importance to the nurse and allows her to administer knowledgeable and thoughtful nursing care as well as suggest possible alternatives to the physician responsible for prescribing treatment measures.

Symptoms of Heroin Withdrawal Physical manifestations indicating the onset of heroin withdrawal appear within four to ten hours after the last "fix" (injection) and are dependent upon the potency of this last dose and the extent of the heroin abuse. In general, the greater the habit (number of "bags" or "spoons" per day), the more severe the withdrawal syndrome. The time of onset of withdrawal symptoms for morphine dependence is essentially the same as that for heroin, with individual variations. The actual symptoms of withdrawal from heroin and morphine are also essentially the same. Therefore, reference will be made to the heroin withdrawal syndrome in the remainder of this section.

Withdrawal symptoms associated with heroin dependence are relatively mild when compared with the abstinence syndromes for alcohol and barbiturates, in which seizure activity can occur. These symptoms are usually not considered life-threatening. Many heroin addicts withdraw "cold turkey" (unassisted) several times during their drug abuse career without serious harm. The psychological fears and anxiety generated by impending withdrawal are considered one of the major factors responsible for continued abuse. Thus, such fear and psychological discomfort can often be more disquieting to the user than the actual physical abstinence symptoms. In fact, addicts have often described the syndrome as resembling a bad case of the flu.

Initial symptoms of heroin withdrawal are drug craving, restlessness, yawning, and insomnia. As the syndrome progresses, these symptoms intensify and tearing, runny nose, and sweating appear. Varying degrees of anxiety are generally present. Without treatment these symptoms also intensify while eye pupils react sluggishly and begin to dilate as muscular cramps, twitching, tremors, and joint pains then become evident. There may be abdominal cramping, diarrhea, vomiting, and hot and cold flashes. Elevation in pulse, respiration, temperature, and blood pressure is common. Death may occur if these symptoms become prolonged with resulting acute weight loss, dehydration, and fluid and electrolyte imbalances, especially in the debilitated, malnourished person.

Duration of the withdrawal syndrome varies from four to ten days with a peak intensity of symptoms at twenty-four to seventy-two hours for heroin dependence and thirty-six to forty-eight hours for morphine dependence.[20, 21]

Specific Interventions for Heroin Withdrawal Before initiating specific treatment measures, some physicians will administer an injection of methadone to the patient in order to validate heroin dependence and also determine the extent of the habit. Because methadone is a long-acting, synthetic narcotic, when administered in this way the withdrawal symptoms subside. If they do not disappear with the initial dose, an adjustment can be made in the next dose of the narcotic blocking agent.

Detoxification with Methadone When the test dose of methadone is not used, the drug can be employed in a controlled withdrawal program. Depending on the particular treatment schedule, the initial dose may be fixed at 10 or 20 mg PO or I.M., or calculated on the number of bags of heroin used per day; e.g., five to seven bags would require a methadone dose range from 20 to 40 mg by mouth and it must be maintained for at least one or two days. Then controlled reduction in dose can begin, usually at 5 mg per day.[22] On this kind of schedule, detoxification can be completed in approximately four to ten days. In addition to methadone, some physicians will administer medication to relieve muscle cramps and pains or to promote sleep; other programs rely solely on the narcotic blocking agent.

Symptomatic Treatment of Withdrawal Treatment programs not using methadone emphasize providing symptomatic relief for the discomfort of the abstinence syndrome. Mild, non-dependence-producing muscle relaxants can be given for muscle spasm. Chloral hydrate in large doses, up to 2.5 gm, may be successful in relieving insomnia. The patient experiencing acute nervousness, or "jumpy nerves," may benefit from oral diazepam, phenobarbital, or chlordiazepoxide in usual doses. When nausea and vomiting are present, antiemetic agents may be employed. To decrease pain or general discomfort, propoxyphene hydrochloride (Darvon®) or aspirin is often effective. Supportive therapy may also include mild anticholinergic drugs to alleviate a runny nose.

Following detoxification, the heroin- or narcotic-dependent person must continue with treatment for the underlying problems associated with drug abuse. When follow-up care, counseling, and long-term treatment and rehab-

---

[20] Gay et al., op. cit., p. 132.
[21] I. H. Perkins, "Hospital Treatment of Narcotic Addiction," *Clinical Toxicology,* 3:576–577, December 1970.
[22] Alex Richman, Marcus A. Feinstein, and Harold L. Trigg, "Withdrawal and Detoxification in New York City Heroin Users," *Drug Abuse: Current Concepts and Research,* in Wolfram Keup (ed.), Charles C Thomas, Springfield, Ill., 1972, p. 427.

ilitation are not carried out, relapse rates run as high as 95 percent six months after detoxification.[23] Therefore, although short-term abstinence via detoxification produces benefits for society by temporarily reducing criminal activity, the drug abuser almost inevitably will return to drug use if he is discharged without adequate long-term care.

Treatment of Heroin Withdrawal in the Newborn An extremely high percentage of pregnant heroin abusers give birth to drug-dependent infants. These infants generally have a lower birth weight than nondependent infants, with many born prematurely. Without prompt and specific treatment, the heroin-dependent infant may die.

Onset of withdrawal symptoms in the neonate may occur within hours of delivery. Most babies exhibit symptoms within the first twenty-four hours after birth.[24, 25, 26] Commonly occurring symptoms include a shrill, persistent cry, trembling and hyperactivity, irregular rapid respiration with periods of apnea, difficulty in feeding, incomplete Moro reflex as well as exaggerated reflexes, yawning, short sleep periods, hyperirritability, diarrhea which results in rapid weight loss, and possibly convulsions. The extent and presence of each of these symptoms will very from infant to infant. Because so many of these babies are premature and/or have low birth weights, untreated diarrhea will produce life-threatening fluid and electrolyte and temperature regulation imbalances. Prompt treatment is mandatory and usually comprises detoxifying and sedating medications and supportive therapy to prevent excessive fluid, electrolyte, and nutritional loss and serious respiratory complications.

Drugs used in the treatment of the infant heroin withdrawal syndrome are paregoric, chlorpromazine, phenobarbital, diazepam, and occasionally methadone. Two of the more prevalent treatment schedules are presented below. Keep in mind, however, that different treatment centers may use different drugs.

Paregoric Used for Infant Detoxification Paregoric may be orally administered to the neonate via eye dropper at a dose of approximately five drops every three to four hours. The dose can be increased up to eight drops if the infant does not respond. The baby is maintained on this regimen for up to three weeks and subsequently is started on a controlled, gradual reduction over three to seven weeks. Rapid withdrawal can stimulate a recurrence in symptoms.

[23] E. Leong Way, "Narcotics," in Jack R. Arndt and William L. Blockstein (eds.), *Problems in Drug Abuse,* University Extension, Madison, Wisc., 1970, p. 65.

[24] "The Youngest Addict . . . and Ways to Recognize Him . . .," *Emergency Medicine,* 2:28, September 1970.

[25] Mary Helen Carroll, "Recognizing Narcotic Withdrawal in Newborns," *Journal of Obstetrical and Gynecological Nursing,* 1:23, June 1972.

[26] Evelyn Sprung, "Drug Withdrawal in Newborn Infants," *Bedside Nurse,* 4:12, December 1971.

Chlorpromazine Used for Infant Detoxification Chlorpromazine can be administered by mouth or by intramuscular injection in doses calculated on 0.7 mg to 2.2 mg per kilogram of body weight.[27, 28, 29] The total amount is given in equally divided doses, usually four times a day. After maintenance on this schedule for ten to forty days, the infant is gradually and carefully withdrawn from the medication. An acceptable reduction rate is 0.2 mg per kilogram of body weight every two or three days over a rather lengthy time period of two to six weeks. In general, infants will respond rapidly to chlorpromazine therapy by increasing sleep periods, ingesting offered food, and decreasing hyperactivity and crying.

Supporting Treatment during Infant Withdrawal The acutely ill premature infant who is experiencing heroin withdrawal symptoms requires intensive medical treatment and nursing care. Maintenance of respiratory status and a constant, optimal body temperature are vital. Frequent, nutritious feedings must be carried out. Intravenous fluid and electrolyte replacement are usually not used unless serious dehydration is present.

The infant who is dependent on heroin or other narcotics at birth will respond to rapidly instituted treatment, and after successful detoxification the babies usually have no further drug-related problems.

Treatment of Medical Complications of Heroin Dependence

Many of the medical complications of opiate abuse are found in other drug abuse populations and are associated with drugs given by the intravenous or subcutaneous routes, e.g., hepatitis, recurrent skin infections, and foreign particle emboli. These conditions arise in amphetamine abusers and multiple drug abusers who use two or more illicit drugs by intravenous and oral routes. Treatment for tetanus and bacterial endocarditis is usually needed more often by the heroin addict than by other drug-abusing persons. Because regimens for these conditions are adequately discussed in numerous textbooks, this aspect of drug abuse will not be duplicated here. It should be emphasized, however, that the drug abuser with an acute or long-term medical complication requires skilled and patient medical and nursing care.

Alterations in nutritional patterns are necessary for a large proportion of drug abusers, especially heroin-dependent persons, who tend to seriously neglect this aspect of living. Malnutrition and undernutrition develop within a short time after the abuser begins to devote a substantial or major portion of his time to procuring a drug supply. Hospitalization for a medical condition

[27] Milton C. F. Semoff, "Narcotic Addiction in the Newborn," *Arizona Medicine,* 24:935, October 1967.
[28] "The Youngest Addict . . . and Ways to Recognize Him . . .," loc. cit.
[29] Carl Zelson, "The Infant Addict Can Be Treated," *Consultant,* 11:45, December 1971.

only temporarily serves to provide healthful dietary intake. Thus, the health care team must look for ways to promote long-term changes in nutrition patterns in addition to assisting the addict to control or cease drug-taking behavior.

LONG-TERM TREATMENT FOR HEROIN DEPENDENCE

Following heroin detoxification or in place of it, certain programs employ a chemical maintenance regimen to assist the patient in overcoming or continuing abstinence from opiates. Frequently used approaches are the methadone and the narcotic antagonist programs, and a third plan that utilizes haloperidol in a chemical maintenance framework.

Methadone Maintenance for Heroin Abuse Treatment

Perhaps the most widely publicized and well-known treatment for heroin dependence has been and remains methadone maintenance. Programs using this method are based on the substitution of methadone for heroin. After the maintenance dose is reached, the effects of heroin are blocked when the person uses the opiate while taking methadone. Thus, methadone maintenance is also known as chemical blocking therapy.

Pros and Cons of Methadone Maintenance   Although there are over 450 methadone maintenance programs throughout the United States,[30] this mode of treatment is not supported by all the health professions. A wide divergence in opinion and philosophical stance exists regarding the applicability and efficacy of methadone maintenance. Some of the reasons for its lack of support include the following:

1 Methadone maintenance does not solve the drug-dependent person's basic problem—dependence on a narcotic. It merely substitutes a legal drug for an illegal one. Thus the person is not helped to totally overcome drugs.
2 Legally sanctioned drug dependence serves as a potentially harmful example to non-drug abusers living with the heroin addict being maintained on methadone. Narcotic drug use should not be justified in one situation and forbidden in another.
3 Methadone should not be prematurely touted as the cure-all for heroin dependence. It is too early to make broad claims for its success. This argument emphasizes caution because past mistakes have been made in opiate addiction treatment. For example, years ago heroin was thought to be the best substitute drug for morphine dependence. Later it was found to produce greater problems than the original drug. The question, therefore, becomes:

---

[30] Dorothy Nelkin, *Methadone Maintenance: A Technological Fix,* George Braziller, New York, 1973, p. 3.

Are we being too hasty in accepting methadone as the answer to heroin dependence treatment?

4 Methadone has become a drug of abuse since maintenance programs have become prevalent. Although not as large a problem as heroin dependence, methadone abuse poses an increasingly serious problem in the operation of maintenance programs.

5 Transfer of dependence from heroin to methadone suddenly removes the person's major defense against unpleasant and threatening life problems. When methadone programs make no allowance for initiating intense therapy to help the person learn new coping behaviors, the drug abuser is left unprepared for reentry into society as a functioning participant. If this happens, methadone maintenance is viewed as more harmful than helpful.

Each of these reasons and others are put forth by health professionals who do not believe that methadone maintenance provides optimal treatment for heroin-dependent persons. Advocates of this approach counter with the following arguments in support of their position:

1 Methadone maintenance allows the addict to shift his energies away from drug-procuring criminal behavior. When the craving for heroin is removed by methadone, the person is freed to develop socially contributory behavior patterns.

2 Heroin-dependent persons who are maintained on methadone have no need to resort to criminal activity in order to continue taking the drug. For this reason, addicts on methadone are removed from the criminal arena and are no longer a threat to property and society.

3 By removing the necessity to hustle for illicit drugs, the methadone-maintained person can begin to concentrate on the underlying problems that contributed to the initiation and continuation of drug dependence. All the energy formerly put into securing heroin can be directed to formulation of more appropriate, long-term, problem-solving methods.

4 Methadone maintenance programs are relatively inexpensive and therefore economically feasible for large numbers of heroin-dependent persons. In order to treat the ever increasing number of heroin addicts, methadone offers a feasible alternative to expensive, limited psychotherapeutic programs.

5 While methadone maintenance is continued, the drug abuser can become employed, reassume family responsibilities, and stay out of prison. He is capable of assuming responsibility for himself and of developing an independent, self-actualizing life.

6 Once the person has reached his maintenance dose, he generally does not experience euphoric, perception-altering feelings. If the abuser should inject heroin while on methadone, he will not experience any euphoric response formerly attributed to heroin.

Methadone maintenance has not been completely accepted as the best solution to the problem of heroin dependence, but it has succeeded in helping many addicts to remain opiate-free and lead useful lives. Such success, although not overwhelming, is significant and has provided the solution to a life-threatening problem for people who have never been able to remain drug-free before. For this reason alone, methadone maintenance offers a valuable alternative in the long-term treatment of heroin dependence.

Characteristics of Methadone Programs   Variations in methods, goals, admission policies, dosage schedules, and counseling services are characteristic of methadone maintenance programs throughout the United States. Methods for implementation of methadone programs can include the use of hospital outpatient clinics, privately financed foundations, community clinics, and innovative publicly financed treatment centers. Regardless of the method of implementation, methadone maintenance programs are subject to complex federal and state regulations that require them to follow certain procedures in their organization, the dispensation of methadone, and the security of this treatment method.

Goals of different programs may emphasize long-term continuous participation, eventual withdrawal from methadone, combinations of methadone and counseling, or dispensation of methadone without follow-up or counseling. The goal of each program will determine staffing needs, size of facilities, policies of treatment, and the nature of the heroin-dependent population. These factors and others influence admission criteria, often narrowing them. For example, certain programs establish age limitations and a minimum number of addiction years which must be met before the heroin-dependent person can be accepted. Programs with such criteria often have long-term counseling services and residential rehabilitation services and employ numerous lay and professional staff to implement therapy sessions. Other programs do not have such restrictions; i.e., heroin addicts are accepted regardless of the number of years of drug dependence, past treatment, number of relapses, and criminal record. Additional criteria that restrict admission to some programs include multiple drug abuse and the presence of psychiatric illness. Many programs simply are not equipped to adequately treat the complex problems such drug abusers present and consequently do not attempt to do so. Persons are accepted into methadone maintenance programs on a voluntary basis, or may be referred to such centers on a mandatory basis in lieu of a jail sentence.

Methadone Administration and Dosage   Methadone hydrochloride is given orally in orange juice or in an orange-flavored liquid to mask both its bitter taste and the amount of the dose. Some maintenance programs dispense only a fixed dose. The majority of the programs, however, adjust the schedule to meet the person's response. In this way, a dose that is not sufficient to block heroin withdrawal symptoms can be increased.

Persons accepted to a methadone program are slowly brought up to their maintenance dose, usually over a three- to four-week period. Maintenance doses range from 30 mg to 120 mg per day but can be increased to a maximum of 180 mg per day. The dose is administered once daily, usually in the morning because the duration of methadone is approximately twenty-four hours. An initial dose may be 40 mg per day maintained for several days up to a week. The dose is then increased at 10 to 20 mg increments each week until the person's maintenance level is reached.

Daily dispensation of methadone requires only one clinic visit per day for most drug abusers. Other drug abusers find that the dose is more beneficial when received in two equal doses, one in the morning and the other in the afternoon or early evening. Several times a week or daily, supervised urine specimens are required of participants. These specimens are analyzed to determine if the person has taken opiates, barbiturates, or other chemicals of abuse while on methadone. Repeated evidence from urine analysis that the person has taken such drugs may result in his dismissal from the program or other disciplinary action. Sometimes no action is taken and the abuse of other chemicals is considered an expected hazard with heroin abusers.

Programs that include a long-term plan for continued outpatient treatment may be designed to extend increasing degrees of trust in the heroin addict's ability to regulate his own methadone. In these instances, after the person has clearly demonstrated his capability to respond to treatment and has not evidenced further drug use, he may be given several doses of methadone to take unsupervised. If he continues to demonstrate such capability, he is given more independence in controlling and administering his own regimen. One means of exhibiting trustworthiness and capability is participating in the program's group therapy sessions and other treatment efforts. When the person backslides, or is unable to continue independent methadone self-administration, he begins daily visits to the clinic to receive the medication, participate in therapy sessions, and again develop the ability to assume responsibility for the intake of the blocking agent.

Problems Associated with Methadone Maintenance Numerous physiological and psychological side effects have been reported by those on methadone maintenance regimens. Among the most prominent of the physical side effects are disturbances in sleep patterns, increased perspiration, constipation, muscle cramps, and sexual dysfunction, such as impotence. Significant psychological side effects include the development of different drug dependencies—alcohol or barbiturates—and the emergence of psychiatric problems. For some persons, methadone maintenance causes the appearance of serious personal problems, personality disorders, or major psychotic illnesses. Many of these problems can assume crisis proportions. While the abuser was dependent on heroin, these problems could be partially or wholly submerged. When he is freed of heroin dependence, the "shelter" of the heroin "nod" is no longer available.

Persons on methadone maintenance regimens should never receive Talwin® for the relief of pain. This drug blocks the action of methadone and therefore can precipitate immediate withdrawal symptoms. Withdrawal from methadone takes longer than withdrawal from heroin and may have greater or less discomfort associated with it. Infants born of mothers who are on methadone maintenance therapy during pregnancy can develop withdrawal symptoms on the first day of life. The tremors and irritability of the syndrome last longer than those from heroin withdrawal in the neonate.[31]

Methadone overdose is becoming more prevalent, especially in children who unknowingly consume the drug premixed in fruit juices.[32] Death from overdose may also occur with non-heroin-dependent persons who ingest the drug without having built up a tolerance to it.

In summary, methadone maintenance has proven a boon to many drug abusers who could not otherwise succeed in various treatment programs. On the other hand, further study and research into the long-term physical and psychological effects of methadone is required before any permanent commitment to the drug can be made.

Narcotic Antagonists for Heroin Abuse Treatment

In recent years, modest success has been obtained by the use of certain narcotic antagonists with heroin-dependent persons who have been withdrawn from the narcotic. It is hypothesized that the narcotic antagonists prevent heroin or other narcotics from reaching specific receptor sites in the brain. Thus, heroin would have no effect when injected after an antagonist had been ingested.

Two of the more frequently used narcotic antagonists are cyclazocine and naloxone. Cyclazocine is a nonnarcotic with action lasting from twelve to twenty-four hours. It is given orally in initial doses of 0.2 mg and gradually increased over a two- or three-week period until the maintenance level of 4 mg to 6 mg is reached. When the drug is taken before an injection of heroin, the abuser will not experience the effects of heroin. Unfortunately, cyclazocine has several uncomfortable side effects and is therefore not actively sought by most heroin addicts. The main side effects include nausea, dizziness, headaches, delusions, thought disturbances, and hallucinations. Tolerance to these discomforting side effects develops over time, but tolerance to the drug's blocking effects does not also develop. A mild abstinence syndrome may develop when cyclazocine intake is stopped.

---

[31] B. K. Rajegowda et al., "Methadone Withdrawal in Newborn Infants," *The Journal of Pediatrics,* 81:533, September 1972.

[32] Nelkin, op. cit., p. 39.

Naloxone is also a non-drug-dependence-producing chemical with a duration of approximately four to six hours. The short duration of action is one of the primary drawbacks to its wider use. Naloxone does not require gradual build-up of dosage as does cyclazocine. However, larger doses are required per day than for the other antagonist. Doses of greater than 200 mg per day, up to 2,400 mg per day, of Naloxone have been reported.[33] Side effects are mild compared with those of cyclazocine.

To date, use of these narcotic antagonists to help former heroin addicts maintain abstinence has not been widespread. Vigorous research continues to determine optimal uses for the narcotic antagonists in heroin abuse treatment. Thus far, success has been most often associated with long-term residential treatment programs in which the antagonist is used as one component of the therapy regimen.

Maintenance Treatment with Haloperidol

Haloperidol, a nonaddictive and nonnarcotic tranquilizer, has been successfully employed in preliminary studies in which heroin addicts' abstinence symptoms were prevented by maintenance doses of this drug.[34] Further research into its effectiveness and appropriateness is required before the drug can receive wide acceptance.

Treatment of heroin dependence presents a vital and often frustrating challenge to the health professions. The approaches presented in this chapter have centered on immediate and specific long-term treatment methods. Long-term rehabilitation programs are discussed in Part Three of this book. Also included in Part Three are many of the psychologically oriented methods of treatment indigenous to the rehabilitation program.

TREATMENT OF DEPENDENCE ON HALLUCINOGENS

People who abuse the hallucinogen drugs do not develop physical dependence and craving, nor do they experience a physiological abstinence syndrome when intake is discontinued. Hallucinogen dependence is primarily associated with psychological dependence. For these reasons, treatment of persons who abuse hallucinogens focuses on two areas: adverse reactions to the drug experience and long-term group or psychotherapy dealing with complex underlying psychological problems. Treatment methods that address adverse reactions are discussed in the following section. Long-term therapeutic approaches are discussed in Part Three.

---

[33] James R. Gamage, and E. Lief Zerkin, "Narcotic Antagonists," *Report Series: National Clearinghouse for Drug Abuse Information,* ser. 26, no. 1, p. 9, October 1973.

[34] John Karkalas, and Harbans Lal, "Haloperidol in the Treatment of Heroin Addiction," in Jasbir M. Singh et al. (eds.), *Drug Addiction: Clinical and Socio-Legal Aspects,* Futura Publishing Company, Inc., Mt. Kisco, N.Y., 1972, p. 251–256.

Treatment for Adverse Reactions to Hallucinogens

Overdose with hallucinogens is not a major problem with the abuser of psychedelics. When death results, it is from the distorting effects of the drug experience; e.g., the person may believe he can accomplish superhuman feats and leap from a great height to his death, or he may try to escape from hallucinatory threats during panic states and cause his own destruction. Treatment efforts are designed to prevent such deaths from occurring.

Treatment of the "bad trip" phenomenon attempts to reduce panic states, refocus the drug experience into nonthreatening directions, help the panicked person regain control of the hallucinogen experience, or reverse the bad trip via use of chemical agents. To accomplish these goals, the care givers (whether lay or professional) use numerous approaches. The first necessary step is to establish a quiet, secure, and nonstressful environment in which the drug abuser will not be bombarded by external stimuli. The care giver should be calm, use a normal or low tone of voice, and display an attitude of caring.

Establishing communication with the person experiencing panic or a bad trip after hallucinogen ingestion is of vital importance. Continuous verbal orientation by telling him his name and location and assuring him of his safety provide a link with reality and help the person realize that his hallucinogenic perceptions are not real. When possible, it is most beneficial to have one care giver remain with him throughout the treatment process. It does not necessarily have to be the same person. As the care giver reorients the person, he should encourage him to discuss the content of what he is perceiving. Understanding what the bad tripper is undergoing allows the care giver to emphasize the relationship to drug action only, not to reality. Clarifying that what the drug user is currently experiencing is transitory can help him accept the continued distortion and alleviate feelings of panic and terror.

Discussion of the bad tripper's hallucinogen experience also can act as the catalyst for his reassuming control of the situation. Identifying threatening perceptions as drug-oriented, when coupled with efforts to redirect such perception into acceptable channels, often helps the drug user to gain control of the experience. The care giver should also provide anticipatory guidance regarding the probable course of the trip. For example, it often helps to know that as the drug effects begin to wear off, the person will experience alternating periods of awareness and confusion. As the trip reaches its conclusion, periods of awareness increase—the experience passes.

When it is not possible to have a one-to-one ratio of care giver to drug abuser, chemical agents have been employed to reverse or control panic and bad trip reactions. Phenothiazines, specifically chlorpromazine, have been effective in controlling or blocking the LSD bad trip but can intensify and prolong a negative hallucinogen experience when given to persons who have taken other psychedelic drugs. An appropriate dosage of chlorpromazine ranges from 50 to 100 mg PO or I.M., which may be repeated as needed.[35, 36] When the adverse reaction is due to LSD ingestion, administration of chlorpromazine is usually very effective in alleviating many of the unpleasant, frightening sensations. Short-acting barbiturates have also been used with some success as have drugs such as diazepam.

Treatment of the bad trip experience related to hallucinogen ingestion emphasizes interpersonal support, reassurance, and the maintenance of contact with reality. Chemical agents are often successful as an adjunct to the personal approach, which is the key to uncomplicated resolution of a bad trip or panic reaction.

TREATMENT OF DEPENDENCE ON VOLATILE SUBSTANCES

To date, there has been no definite demonstration of physical dependence, craving, or withdrawal syndrome associated with the abuse of volatile substances. Treatment of the person psychologically dependent on volatile inhalants centers on emergency intervention in an overdose situation and long-term therapy aimed at helping him learn to face the problems that contributed to drug-abusing behavior. Specific treatment measures appropriate to overdose with volatile inhalants are generally the same as those for barbiturate overdose, which was discussed in the second section of this chapter. In addition to these measures, the overdosed person may benefit from the inhalation of fresh air, or a combination of 95 percent oxygen and 5 percent carbon dioxide.[37] Intense physiological supportive measures are required to prevent total respiratory collapse in the overdosed volatile substance abuser.

REFERENCES

Abramson, David H.: "Bigeminy and Heroin Intoxication," *New York State Journal of Medicine,* 72:2888–2890, December 1, 1972.

Arndt, Jack R., and William L. Blockstein (eds.): *Problems in Drug Abuse,* University Extension, Madison, Wisc., 1970.

Blachly, Paul H. (ed.): *Progress in Drug Abuse,* Charles C Thomas, Springfield, Ill., 1972.

Drug Dependence: A Guide for Physicians, American Medical Association, Chicago, 1970.

---

[35] Charles Clay Dahlberg, "Treatment and Rehabilitation of Abusers of Hallucinogens and Amphetamines," in Jack R. Arndt and William L. Blockstein (eds.), *Problems in Drug Abuse,* University Extension, Madison, Wisc., 1970, p. 132.

[36] Robert L. Taylor, John I. Maurer, and Jared R. Tinklenberg, "Management of 'Bad Trips' in an Evolving Drug Scene," in Paul H. Blachly (ed.), *Progress in Drug Abuse,* Charles C Thomas, Springfield, Ill., 1972, p. 309.

[37] *Desk Reference on Drug Abuse,* op. cit., p. 5.

Duberstein, Joel L., and David M. Kaufman: "A Clinical Study of an Epidemic of Heroin Intoxication ahd Heroin-Induced Pulmonary Edema," *The American Journal of Medicine,* 51:705–714, December 1971.

Fink, Max et al.: "Narcotic Antagonists: Another Approach to Addiction Therapy," *American Journal of Nursing,* 71:1359–1363, July 1971.

Gamage, James R., and E. Lief Zerkin; "Narcotic Antagonists," *Report Series National Clearinghouse for Drug Abuse Information,* ser. 26, no. 1, October 1973.

Gay, George R.: "Outpatient Barbiturate Withdrawal Using Phenobarbital," *The International Journal of the Addictions,* 7:17–26, 1972.

Gay, George R., David E. Smith, and Charles W. Sheppard: "The New Junkie," *Emergency Medicine,* 3:117–133, April 1971.

Hadden, John et al.: "Acute Barbiturate Intoxication," *Journal of the American Medical Association,* 209:893–900, August 11, 1969.

Hammond, Allen L.: "Narcotic Antagonists: New Methods to Treat Heroin Addiction," *Science,* 173:503–506, August 6, 1971.

Lennard, Henry L., Leon J. Epstein, and Mitchell S. Rosenthal: "The Methadone Illusion," *Science,* 176:881–884, May 1972.

Perkins, I. H.: "Hospital Treatment of Narcotic Addiction," *Clinical Toxicology,* 3:571–578, December 1970.

Rich, Joseph D.: "Medical Aspects of Drug Abuse," *Bedside Nurse,* 29–32, July 1972.

Robinson, Roscoe R., J. Caulie Gunnells, Jr., and James R. Clapp: "Treatment of Acute Barbiturate Intoxication," *Modern Treatment,* 8:561–579, August 1971.

Scher, Jordan M.: "Oral Methadone Maintenance," *Journal of the American Medical Association,* 222:488, October 23, 1972.

Semoff, Milton C. F.: "Narcotic Addiction in the Newborn," *Arizona Medicine,* 24:933–936, October 1967.

Shubin, Herbert, and Max H. Weil: "Shock Associated with Barbiturate Intoxication," *Journal of the American Medical Association,* 215:263–268, January 11, 1971.

Smith, David E., and Donald R. Wesson: "Phenobarbital Technique for Treatment of Barbiturate Dependence," *Archives of General Psychiatry,* 24:56–60, January 1971.

Smith, David. E., et al.: "New Developments in Barbiturate Abuse," *Clinical Toxicology,* 3:57–65, March 1970.

Stimmel, Barry, Morris Bernstein, and Hillel Tobias: "Methadone Maintenance Program," *New York State Journal of Medicine,* 72:2673–2677, November 1, 1973.

"The Youngest Addict . . . and Ways to Recognize Him . . ." *Emergency Medicine,* 2:28–29, September 1970.

Vogl, A. J.: "Better Treatment Through Chemistry," *Medical Economics,* 93–96, May 28, 1973.

Vogl, A. J.: "From Epidemic Thinking to Realistic Goals," *Medical Economics,* 86–89, May 28, 1973.

Watson, Robert, Ernest Hortmann, and Joseph J. Schildkraut: "Amphetamine Withdrawal: Affective State, Sleep Patterns, and MHPG Excretion," *American Journal of Psychiatry,* **129**:263–269, September 1972.

Wikler, Abraham: "Diagnosis and Treatment of Drug Dependence of the Barbiturate Type," *American Journal of Psychiatry,* **125**:758–765, December 1968.

Zelson, Carl: "The Infant Addict Can Be Treated," *Consultant,* **11**:45, December 1971.

Chapter 14

Nursing Care
of the Drug Abuser
in the General Hospital

In recent years, the role of the general hospital in the treatment of drug abusers has greatly expanded. Numerous large urban community hospitals have served as the main focus for innovative programs with varying degrees of success and involvement. Unfortunately, a significant number of general hospitals will not accept acknowledged or diagnosed drug abusers for treatment. Like alcoholics who require inpatient hospital services, many drug abusers are admitted under secondary diagnoses (hepatitis, circulatory dysfunction, etc.).

As mentioned earlier, there is a trend to liberalize admission policies, and the American Hospital Association supports not only the acceptance of drug-dependent persons for treatment but also the development of programs designed to meet the unique needs of these people.[1] Now that certain insurance policies include coverage for hospital treatment of drug dependence more services will be extended to larger numbers of the drug-abusing population.

[1]"Statement on the Admission to the General Hospital of Patients with Alcohol and Other Drug Problems," American Hospital Association, Chicago, revised November 19-20, 1969, pp. 3-4.

As the admission policies of the general hospital are modified to include persons with a primary diagnosis of drug dependence, the role of the nurse will also be modified. Nursing interventions and strategies will be needed for the various aspects of treatment that are unique to the drug abuser. In this and the following two chapters, the approaches discussed can serve as guidelines in most of the settings in which the nurse will come in contact with the drug-dependent person.

REASONS FOR HOSPITALIZATION

The drug-dependent person may be hospitalized for one of the following reasons:

1 For emergency treatment for overdosage
2 For withdrawal from the dependence-producing chemical
3 For treatment of complications of drug addiction, for example, hepatitis, respiratory infections, and dermatological infections
4 For protection from self-inflicted injury or suicide
5 For immediate crisis intervention

The length of stay depends on the reason for admittance. For example, the heroin-dependent person may be physically withdrawn from the drug or treated for overdose but continue to require extensive general hospital services for serious medical illnesses.

HOSPITAL SERVICES USED BY THE DRUG ABUSER

The emergency room of the general hospital sees perhaps the greatest number of drug abusers requiring intensive care. Persons overdosed on opiates or barbiturates or on bad trips with hallucinogens are often brought here. Nurses working on general medical-surgical nursing units may come in contact with the drug abuser admitted for a secondary diagnosis or for an elective or emergency surgical procedure.

Pregnant drug-dependent women who become in-hospital obstetrical patients represent especially challenging problems. Labor and delivery for the heroin- or barbiturate-dependent mother can become complicated if the drug abuse history is not known. Also, the neonate can experience withdrawal symptoms within a short time after birth, which necessitates prompt and knowledgeable nursing assessment and intervention.

The outpatient department of the general hospital frequently serves as the site for dispensation of methadone for heroin addicts. For this reason, the hospital clinic becomes a vital part of the overall program for treatment and rehabilitation. Outpatient clinics can also care for drug abusers' long-term physical problems that no longer require acute care facilities but do require periodic checkups or treatments.

Many of the nursing interventions discussed in this chapter are applicable to more than one hospital service. For example, nursing care for the overdosed heroin addict will be basically the same whether in the emergency room or on the general nursing unit. (Nursing care appropriate to the outpatient department will be covered in Chapter 16.) After the drug abuser has been hospitalized, he will be assigned to the care unit that can best meet his immediate needs. Therefore, the patient acutely or critically ill will be admitted to an intensive care unit, a detoxification unit, or a general nursing unit equipped for such situations. It must be emphasized that since nursing actions applicable to one unit are also applicable to other units, interventions designed for the acute physiological crisis can be used in settings other than the emergency room. In addition, although psychiatric nursing or interpersonal techniques are covered in Chapter 15, they are not confined to that setting—in fact, they must not be restricted. The drug abuser requires a comprehensive nursing care plan of action.

THE NURSING ASSESSMENT

Much of the nursing assessment of the drug abuser parallels that of the alcoholic patient. As the nurse evaluates the drug abuser's physical, psychological, and social needs, she can record pertinent information on the history report. Many of the situations are so acute, however, that actual recording of assessment data is neither reasonable nor necessary. In noncrisis situations, use of assessment data for design of the nursing care plan will facilitate and individualize nursing interventions and ensure continuity.

Assessment of the drug abuser takes into consideration the specific characteristics and actions of the primary drug of abuse, and specific points of nursing care appropriate to certain drugs.

Physical Assesment

The goal of the nurse's physical assessment consists of identifying (1) symptoms and behavior that indicate ongoing or impending drug withdrawal, (2) symptoms and extent of central nervous system depression, (3) the presence of adverse drug reactions, and (4) the presence of physical complications. In order to evaluate the patient in these areas the nurse should consider the following points.

Symptoms Indicative of Withdrawal Observations of behavior will often provide significant information about the initial stages of withdrawal even if the person denies the possibility. When considering withdrawal from heroin, the nurse can observe for restlessness, runny nose, tearing, sweating, and general anxiety. Observable evidence of needle marks, or "tracks," on the extremities are an obvious clue to self-administration of heroin intravenously. Since this is the major route of heroin injection, hospitalized patients, clinic patients, or emergency room patients may exhibit these symptoms. The patient may also complain of diarrhea, vomiting, nausea, and abdominal cramps. Elevation in pulse, respiration, temperature, and blood pressure is common. Rapid identification of the significance and potential harm of these symptoms is necessary.

Persons experiencing uncontrolled withdrawal from barbiturates will present with different behavior and physical symptoms, many mimicking alcohol withdrawal. The nurse should assess the presence, extent, and severity of muscular weakness, anorexia, nausea and vomiting, and psychomotor hyperactivity as evidence of initial withdrawal symptoms. If the syndrome has progressed, the nurse observes and evaluates the patient for more severe central nervous system responses such as hallucinations and delusions.

If the patient is delirious and shows disorientation, confusion, severe tremors, and hallucinations, he has progressed to a severe stage of withdrawal. The nurse must be aware that these symptoms precede the appearance of seizure activity and implement nursing actions to prepare for and assist in the prevention of this life-threatening condition.

Hospitalized patients who are extremely nervous, jittery, and restless, have needle tracks on their extremities or other body parts, or crash (sleep) for long extended periods of time should be evaluated for possible amphetamine withdrawal. Although they do not produce physical dependence, amphetamines do precipitate observable behaviors when withdrawn.

Symptoms Indicative of Overdose Nursing assessment of the physical status of the person overdosed on heroin, barbiturates, or volatile substances includes astute observations of response, and intense and continuous evaluation of patient status.

The barbiturate-overdosed patient will be comatose, with variation in the depth of the coma. Pupil reactivity should be evaluated because dilated pupils are a characteristic symptom of barbiturate overdose and consequent central nervous system depression. Vital sign and reflex responses will correspond to the depth of the coma and for this reason are an important evaluative tool. (Chapter 13 gives a more detailed discussion of physical manifestations.) The overall assessment the nurse makes of the comatose patient becomes vital information to the physician who must determine immediate medical intervention. At the same time, the nurse's physical assessment guides her immediate interventions in preventing death and nurturing the patient back to physiological equilibrium.

Heroin overdose consists of many characteristic physical symptoms that the nurse can observe while evaluating the overall physiological status of the patient. Pupil reactivity and respiratory status are important clues. If the patient has overdosed, the pupils will be pinpoint, respirations will be depressed, and vital signs may be depressed or deceptively strong. Pinpoint pupils and respiratory depression and irregularity are major distinguishing features of heroin overdose as opposed to barbiturate overdose. Patients who are experiencing tremors, convulsions, muscle twitches, and dilated pupils may be victims of meperidine overdose and should not be mistaken for persons overdosed on barbiturates.

The patient who has overdosed on volatile substances will generally exhibit physical symptoms similar to those from barbiturate overdose. However, the nurse should also determine by smell the type of agent used—glue, gasoline, or sprays.

Extent and Type of Dependence　A major part of the physical assessment must include observations for the extent and type of drug dependence. Certain abused drugs are not associated with physiologically life-endangering overdose phenomena, but the nurse must be able to assess physical responses and changes as they relate to these different drugs. For instance, the person using hallucinogens will not have severe central nervous system depression. He will present with certain fairly characteristic symptoms: increased pulse rate, fluctuations in blood pressure, irritation and reddening of the eyes or dilated pupils; if the drug is marijuana, a sweet, smoky odor will be on the patient's clothing.

Inspection of the body for puncture sites, scar tissue over veins, and needle tracks can indicate the type and length of the patient's drug history. With this information, it is often possible to hypothesize the extent and nature of the drug dependence. Such information aids the physician in designing reasonable treatment regimens and follow-up care. The nurse should look for puncture sites and scarring at all major, visible vein sites—in the antecubital spaces, beneath the tongue; in the groin area; along the arms, hands, legs and feet; between the fingers and toes, and on the penis in the male patient. The nurse should also consider methods the patient may have used to hide drugs and "works" (drug injection paraphernalia) on the body, especially when evaluating the heroin addict. Careful inspection of clothing and hair may reveal drugs or works. Other sites used to hide drugs include the vagina, the anal canal, beneath pendulous breasts, and the armpits.

The nurse should also examine the patient's skin for evidence of abscesses. Scar tissue and open areas indicate that the mode of administration has included skin-popping, or subcutaneous injections. This method is used by heroin-dependent persons. If there is evidence of skin-popping only, the extent and length of the dependence may be less than that of the abuser who injects heroin intravenously.

Nutritional and Hygienic Status   The long-time drug abuser usually neglects personal health care and maintenance. Heroin-dependent persons characteristically neglect proper eating habits. The nurse can check the patient's weight distribution, muscular development or wasting, and mouth for evidence of vitamin deficiency. Dryness, flaking, and cracking of the skin is indicative of fluid and nutrition deficit. Amphetamine abusers who use their drug in binges also neglect nutrition and personal hygiene measures. Dulled hair and soiled clothing are specific signs of personal neglect. Foul breath associated with decayed teeth, gum disease, and numerous dental caries is frequently found in the heroin addict. Unhealed sores, cuts, and multiple bruises also suggest poor nutritional intake and tissue regenerative ability as well as physical abuse.

Identification of Physical Complications   Physical assessment of the drug abuser includes identifying signs of physical complications. The nurse should look for evidence of infection in open, draining wounds or injection sites, or in excessive or tenacious respiratory secretions and congestion. Use of the stethoscope to listen to the chest is a necessary part of the assessment process. Dulled or jaundiced skin color, decreased tone, and lack of resiliency indicate hepatic dysfunction and should be noted.

Due to the sedating, sensory numbing actions of certain abused drugs, the patient is often not aware of injuries or illnesses. Therefore, the nurse must carefully record and communicate her findings to the physician, who can then emphasize them during the thorough physical examination. In general, assessment for physical complications takes into account all the observations and measurements the nurse makes that are not within normal limits.

Psychological Assessment

The primary goals of the initial psychological assessment are to validate the presence and extent of drug abuse and its impact on the individual. Methods and approaches employed to attain these goals can include nurse-patient interaction and observations as well as nurse-family and nurse-friend interactions and observations.

Orientation and Level of Consciousness   Depending on the drug of abuse and the patient's immediate status, it may or may not be possible for the nurse to verbally interact with him. When the patient is awake, the nurse can determine his level of consciousness by questioning him. Of equal importance is the degree of orientation to reality and current surroundings. The patient who is actively hallucinating, incoherent and confused, or frightened will require immediate planned intervention. Verbal interaction with the patient can aid in determining if these behaviors are from barbiturate withdrawal or an adverse experience with hallucinogens.

An integral part of the psychological assessment is determining the patient's level of understanding of his hallucinations. Does he understand that they are due to drug intake? Finding the answer to this question is a key purpose of assessment because if the patient is unable to maintain or accomplish such recognition, more serious psychological disruption may result.

Validation of Drug Abuse History   An important aspect of the psychological assessment process is the validation of the patient's drug history through his family or friends. Often this must be quickly accomplished after the patient is admitted. Friends of the drug abuser, who are often drug-dependent themselves, tend to fade away once the patient is in the care of the hospital. The nurse should validate the existence and extent of drug use: What is the pattern of abuse? What drug is taken? How much drug is used daily? Is more than one drug abused? What time did the patient take the last dose? What did it consist of? When did the patient begin to react unfavorably? All these questions and many others can help in obtaining an accurate history. Use of slang terms for drugs by the nurse will help in gathering this information, which not only aids in the immediate treatment but also serves as baseline data in formulating a controlled detoxification and maintenance program after a life-threatening crisis is over.

Determination of Motivation for Treatment   At the time of admission for treatment of an acute physiological crisis, the drug-dependent person is not truly able to commit himself to further treatment. Therefore, assessment of and determination of motivation for continued treatment should not be emphasized. Vows made by the patient at this time generally prove to be invalid due to the stress he experiences at the time of hospitalization. The nurse can, however, try to determine the patient's interest in continuing treatment and communicate this information to the physician and social worker after the physical condition has stabilized.

In establishing a positive nurse-patient relationship, an honest, straightforward approach makes it possible to learn the behavior patterns of the drug abuser, evaluate his needs for treatment, and establish an open, "up front" communication channel between the nurse and the patient, which may be used at a later time.

Social Assessment

It often becomes very difficult or very challenging to adequately evaluate the social needs of the drug abuse patient. Frequently the person is in the hospital emergency room only several hours, and never formally admitted for inpatient care. Under these circumstances, the nurse needs to quickly assess the patient's resources outside the hospital. For example, a person who has a bad trip with hallucinogens and who is brought to the meergency room and cared for during the period of the experience can be discharged to the care of a relative or friend before the trip is completely over. But the nurse must first be sure of the friend's or relative's ability to care for the patient. A person who is coming down from amphetamines does not usually require in-hospital care if someone he knows and trusts can remain with him constantly during the depression phase after cessation of drug intake. In this case, the nurse's assessment of the friend's capability and willingness to assume this responsibility crucial to the patient's care and safety.

People dependent on drugs who become in-hospital patients have to be assessed for financial resources, living accommodations, and employment status. The information need not be obtained immediately after admission but should be covered at some time during the course of treatment. Early referrals to the social worker are highly beneficial in initiating continued care and rehabilitation.

The assessment process should succeed in obtaining physical, psychological, and social data that will guide the formulation of the drug abuser's nursing care plan. Continual revision of the plan may be required to meet the fluctuating needs of the patient. Nurses in different settings with different educational backgrounds and different patient needs will devise individualized ways to accomplish this purpose. The important point is that nursing care for drug abuse can be more easily and clearly defined when it is based on a thorough patient assessment. Table 14-1 summarizes this assessment process.

Table 14-1   The Nursing Assessment Process for the Drug Abuse Patient

Assessment component	Focus of assessment
Physical assessment	Symptoms indicative of withdrawal Symptoms indicative of overdose Extent and type of dependence Nutritional and hygienic status Identification of physical complications
Psychological assessment	Orientation and level of consciousness Validation of drug history Determination of motivation for treatment
Social assessment	Determination of sources of support: Family and friends Financial means and employment Living accommodations

APPROACHES TO THE NURSING CARE OF THE DRUG ABUSER

The person admitted to or treated in the general hospital will need medical and nursing intervention for many different problems. This section discusses specific approaches in meeting immediate needs. (Long-term nursing care measures are discussed in Chapter 15.)

The format of the nursing care plans to be presented parallels that used in Part One, Chapter 5, and will consist of patient problems, goals or objectives for nursing actions, and nursing approaches or actions necessary to achieve the identified goal. Rationale (R) for certain nursing actions will be included. In addition, actions that apply only to a particular drug category are identified by the name of the drug in parentheses following the statement of the approach.

Many of the actions presented here are applicable to more than one setting. i.e., emergency room, detoxification unit, general nursing units. For this reason, the identified patient problems are stated in such a way that they can apply to more than one type of drug dependence and setting. To clarify specific types of drug dependence, the name of the principal drugs associated with each problem will be included in parentheses or within the context of the problem statement. Nursing care for unusual patient problems is integrated into the overall care plan and clearly identified, e.g., the drug-dependent newborn.

Problem

Excessive drug intake bringing about life-threatening central nervous system depression—overdose (opiates, barbiturates, volatile inhalants).

Goals

To maintain circulatory-respiratory function; to prevent circulatory-respiratory collapse; and to closely monitor patient response to detect detrimental and beneficial physiological changes in condition.

Nursing Approaches

1 Establish an open airway if respiratory function is severely depressed. Clear mouth of foreign matter and vomitus if present. Insert an oral airway or initiate mouth-to-mouth, mouth-to-nose, or mechanical respiratory assistance. R: The overdosed patient often has profound depression of the respiratory mechanism. If immediate assistance is not provided, death is inevitable.

2 Immediately initiate external cardiac compression resuscitation procedures if cardiac arrest occurs or cardiac function is inadequate to meet the body's minimal needs for perfusion. R: Heroin or barbiturate overdosed patients may arrive at the hospital with absent or inadequate cardiac function.

3 Periodically suction secretions from mouth, pharynx, and bronchial tree. R: Excessive secretions from pulmonary edema associated with heroin overdose can occlude the respiratory passages.

4 Prepare equipment for endotrachial intubation by the physician with a cuffed tube. R: A more stable airway can be established via intubation, which also allows for mechanically assisted and consistent ventilation via positive pressure breathing equipment.

5 Insert a nasogastric tube as ordered when endotrachial tube is in place and the cuff is inflated. R: Gastric lavage can aid in removing barbiturates from the body but is of no help if the patient has overdosed on injected opiates or inhaled solvents. In order to prevent pulmonary aspiration of gastric contents, the nasogastric tube should be inserted only when the endotrachial cuff is inflated.

6 Do not provide oral fluid or food intake. R: Food or fluids may occlude the pharynx or esophagus and precipitate vomiting and resulting aspiration of ingested material into the lungs.

7 Establish an intravenous infusion as ordered or prepare equipment and assist the physician with this task. R: The patient overdosed on barbiturates is likely to have palpable veins that can be more easily used for intravenous infusion than the heroin addict, who usually has excessive scar tissue over main vein puncture sites. In the latter instance, the physician may request a cutdown or minor surgery tray to establish an intravenous channel.

8 Monitor vital signs and blood pressure at approximately five- to fifteen-minute intervals. R: The vital signs and blood pressure indicate the patient's response to treatment and ability to tolerate further stress.

9 Prepare appropriate medications to combat the effects of the abused drug. For heroin overdose: Nalorphine hydrochloride (Nalline®), Levallorphan tartrate (Lorfan®), Naloxone hydrochloride (Narcan®). Specific doses will be ordered by the physician. (Refer to Chapter 13 for dose ranges.) For barbiturate overdose: plasma expanders, intravenous solutions, vasopressors (levarterenol bitartrate, metaraminol bitartrate), antacids. R: Narcotic antagonists can immediately reverse the effects of opiate overdose and should be prepared for rapid administration when the diagnosis has been made. Barbiturate overdose requires multiple drug therapy to combat circulatory collapse and elevate blood pressure and prevent acidosis.

10 Insert an indwelling bladder catheter as ordered. R: Accurate measurement of urine output can be maintained. Patient may experience either urinary incontinence or retention, which would adversely influence urine output measurements and treatment measures aimed at maintaining circulatory volume stability.

11 Frequently and accurately monitor fluid intake and output. R: Urine output measurements reveal renal function, circulating volume status, and excretion rates for the ingested drug. The barbiturate-overdosed patient may be given powerful diuretics to promote rapid diuresis—accurate urinary output measurements are mandatory and help in determining further treatment efforts.

12 Ensure that a skilled staff member remains with the patient at all times during the critical phase of treatment. R: The patient overdosed on opiates cannot be left while he is responding to narcotic antagonists because these drugs may wear off rapidly and precipitate a return to profound respiratory depression. Barbiturate-overdosed persons also require intense observation until they have reached physiological stability.

13 Frequently turn the comatose patient and provide conscientious skin care—including placing the patient on air or water mattress. R: The patient who is comatose from drug overdose (especially barbiturates) requires consistent and conscientious basic nursing care to prevent the hazards of immobility—skin breakdown, circulatory stasis, and respiratory stasis with resultant infection.

14 Administer artificial tear solutions as ordered and patch or tape the eyes of the comatose patient. R: The comatose patient is unable to prevent excessive drying of the eyes and corneal damage via blinking and tearing. Therefore, these acts must be carried out by those caring for him. The need for this nursing intervention applies most specifically to the comatose barbiturate-overdosed patient.

Problem

Increased probability of central nervous system instability due to rapid cessation of drug intake (withdrawal) and increased possibility of severe psychomotor hyperactivity (person experiencing withdrawal from barbiturates).

Goals

To prevent the exacerbation of hyperactivity; to prevent the development of convulsions; and to alleviate the discomfort associated with withdrawal.

Nursing Approaches

1 Monitor vital signs and gross neurological reflex responses. R: Fluctuations in vital signs and reflex responses can precede convulsions in the acutely withdrawing patient—barbiturates.

2 Provide a quiet, calm environment. R: The person withdrawing from barbiturates cannot easily tolerate noise or other excessive stimulation. Environmental stimulation will increase his agitation and irritation.

3 Reorient the confused patient to reality and his location. R: The barbiturate-dependent person who is withdrawing can be confused, disoriented, or hallucinatory. Frequent reorientation of the patient helps him gain control and reduce anxiety. Do not support hallucinations if they should occur.

4 Convey an attitude of caring concern consistent with the approach to any ill person. R: The drug abuser is acutely sensitive to the attitudes of health professionals and will quickly perceive negative feelings toward him. His desire to cooperate in treatment can be adversely affected when he believes care givers are not sincerely interested in his problem.

5 Administer medication, carefully following the prescribed withdrawal regimen. R: In order to prevent excessive withdrawal reactions (confusion, hallucinations, convulsions), the prescribed barbiturate must be given as scheduled. Patient agitation and discomfort increase when medication is not dispensed on time.

6 Institute physical protective measures when convulsion is likely to occur. See the section in Chapter 5 on Nursing Care for Acute Hallucinosis and Delirium Tremens for specific nursing actions that are also appropriate to the acutely ill barbiturate-dependent patient undergoing withdrawal.

7 Provide opportunities for the patient to express his feelings and fears about his drug dependence and current treatment. R: Patients withdrawing from barbiturates are often not ready to seriously discuss deep-seated problems leading to abuse. They can, however, benefit by expression of immediate fears and concerns, and by realistic reassurance from the nurse. Reassurance should be hopeful, with emphasis on the fact that treatment facilities and supportive services are available.

8 Observe patient response to the withdrawal regimen, paying particular attention to any behavior indicating unusual sedation or an increase in psychomotor hyperactivity. R: Many barbiturate abusers do not or cannot give accurate drug use histories. Consequently, the initial withdrawal regimen may oversedate the patient and must be adjusted when such reactions set in.

9 Provide adequate recreational or work activity. R: The patient undergoing controlled withdrawal can often benefit from participation in various activities that help in occupying his time, distracting him from physical discomfort, and directing excess energy into appropriate channels of expression.

Nursing Approaches for Newborn Withdrawal

1 Observe the newborn delivered from a barbiturate-dependent mother for excessive shrill crying, vasomotor instability, disturbed short sleep periods, tremors, voracious appetite, overactivity, and diarrhea. R: These symptoms are associated with withdrawal in infants delivered from barbiturate-dependent mothers. The significance of the symptoms must be noted and reported quickly to prevent convulsion and death. The onset of symptoms varies from one or two days up to a week or more after birth.

2 Consider transferred drug dependence in the neonate who exhibits bizarre behavior even when the mother is not known to be drug-dependent. Report observations to the physician promptly and seek more data from the mother regarding drug use.

3 Frequently monitor vital signs, fluid balance, and duration of diarrhea. R: The newborn has poor tolerance of electrolyte imbalance and vital sign instability, especially fluctuations in temperature.

4 Administer prescribed medication according to the schedule for controlled withdrawal: paregoric or chlorpromazine. R: The barbiturate-dependent neonate can be withdrawn on a gradually decreased medication regimen.

5 Implement prescribed fluid and electrolyte replacement therapy.

6 Instruct the infant's mother to observe for unusual crying, eating, sleeping, and eliminative behavior prior to discharge and to bring the infant to the hospital or seek medical help should such behavior occur. R: The neonate barbiturate withdrawal syndrome may not begin until after the mother and baby are discharged from the hospital.

Problem

Increased physical discomfort due to cessation of opiate intake—withdrawal syndrome. (Nursing approaches in methadone maintenance to block opiate withdrawal are discussed in Chapter 16.)

Goals

To decrease physical discomfort, allay anxiety, and prevent complications of withdrawal.

Nursing Approaches

1 Do not allow visitors during the period of controlled or symptomatic withdrawal treatment. R: Contact with persons associated with the addict's drug-using environment makes it extremely difficult for the patient to maintain abstinence and remain in treatment. Visitors may secretly bring drugs to the patient or administer opiates to him while visiting. It is essential to break the ties the patient has with other drug users and his source of supply if he is to achieve any sustained recovery.

2 Observe for symptoms and behavior changes associated with opiate withdrawal: agitation, anxiety, yawning, drug craving, runny nose, tearing, and sweating. More severe symptoms include insomnia, muscle cramps, tremors, joint pains, diarrhea, vomiting, elevation in vital signs and blood pressure, and hot and cold flashes. R: Many treatment regimens for opiate withdrawal are not instituted until the individual begins to exhibit abstinence symptoms. Knowledge of the nature of opiate withdrawal symptoms should guide the nursing assessment of patients when drug dependence is not known or acknowledged.

3 Administer prescribed medication (methadone) per the treatment regimen. R: Once abstinence symptoms have appeared and medication has been started, the regimen must be carefully followed to maintain control of the withdrawal process.

4 Observe the patient for symptoms of oversedation—euphoria, unusual relaxation, decreased concern with surroundings, sleepiness, nodding.

5 Administer prescribed non-dependence-producing medication for symptomatic relief of withdrawal discomfort. R: When controlled withdrawal is not used, various medications can be helpful in alleviating physical discomfort: muscle relaxants for cramping, diazepam for nervousness, chloral hydrate for insomnia, and mild pain relievers for general discomfort.

5 Convey a nonjudgmental, straightforward, but caring attitude to the heroin-dependent patient. R: Like other drug abusers, the heroin addict is acutely sensitive to the attitudes and biases of those caring for him. It is important for heroin addicts to perceive the nurse as one who wishes to help him

overcome drug dependence but who cannot be manipulated or conned by his stories and evasions.

7 Secure all narcotics, syringes, and needles and other medication in locked containers or cabinets and consistently control medication dispensation and accounting. R: The heroin addict will usually take advantage of any laxity that allows him access to narcotics, sedatives, injection equipment, or other salable and usable medications. Addicts will self-administer narcotics while in the hospital if the opportunity presents itself, especially when withdrawal is not a personal objective.

8 Offer comfort measures such as back rubs, sponge baths (assist the patient or encourage self-bathing), and warmed blankets when the patient is chilled.

9 Do not use the street drug-oriented jargon of the patient. R: Using terms that the drug abuser uses only strengthens his ties with the drug-oriented lifestyle and reinforces such behavior by validating its acceptability. (It is important, however, that the nurse know the meaning of the street terms so she can understand what the patient says as well as correctly assess immediate needs. For this reason, terms such as "bags," "spoons," "junk," "shooting," etc., have been included throughout Part Two.)

10 Make initial plans for continuing treatment by contacting available programs and discussing with the patient his plans following withdrawal. R: During the withdrawal process, the nurse is frequently responsible for initiating arrangements for patient transfer to a long-term treatment program. Before these plans are made final, it must be determined whether or not the patient will follow through with them. Often the nurse can only inform the drug abuser of the available long-term treatment resources and encourage him to make a commitment on his own after withdrawal is completed.

Problem

Critical physiological instability in the heroin-dependent neonate undergoing withdrawal.

Goals

To monitor infant reactions to withdrawal symptoms; to prevent life-threatening physiological responses to withdrawal; and to support the infant through withdrawal.

Nursing Approaches

1 Confirm suspicions of maternal heroin dependence before delivery by looking for visible signs of needle marks, abscesses, cellulitis, or withdrawal symptoms. The mother may not admit to drug abuse, but it can be confirmed by physical evidence as well as urine analysis. Once heroin dependence is suspected, the nurse should be prepared to care for the withdrawing infant.

2 Observe the newborn for symptoms associated with heroin withdrawal: shrill, persistent cry, hyperactivity, trembling, fluctuations in respiratory activity, difficulty in feeding, unusual reflex responses (exaggerated Moro reflex), diarrhea, vomiting, disrupted sleep periods, hyperirritability, occasionally convulsion. R: Onset of symptoms can occur within twenty-four hours after birth. Rapid identification of symptoms is imperative. Treatment must be initiated immediately.

3 Closely and frequently monitor fluid balance, vital signs, and diarrhea pattern. R: The birth weight of the heroin-dependent infant is usually lower than that of the non-drug-dependent neonate. As a result, the infant cannot tolerate fluctuations in electrolytes and vital signs (especially elevated temperature, a common symptom) well and can become seriously dehydrated with accompanying severe weight loss.

4 Provide a quiet, nonstimulating, dimly lit environment. R: Decreased stimulation lessens infant irritability and induces sleep.

5 Keep the infant warm by swaddling and providing a temperature-controlled environment. R: Warmth helps to reduce excessive heat loss and discourages excessive energy-draining activity.

6 Administer prescribed medication according to the withdrawal regimen: paregoric, chlorpromazine, methadone, diazepam. (See Chapter 13 for dose ranges.) R: An infant can be withdrawn over several weeks' time via a gradually decreased medication schedule.

7 Administer prescribed supportive measures: intravenous fluid and electrolyte replacement, nutritional intake. R: Many withdrawing infants will not require intensive therapy; however, the underweight infant can quickly become dehydrated. Therefore, therapy measures for preventing untoward complications can be instituted. Frequent, nutritious feedings must be patiently given to the infant who often has impaired or exaggerated sucking reflex.

8 Encourage the mother to return for well-baby clinic visits and evaluations. R: Although the drug-dependent mother often fails to attend well-baby clinics, the effort to convince her of its importance should still be made.

9 Counsel the mother on drug treatment facilities available to her. R: This can be done directly with the mother or by referral through the hospital social worker. In any event, the mother must be told about the importance of treatment for herself. Encouragement of this type can also help to ensure that the infant will receive continued health care.

Problem

Disruption in sensory input interpretation, which can lead to lowered ability to self-protect from psychological or physical harm (hallucinogens, amphetamines)—the bad trip reaction.

Goal

To decrease the possibility of self-inflicted injury.

Nursing Approaches

   1   Arrange the treatment environment so that it is quiet, secure, and non-stressful. Often a small, separate room with adjustable lighting is most beneficial. R: The person experiencing a bad trip on hallucinogens or recovering from an amphetamine jag can misinterpret multiple external stimuli. The subjective experience can then become more intensified and frightening.
   2   Remove potentially harmful objects from the immediate environment, e.g., syringes, medication, and mechanical equipment. R: The patient may misinterpret the significance of such objects. Physical behavior as a result can become unpredictable—attempting to flee, attacking inanimate objects, inflicting self-injury, or striking out at care givers. Such reactions are unusual but should be taken into account when caring for the person experiencing an adverse hallucinogen trip.
   3   Remain with the patient or have a knowledgeable person remain with him throughout the treatment process. R: The subjective experience of the drug's action is unpredictable—the patient may appear to be in control and calm. While left alone in this state, he may again perceive threatening stimuli and harm himself in an effort to escape the hallucinatory or delusional threat.

Problem

Excessive terror or paniclike reaction.

Goal

To alter the person's drug-induced perceptual experience from one of terror to one of a more positive and comforting nature.

Nursing Approaches

In addition to the procedures presented above, also consider the following:

   1   Initiate a one-to-one nurse-patient interaction using a calm, relaxed approach and a moderated tone of voice. It sometimes helps if the nurse is dressed in casual clothing rather than a white uniform, and cap. R: The patient usually can respond to a low-keyed, calm approach by one consistently present person.
   2   Do not touch the person unless the motion's intention is absolutely clear to him. R: These patients are usually quite fearful, often paranoid about the actions of others toward them, and can therefore react violently or excessively when surprised by physical contact (especially amphetamine abusers).
   3   Gentle touch may be offered in a caring, sincere manner to the hallucinogen bad tripper. R: These people usually respond favorably to indications that they are secure and cared for. It reinforces reality for them.
   4   Encourage the patient to discuss what he is perceiving. Clarify miscon-

ceptions and misinterpretations; do not support negative hallucinatory content. R: Knowing what the patient is perceiving allows the nurse to clarify his experiences and relate them to reality. Support of negative hallucinatory content can intensify the experience.

5 Reassure the patient that he is in a safe, secure environment and will be cared for.

Problem

Loss of control over drug experience.

Goals

To assist the person undergoing a bad trip on hallucinogens to regain control of the experience. Accomplishment of this goal will help to achieve a second goal: to prevent long-lasting adverse psychological reaction following a bad trip.

Nursing Approaches

1 Frequently orient the patient to where he is and who is with him.

2 Emphasize the transitory and drug-related nature of the current, frightening perceptions. R: If the bad tripper can realize that his fearful perceptions are from the drug, he can generally start to regain control of the experience. Panic reactions and subsequent loss of control are related to the undefined and overwhelming sensory stimulation characteristic of the bad trip.

3 Offer objects to the person to handle and describe them. R: This action reinforces reality and the transitory nature of the hallucinatory experience and provides a source of temporary diversion.

4 Continue to encourage verbal expression of perceptions.

5 Encourage the person to contemplate pleasant, relaxing thoughts.

6 Continue the "talk down" of the patient while remaining with him. R: Consistent contact with the same person during the talk-down process sometimes takes six to eight hours. Verbal contact provides the key link to reality, security, and comfort for the person undergoing a fearful, threatening experience.

7 If the patient is to be discharged before the entire trip is completed, counsel the patient's friends or relatives on appropriate interpersonal approaches and the importance of remaining with the patient. R: Nonprofessionals are often quite adept at talking down the bad tripper and caring for him. It is frequently necessary to entrust these responsibilities to lay care givers.

Problem

Disruption in nutritional patterns due to lifestyle changes associated with drug abuse behavior.

Goals

To provide optimal nutritional intake while the patient is hospitalized and initiate follow-up care for nutritional well-being following discharge.

Nursing Approaches

In general, the drug-dependent person suffers from many of the same dietary deficiencies as the alcoholic. Undernutrition and malnutrition are common.

1 Provide small, frequent, high-protein, high-calorie, and vitamin-enriched meals according to dietary limitations and goals. R: This method may be more palatable and acceptable than the three, large meals per day that are customary for the well person.

2 Provide nutritious snacks or make them easily available to the patient. R: Drug abusers are not accustomed to eating at set times—they eat when the need arises, regardless of time. It therefore becomes more realistic to adapt to this pattern rather than forcing a regimented eating schedule on a person who is currently physiologically unstable.

3 Administer oral vitamin supplements as prescribed. R: The oral route of drug administration is preferred when feasible. It does not reinforce or fill the need for injections and thus may help to break needle-oriented habits.

4 Emphasize the importance of nutritious food intake during the treatment process and encourage adherence to beneficial eating habits.

Problem

Neglect of health care and increased incidence of medical complications related to the method of drug administration.

Goal

To nurture a return to an optimal health status.

Nursing Approaches

Specific nursing measures applicable to the care of drug abusers with hepatitis, respiratory infections, dental problems, systemic infection, or other complications of drug dependence can be studied in general medical-surgical nursing textbooks. For this reason, these measures are not repeated here. Additional nursing considerations include the following:

1 Implement treatments that promote closure and healing of skin abscesses and infections: frequent change of moist, sterile compresses, use of fine mesh gauze to debride necrotic tissue, application of antibiotic ointments or solutions, and prevention of cross infection or introduction of other microorganisms into the wounds.

2 Instruct the patient or other person living with him in the techniques for care of skin infections. R: The drug abuser is often discharged after an acute episode but before the skin infection is entirely healed. If the patient is not interested in or capable of caring for the infected wound, another person close to him may be enlisted to provide this aspect of continuing care.

3 Make appointments for the patient with the outpatient department or clinic to check the progress of wound healing and general health status and recovery. R: The drug abuser who is recovering from an illness or local infection often will not return for follow-up evaluation or continuing care unless he is acutely ill. One way of encouraging a return to the clinic is to make a specific appointment and provide the patient or his friend with a written appointment card.

4 Instruct the patient in the relationship between the method of drug administration and the development of infection and potentially life-threatening complications. R: Although scare tactics rarely are effective in deterring the abuser from continuing drug use, honest and straightforward information presented in a nonjudgmental fashion may help to increase the patient's awareness of potential dangers after discharge.

Problem

Difficulty in making a meaningful commitment to long-term treatment for drug dependence.

Goal

To assist the abuser in making a commitment to continued treatment.

Nursing Approaches

1 Discuss with the patient the available treatment programs.

2 When feasible, arrange to have a recovered drug abuser from a selected program visit the patient. R: The ex-drug abuser can use a realistic, no-nonsense approach with the drug-dependent person. He can often succeed where health professionals cannot because of his personal insight into the dynamics of drug abuse. Also, the ex-drug abuser serves an an example that drug dependence can be overcome.

3 Offer realistic, goal-directed encouragement. R: False reassurance about the patient's ability to easily overcome dependence is inappropriate with someone who has failed on numerous occasions to remain drug-free. Short-term goals for continued treatment are much more meaningful; i.e., aim for acceptance into a treatment program, then focus on each day of treatment that leads to abstinence, then each day of maintained drug-free living.

4 Make arrangements for transfer directly from the hospital to the treatment program when possible. R: An unbroken sequence of treatment is crucial

to the abuser, who is not yet capable of resisting drug use. Abusers who are discharged from the hospital, returned to the street, and not quickly admitted to long-term treatment programs resume drug abuse behavior, with rare exception.

5 When appropriate or a part of the hospital's services, implement drug blockade treatment as ordered before the patient is discharged. R: Initiation of methadone maintenance for heroin-dependent persons while still in the hospital provides a beneficial transition from hospital to community. Usually, the maintenance regimen can then be continued on an outpatient basis. The crucial point is that treatment not be interrupted.

6 Interact with the patient in a nonjudgmental and accepting manner, even when he has suffered relapses. R: The high relapse rate is quite discouraging to those who repeatedly care for the drug abuser, but the nurse must realize the importance of short-term goals and accept relapses as a part of the illness.

The patient problems, goals, and approaches presented in this chapter are not all-inclusive. Nurses working with drug abusers in different programs and hospitals can devise effective, creative approaches not included here.

Problem of Nurse Drug Dependence

Although they constitute a small percentage of the drug-dependent population, nurses do need to be acutely aware of the dangers of drug abuse within the profession. The relative accessibility of narcotics, barbiturates, and other abused substances make drug dependence a potential hazard for nurses. When dependence does develop, the nurse often depends on hospital drug supplies to maintain her dependence. As a result, she may divert drugs prescribed for patients to her own use and cover the acts with false drug loss or damage reports, falsified patient records, or forged physician signatures on prescription blanks.

Nurses must not assume that they possess a superior ability to control drug abuse behavior. Loss of control as well as physical and psychological dependence can occur as easily in the nurse as in any other drug abuser. As a matter of professional ethics, concern for the well-being of patients, and a desire to help a colleague, nurses who suspect or know of drug dependence in a nurse must not shelter the person. As with any ill person, the nurse who is drug-dependent needs prompt and professional intervention if she is to recover.

PROBLEMS RELATED TO NURSING CARE

The drug abuser who becomes a patient in the general hospital presents the nurse with many unique problems and challenges. For example, the nurse must learn to relate to people who are usually labeled as society's outcasts. Heroin addicts engage in various forms of criminal activity ranging from prostitution to petty thievery. The nurse may find it discouraging and disillusioning to care for such people. As a way of overcoming personal judgments against this patient group, she may find it helpful to remind herself that drug dependence *is* an illness, a devastating illness. The criminal activity is necessary to support the illness but it is not usually an end in itself.

The personality of many drug abusers presents another challenge. A highly developed ability to manipulate others is a major component of the personality structure of most drug-dependent people. Knowing this to be true, the nurse can take it into account when evaluating the person's requests or demands. Over time, she will develop skill in discriminating between genuine complaints and exaggerated ones aimed at achieving an unrelated goal.

Unfortunately, the friends of drug abusers may bring drugs to the patient while he is hospitalized. They may also administer the drugs to the patient as a "helpful" gesture to ease his discomfort. For these reasons, it is imperative that the nurse prohibit visitors and closely supervise gifts for patients. She should realize that even though the patient is being treated for a drug-related illness or for drug dependence voluntarily he may still be unable to break the ties with old behavior patterns.

Perhaps the most tragic aspect of drug abuse is the tremendous waste of human resources. Drug addicts lose precious years of their life to drug-related behavior and many lose life itself. Young children and adolescents become enmeshed in drug-using patterns before they can realize the significance of their actions. Without a doubt, this fact is discouraging. But treatment programs are increasing, public education on the subject is improving, and the knowledge base of health professionals is expanding daily in relation to the dynamics of and approaches to drug dependence. The nurse must maintain a hopeful attitude toward this pervasive health problem and seek to inform those she associates with of its significance and potential dangers. Viewing the problems as challenges may help her devise new approaches and methods of care that will contribute to the evolving body of knowledge related to drug abuse nursing.

REFERENCES

Berman, Joseph I.: "Treatment of the Opiate Addict in Maryland. Does the General Hospital Have a Role?" *Maryland State Medical Journal,* **19**:65–67, November 1970.

Carroll, Mary Helen: "Recognizing Narcotic Withdrawal in Newborns," *Journal of Obstetrical and Gynecological Nursing,* **1**:23–24, June 1972.

Fleming, Juanita W.: "Recognizing the Newborn Addict," *American Journal of Nursing,* **65**:83, January 1965.

Foreman, Nancy Jo, and Joyce V. Zerwekh: "Drug Crisis Intervention," *American Journal of Nursing,* **71**:1736–1739, September 1971.

Freedman, Alfred M.: "The Narcotic Addict in the General Hospital," *Mental Hospitals*, **16**:230–232, August 1965.

Imhof, John E. et al.: "The Emerging Role of the Hospital in Drug Abuse Education and Prevention," *The Journal of School Health*, vol. XLII, no. 8, October 1972.

Sprung, Evelyn: "Drug Withdrawal in Newborn Infants," *Bedside Nurse*, **4**:11–12, December 1971.

Chapter 15

Psychiatric Nursing and the Drug Abuser

Drug-dependent persons require, with rare exception, in-hospital or outpatient psychiatric intervention in order to overcome deep-seated problems that contribute to drug abuse behavior patterns. Abusers are seldom able to maintain drug-free behavior permanently until they have evolved new methods of coping with their problems, daily anxiety, and the common frustrations of living. Entrance into a psychiatric program may follow detoxification or may precede controlled withdrawal. In either instance, the drug abuser can benefit from many of the services provided in a psychiatric setting.

CHARACTERISTICS OF PSYCHIATRIC TREATMENT PROGRAMS

Facilities for the psychiatric care and treatment of various drug abuse problems are located in (1) the general hospital setting—inpatient short-term care, depending on extent of services; (2) public financed psychiatric institutions—inpatient short-term and long-term residential programs; (3) privately financed psychiatric hospitals or clinics—short-term and long-term inpatient residential services; and (4) outpatient clinics—short-term or long-term day care and related drug treatment programs. Variations in these basic classifications are common. Individual programs are devised to meet identified needs of their specific patient population, and special attention is paid to the cultural needs of different patient groups.

Psychiatric treatment and counseling can consist of just a few intensive counseling sessions or continue for up to a year or more. The length of time is determined by the program's financial resources, staff-to-patient ratios, specific patient needs, goals of the program, and location of the program. For example neighborhood clinics are not able to provide inpatient services but can offer day care programs, health appraisal, and immediate crisis intervention. Psychiatric programs in the general hospital can provide a multitude of patient services ranging from crisis intervention to occupational therapy. In general, then, psychiatric programs offer a wide variety of services: short-term individual psychotherapy, crisis intervention, educational and family counseling, encounter groups, sensitivity or self-awareness groups, and recreational and occupational therapy, to name the most prevalent.

A current trend in the treatment of drug abuse problems is long-term residential programs. These programs focus primarily on gradual, controlled rehabilitation over a rather long period of time. Depending on the resources of the particular program, the drug abuser may be accepted before he has undergone withdrawal and remain in the program until he is ready for final reentry into the community. Many of the approaches used in these residential programs rely heavily on psychologically or psychiatrically based principles. An in-depth discussion of the design and objectives of the residential rehabilitation program is given in Part Three of this book.

Criteria for Admission

Depending on financial and facility limitations, staff resources, and current community needs, the criteria for admission into a given psychiatric program may be highly restrictive or open to all who apply. Many hospitals and privately financed programs, for example, will not accept the heroin-dependent person. This restriction is based on the fact that heroin abusers require a long-term investment of time and effort and frequently return to drug use after discharge. Restrictive admission policies, although prohibiting services to a needy patient population, allow for greater extension of services to other patient groups requiring a lesser investment of financial and personnel resources.

The admission policies may include any of the following criteria. A brief discussion of the underlying rationale for the policy is included.

1 Drug abusers will be accepted only following detoxification. In most cases, this is a necessary criterion when the program has neither the equipment nor the personnel to supervise detoxification.

2   Persons dependent on heroin or other narcotics will not be admitted. As mentioned previously, certain programs do not have the resources required for long-term residential treatment of heroin addicts. In addition, many are not prepared to cope with the challenges associated with treatment of heroin-dependent persons, i.e., the high rate of relapse or refusal to accept and follow treatment.

3   Patients experiencing acute or life-threatening drug-related episodes will not be accepted, e.g., overdose or barbiturate withdrawal. In order to adequately care for these patients, the psychiatric program would need sophisticated medical facilities. Since psychiatric treatment focuses on the personality of the drug abuser, patients acutely ill from physiological dysfunction cannot be accepted. Generally, these patients are considered for admission after they have recovered from the physical insult. Psychiatric programs located within the general hospital may be able to accept these ill patients by calling upon medical personnel to manage the acute episode.

4   Drug abusers experiencing acute psychological instability are admitted for crisis therapy and intervention. Hallucinogen- or amphetamine-induced panic states, bad trips, acute anxiety reactions, or drug-related psychosis can receive immediate crisis intervention in most psychiatric programs. Patients with these problems are immediately admitted and cared for.

5   All persons in need of psychiatric care and treatment because of drug abuse or drug dependence are accepted (regardless of the number of previous admissions). Many of these programs provide short-term care and treatment because of the rapid patient turnover and the volume of persons using program services.

6   Patients will be admitted on a voluntary basis. Voluntary entrance into a psychiatric program is a common criterion. Patients usually may request discharge themselves or leave the program without approval. In general, voluntary entrance will consist of an agreement between the patient and the staff to remain for a specified minimum period of time.

7   Each potential patient will be interviewed before acceptance. The interview is conducted by staff members and is aimed at determining the applicant's suitability and ability to benefit from treatment. Not all psychiatric programs have such a preadmission requirement.

8   The person seeking admission must be currently drug-free. This requirement is a necessity for those programs that are not equipped to handle withdrawal. Also, by accepting only the drug-free person, the program can emphasize rapid entrance into intensive group therapy. A third benefit is elimination of those patients who are multiple drug abusers, patients that create unpredictable and critical problems for the care givers.

9   Drug abusers who have previously participated in numerous programs, only to return to drug use after discharge, will not be accepted. Many psychiatric programs emphasize availability of services to the largest number of persons who can benefit optimally from efforts made in their behalf. Unfortunately, heroin abusers (primarily) are often unable to abstain from drugs after initial treatment efforts, and thus they may be denied subsequent treatment. On the

other hand, a significant number of heroin abuse programs have no such restriction.

10 Persons younger or older than a certain age will not be accepted. Due to limited services and personnel skilled in the unique needs of certain age groups, drug abusers of a specific age may not be accepted into some programs.

11 Drug abusers having active, acute psychiatric illness will not be accepted. Some programs will not accept the person with a chronic or acute psychiatric illness not related to drug abuse. However, there is a problem in differentiating between the preexisting illness and the illness developed as a result of drug abuse.

In establishing admission policies, staff attempt to consider the major variables impinging on their ability to treat and care for the drug abuser as well as the patient's individual needs. The criteria presented here represent a brief summary of some of the major points considered before admission.

Patient Population

Psychiatric programs provide services for varied patient populations. Some programs concentrate on certain ethnic minority groups and place the treatment facility within the patient community. Such specifically designed programs are able to meet the individual needs of certain cultural groups better than programs designed to meet the needs of the dominant patient population.

The patient population of a particular program may consist of adolescents, young adults, mature adults, and occasionally elderly persons. Depending on the resources of the program, both males and females will participate in treatment together. At times this arrangement may pose problems for the care givers due to different needs of the male and female parent.

Programs that restrict admission may have patient populations whose drug of dependence is the same, e.g., heroin addicts. In these cases, the procedures adopted can achieve uniformity to some degree. Patients are more apt to receive meaningful therapy when the number of different drug dependencies is limited.

CARE GIVERS: PROFESSIONAL OR NONPROFESSIONAL

The composition of staff will vary according to the program's philosophy and goals. Many long-term treatment and rehabilitation centers include ex-drug abusers as members of the staff. These nonprofessionals make vital and significant contributions to the recovery of the active drug abuser. They possess a kind of insight and in-depth understanding of the nitty-gritty aspects of drug abusers' personalities and problems that the professional cannot match. Drug abusers tend to trust ex-addicts although they cannot easily be manipulated as can most inexperienced professionals. Often the ex-addict joins the staff of his treatment program after recovery. (Unfortunately, this is one of the few types of employment open to the ex-drug abuser.)

The ex-addict may fulfill many functions within the long-term program: He may counsel the drug addict participating in methadone maintenance, act as the interviewer or screener of new applicants, assist in crisis situations on a one-to-one basis or via telephone, serve as a major resource person to professional staff members, and act as a role model to the program participants. A drug abuser taking part in the activities of the treatment center is confronted with the role example of the ex-addict counselor. The ex-addict's ability to live without drugs illustrates that dependence can be treated and that with hard work he, too, can someday help others with similar problems.

Numerous professional and lay disciplines are represented on the psychiatric treatment team: psychology, nursing, medicine, and social work. The care team may also include volunteers and representatives of various religious groups. Depending on the financial resources of the particular program, staff members can hold full-time or part-time positions. In addition, many programs do not include the nurse or physician. They are called upon only when specific health problems arise. In general, each staff member has different and often overlapping contributions to make to the recovery of the drug abuser. It is this aspect of a team approach that facilitates comprehensive treatment and rehabilitation. The remainder of the chapter discusses various nursing considerations and actions appropriate to the psychiatric program.

PREREQUISITES FOR UNDERSTANDING DRUG ABUSE AND THE DRUG ABUSER

The nurse who wishes to work with drug abusers in a psychiatric treatment program must understand various aspects of drug abuse and the characteristics of certain abusers before she implements nursing interventions. Achieving such an understanding applies to any nurse who has contact with the drug abuser in the course of delivering health care or in daily living. Knowledge of some of the basic beliefs of drug abusers helps to prepare the nurse for the challenges associated with their treatment and care. It should be pointed out, however, that the insight the nurse gains from a study of drug abuse is no substitute for actual interaction with members of this patient population.

Lifestyle Associated with Drug Abuse

It is important that the nurse carefully assess the patient's lifestyle. The abused drug will in large part determine many aspects of the lifestyle. For instance, the barbiturate-dependent person may be able to maintain his usual manner of living and employment if he is able to get the drug through legal prescriptions. If drugs must be obtained from illegal sources, the barbiturate abuser will have to alter his lifestyle and beliefs to a certain extent in order to sustain his dependence. The heroin-dependent person, on the other hand, must rely exclusively on illegal supplies and usually criminal activities to procure them. Constant hustling to obtain heroin creates a unique subculture and belief system ascribed to by the drug abuser. This particular belief system is also referred to as the "code of the streets" and is based on mutual self-protection, a degree of camaraderie, and various criminal pursuits—prostitution, theft, burglary.

Abusers of hallucinogens or psychedelics and amphetamines have developed a somewhat different lifestyle called the "counterculture," or hippie lifestyle. In the late 1960s this subculture grew and gained a degree of notoriety within society. Currently many members of the counter culture have shifted somewhat to nondrug methods of achieving self-awareness and harmony with the universe. There still remains a significant but perhaps less well publicized number of adolescents and young adults in the psychedelic subculture. Primarily, values ascribed to this group of drug abusers consist of communal living and sharing of minimal material possessions, emphasis on individual needs and freedom, anti-establishment philosophy, and a back-to-nature style of living.

Abusers of volatile substances are primarily adolescents who live at home and who are usually still in school. Adolescents inhaling such substances come from all socioeconomic levels and ethnic groups. In general, the young person stops abusing the volatile inhalants after adolescence.

Drug abusers usually adopt the lifestyle associated with their primary drug of abuse. The nurse who cares for the drug-dependent person should always assess the nature of his current mode of living. In addition, she must be quite careful not to impose her own value system and lifestyle on him. To do so will, with rare exception, only serve to engender his rejection of the nurse's assistance.

Philosophy of Life Associated with Drug Abusers

Lifestyle patterns of drug abusers reflect the underlying philosophy of the drug-using subculture. Many aspects of their philosophy are the opposite of those values held by the rest of society. They often hold beliefs considered to be antiestablishment and antiauthoritarian. Such views are continually reinforced. in the abuser's opinion, by the overtly harsh and punitive legal remedies to the problems of drug dependence and associated criminal activity. The antiestablishment viewpoint is reinforced by the perceived antidrug abuse and antidrug addict beliefs put forth by most members of society. Over time, the drug abuser can rationalize his abuse of drugs as a means of countering antidrug opinions held by the establishment. Such rationalizations allow him to overtly reject society's values and substitute a select set of beliefs that are meaningful only to other drug users. Thus, the so-called subculture seems to evolve in response to societal pressure and serves as a source of cohesion and security to many drug abusers.

The cohesiveness of this subculture fosters a degree of mutual trust and dependence among its members. For example, part of the code of the streets includes a very strict noninformer policy; i.e., one drug abuser will not inform on another to the authorities. Such mutually protective behavior is essential to survival in the drug subculture but poses a tremendous challenge to care givers who work to rehabilitate the drug abuser and consequently try to disrupt the ties he has with former belief systems.

In assessing the belief system adhered to by the drug-dependent patient, the nurse should consider this philosophical beliefs toward treatment and care givers. Although it is neither realistic nor always beneficial to modify interventions so that they blend with the patient's value system, it is necessary to recognize what those values are and assess their importance to the patient. Understanding that most drug abusers reject middle-class values can help the nurse realize that hostile behavior toward her, as a representative of establishment culture and beliefs, is an integral part of the patient's belief system.

THE ROLE OF THE NURSE IN THE PSYCHIATRIC DRUG ABUSE TREATMENT PROGRAM

The nurse's role in a psychiatric program is multifaceted and consists primarily of active and passive supportive actions. In the following sections, the different components of the nurse's role are presented and described. Specific actions applicable to each component are included. Many of the activities relating to one particular component are also applicable to other components. They are separated and correlated with one component only in order to avoid confusion.

Component

Contribute to establishment and maintenance of the therapeutic community or milieu.

Description

The therapeutic milieu is an integral part of long-term psychiatric treatment. It provides a highly structured, secure environment in which the drug abuser can learn new coping behaviors, acquire a sense of responsibility, and prepare for eventual reentry into society as a contributing member. The nurse can foster and facilitate this type of environment via several actions.

Nursing Approaches

1 In some programs, the nurse is responsible for explaining program policies and routines to the new resident. This information may be conveyed on a one-to-one basis or in a group. The nurse can use audiovisual materials and refer to current residents to clarify various points. The nurse may also arrange to have this initial orientation carried out by ex-drug abuser counselors or program residents.

2 It is most important that the communication be characterized by a respectful and caring attitude. A professional but interested manner is required. The drug abuser generally has a very fragile self-image, one that he seeks to protect or conceal by hostile or rejective behavior. By conveying a hopeful but realistic attitude toward the resident's ability to succeed in treatment, the nurse does not reinforce the frequently perceived attitude of inevitable failure so often encountered by the drug abuser.

3 Shortly after admission the nurse opens a conversation with the new resident assigned to her. At this time, she explains her role and its relationship to the patient. Explanations of this nature serve to establish clear limits of performance and expectation for the resident and the nurse.

4 The nurse must continually assess the patient's capacity to handle stress and anxiety. The new environment, recent removal from familiar surroundings, and discontinued drug use all add to the person's anxiety about how he will succeed in the program and maintain abstinence. After determining the resident's status, the nurse can then encourage the resident's interaction with other program members.

5 When feasible, the nurse participates in activities designed to foster increased independence in the resident. For example, supervised shopping expeditions help to gradually reintegrate and reorient the resident to society as a whole. Increasingly complex and demanding work assignments within the program stimulate increased responsibility and self-esteem.

6 In some programs, the nurse is responsible for making work assignments for the resident. When this is done, the nurse takes into account his current status within the program, his capabilities, and the goals of the program. For example, many of the work programs are designed to start the person at very menial tasks and gradually improve the nature of the work, as well as the skill required, according to the resident's improved capabilities.

7 As a member of the psychiatric care team the nurse participates in the periodic or scheduled multidisciplinary conferences held to evaluate the resident's response to and progress in the program. In these conferences, the nurse discusses her observations and assessments of the patient's participation in assigned activities and interpersonal relations.

8 By being available for informal "rap" sessions, or discussions, the nurse can serve as a nonjudgmental sounding board for the drug abuser's feelings and perceptions. In addition, female drug abusers will often interact more freely with a female nurse and discuss health problems or concerns about self-image and appearance. The male drug abuser may simply need someone to listen to his ideas or to talk to regarding his uncertainty about the future and his capabilities to cope with it. It should be remembered, however, that the resident may use these informal rap sessions to try to manipulate personnel and gain sympathy.

9 The nurse conducts staff conferences at established times or in response to specific requests. During the staff conference, the patient's progress and problems are discussed and nursing care plans are devised. Whenever the nurse is having problems with a particular patient, she should feel free to request a staff conference. Thus colleagues can contribute their observations and assessments and suggest interventions that will assist in meeting the identified problems. At the same time, a consistent plan of action is developed that all can follow.

In reality, most of the remaining components are directly related to the maintenance of the therapeutic milieu. They are presented separately to maintain clarity and avoid confusion.

Component

Prevention of the acquisition of drug(s) of dependence or abuse.

Description

Patients will often try to bring drugs with them or make arrangements to have friends bring drugs to them during visits. In order to prevent the resident from ending or disrupting abstinence, the nurse works with other staff members to ensure that the resident cannot obtain drugs while a program participant.

Nursing Approaches

1 The nurse helps to verbally and actively support a no-visitors, no-outside-contact policy. Many programs have such policies, which are based on the premise that the patient (1) is not yet strong enough to control his own desires for drugs of abuse, (2) is not able to prevent friends from bringing drugs to him, and (3) has not yet permanently broken former drug-oriented interpersonal ties. The rule includes a no-telephone-call and no-mail-receipt policy.

2 Depending on the staff resources, the nurse may be responsible for issuing the new resident clothing in exchange for his garments and possessions. The rationale for this exchange is that the clothes the drug abuser wears usually reflect, to some degree, his drug-oriented lifestyle. In addition, he may hide drugs in his clothing and possessions.

3 The nurse carefully assesses the resident's behavior for signs and symptoms of drug use. (Physical manifestations of drug use are discussed in Chapter 11.) When the person appears to be under the influence of a drug, the nurse questions him to determine the drug taken and prepares for any possible adverse reactions. Since the patient now has a low drug tolerance as a result of abstinence, such behavior is then reported to the physician or other program staff member for appropriate action.

Component

Foster and facilitate healthy interpersonal relationships.

Description

Most drug abusers have to learn new interpersonal behaviors to interact with others. These new methods are compatible with society as a whole and, therefore, facilitate the person's rehabilitation and eventual reentry into society. The interpersonal relationships the drug abuser was formerly associated with are incompatible with rehabilitation and drug-free living. Thus, healthy new relationships are based on common interpersonal understanding, value for another human being, self-respect and esteem, and a desire to alter detrimental behavior patterns.

Nursing Approaches

1 The nurse should acquire the ability to identify and cope with manipulative behavior. The drug abuser, as previously stated, tends to be highly skilled in "conning," that is, controlling other people's behavior to one's own ends. Behavior of this nature is disruptive to treatment goals and impedes recovery.

One form of manipulative behavior is game playing. In these games, the addict tries to manipulate the therapist or staff member in order to avoid disciplinary action for unacceptable behavior, to avoid program activities, or to avoid confrontation with his own behavior. Behavior that pits the nurse against other patients or staff, or aims at forming a nurse-patient bond against the "others," must be identified and labeled for what it is—a con job, or game. In some cases, the drug abuser is not overtly aware of the nature of the game.

2 When manipulative behavior is encountered, the nurse can confront the person with it and reinforce established limits for acceptable behavior. Trends or patterns of manipulative behavior can also be discussed in the staff conference and uniform staff plans for intervention can be developed for implementation by all. The drug abuser will then be less successful in playing off one staff member against another and thereby deflecting attention from himself.

3 Reinforcement of the healthy aspects of the patient's personality is also an important part of the nurse's role. Although these may be difficult to verify, due to the person's ability to project images, the nurse can concentrate on validation and subsequent realistic praise. The drug abuser needs to build self-esteem and self-worth based on achievable goals and developed abilities.

4 As the resident progresses in the program, he can be given more responsibility for the guidance of new residents. Extending such trust further increases his self-respect while encouraging communication skills that aid in achieving program goals.

5 As previously stated, the nurse should not use the street jargon of the drug abuser when interacting with him. To do so only reinforces and legitimizes drug-oriented behavior. Over time, as the nurse verbally interacts with the patient, she can foster and reinforce more acceptable communication skills.

6 The nurse can facilitate the development of healthy interpersonal communication skills and relationships in the group therapy and encounter setting. In this situation, the resident is placed in a context in which he cannot, or is not allowed to, avoid his behavior. After a while, as he gains experience in the sessions, he develops the ability to relate to others in a forthright manner while taking into account their needs and reactions.

Component

Encourage or require participation in the group therapy setting.

Description

Various kinds of group therapy are employed in psychiatric settings: activity groups, social groups, educational groups, psychotherapy groups, or encounter groups, to name a few. The drug abuser often resists participation in group sessions or is overly eager to attend them. In either case, he usually will experience, at one time or another, feelings of threat, anxiety, frustration, and anger in the group setting, depending on the focus of the interaction. It is often in the group environment that he gradually learns to understand his behavior and how it influences others. He also learns new behavior patterns that are acceptable and mature and that acknowledge others' feelings and needs.

Nursing Approaches

1 In many psychiatric settings, the nurse acts as cotherapist with the psychiatrist, psychologist, or other therapist. In this role, the nurse tries to facilitate and stimulate the residents' interaction. She may identify problem areas, present them to the group, and then moderate group discussion. Her ability to pinpoint expressed feelings and deflect them back to the group or the individual helps the members to gain self-awareness as well as discourage manipulative reactions and behavior.

2 The nurse participates in encounter therapy in the group as well as on the ward. She challenges the drug abuser's self-defeating statements and identifies manipulative behavior. He is then challenged to reconcile discrepancies in his behavior and interaction. He receives the group's and the nurse's input regarding how he is perceived by others. In daily nongroup interaction with the drug abuser, the nurse continues to clearly identify contradictory behavior, thereby providing consistent input. At the same time, she should assess the person's tolerance of confrontation and challenge, to ensure that he is not in danger of becoming overstimulated by increasing, intolerable levels of anxiety.

3 As a member of the therapy group, the nurse tries to nurture participation, reflect feelings and ideas, and stimulate new problem-solving methods, The drug abuser needs considerable guidance in learning appropriate problem-solving approaches—something he must acquire in order to survive in a drug-free environment. For example, the nurse may identify a particular problem and ask the group member how he usually solves it. The next step is to ask the member and the group as a whole whether the solution is valid and appropriate for a recovered drug abuser. Requests for alternative solutions are also made. Thus each member learns new problem-solving behaviors and acquires an understanding of another person's problems, which frequently mirror their own.

4 Periodically or on a scheduled basis, the nurse may conduct educational group sessions. In these gatherings, the nurse discusses health care and maintenance in addition to giving short talks on health-related topics.

5 On occasion, the nurse may find herself acting as a group leader in an informal group session. It may take the form of a general rap session or a gripe session. Usually the nurse acts as a listener and clarifier and tries to identify specific problems without injecting opinion or being conned by the group—a difficult task.

6 In the group therapy setting, the nurse strives to establish an open and accepting atmosphere. Such an environment provides the drug abuser with an opportunity to freely express his feelings within established boundaries.

Component

Facilitate establishment of a full schedule of activities.

Description

The drug abuser, when still dependent on drugs, was accustomed to almost continuous activity aimed at procuring drug supplies. Once he is in a treatment program, he no longer needs to hustle for drugs and, consequently, time hangs heavy on his hands. It is during prolonged periods of inactivity that the patient begins to experience doubts about his ability to stay off drugs and make it in a "straight" world. To compensate, and hopefully prevent these feelings from overwhelming the person, the nurse assists other care team members in providing meaningful activities for the resident.

Nursing Approaches

1 As previously stated, the nurse may be responsible for making the patients' work assignments, including maintenance jobs within the hospital or treatment center, and maintenance of their rooms or cubicles.

2 The nurse may schedule some group sessions so as to provide a routine for the drug abuser, placing them on certain days, at certain times, and members are held responsible for attending as scheduled.

3 Along with other staff members, the nurse may be responsible for planning and implementing various recreational activities. These can consist of films, creative educational presentations, physical activities and sports, or intellectual pursuits, to name a few. The drug addict is not to be entertained per se but, rather, stimulated to become involved in available activities. If the drug abuser tends to be an isolationist, or a "loner," this is quite a challenge.

4 The psychiatric nurse should provide the resident with uninterrupted time to be alone or to pursue personal interests. It must be remembered that the psychiatric setting is an intensive milieu that requires in-depth involvement of the drug abuser while challenging his basic beliefs and values. The patient, therefore, needs free time to begin to assimilate and integrate new concepts and to work through contradictory feelings and desires.

Component

Support and evaluate rules and behavioral limitations.

Description

Psychiatric programs devise rules and behavioral limitations designed to support the therapeutic milieu. These regulations establish a degree of constancy regarding behavioral expectations and staff approaches, and they define goals of treatment.

Nursing Approaches

1 The nurse should be consistent in supporting the rules and behavioral limitations. The drug abuser may test the rules by repeatedly challenging their constancy. By consistently reinforcing the rules and its objectives, the nurse is less likely to be manipulated by the resident while at the same time reflecting a unified plan of treatment.

2 In order that rules not become unrealistic or unreasonably inflexible, the nurse should also evaluate and assess their validity. The patient's recovery should not be held back by inflexible rules. It becomes necessary in such situations to bring the problem to the attention of other care team members and determine if modification is appropriate.

Component

Evaluate physical health status.

Description

While a member of a psychiatric program, the drug abuser may require health assessment and evaluation of specific physical complaints. The nurse must be aware of physical problems and make referrals as needed.

Nursing Approaches

1 Objective evaluation of patients' physical complaints is essential. The patient will often attempt to elicit the nurse's sympathy and compassion with exaggerated complaints of pain and discomfort. Therefore, taking vital signs and blood pressure and making careful observations of physical reactions will help the nurse in sifting through valid and invalid complaints. When in doubt, the nurse should seek assistance from the physician.

2 Because nutritional deficiencies are common in the chronic drug abuser, the nurse should ensure that the patient's dietary intake is as ordered and that they are consuming the food required. As a means of facilitating nutritional intake, the nurse can also see that in-between-meal nourishments and snacks are made available to the residents.

3 Patients who enter the program with localized skin infections from poor injection technique or trauma will usually need periodic treatment of the affected area. The nurse is generally responsible for carrying out and supervising the treatment. She should evaluate the progress of healing as well as note and report any complications that may arise.

4 When program participants are being maintained on certain regimens, the nurse is usually responsible for evaluating the patient's response to the drug(s). Unusual behavior must be quickly noted and the cause determined. For example, someone who responds adversely to his methadone dose may become over-sedated and require dose adjustments.

Component

Maintain prescribed medication regimens.

Description

Long-term psychiatric programs may include the dispensation of chemical block-ade medication in the form of methadone. In addition, the drug abuser may require various other medications that decrease anxiety, nervousness, or verified physical discomfort.

Nursing Approaches

1 The nurse is usually responsible for dispensing methadone in an oral orange-flavored liquid.

2 Depending on the program's policies, a urine specimen is required from each patient before receipt of the prescribed dose. When necessary, the nurse may be responsible for supervising specimen collection.

3 Each request for PRN medication must be carefully evaluated before it is administered. The drug abuser is frequently quite adept at feigning pain and other physical complaints as a ploy to receive additional doses and sympathy.

4 The nurse must be alert for any signs of adverse reaction attributed to drug action and patient response.

5 After dispensing any medication, the nurse observes the person as it is consumed. Supervision is necessary with people who attempt to hoard medica-tion and take it all at a later time to get a "buzz," or achieve a degree of euphoria. It must be remembered that after detoxification, the drug abuser has a low tolerance for intake of large doses of drugs.

6 Whenever possible and appropriate, prescribed medication should be given by the oral route. Certain drug abusers' lifestyle includes use of hypodermics, and thus continued use of such equipment in a treatment setting can reinforce and legitimize use of needles—something to be discouraged and prevented if possible.

Component

Act as a role model for the drug abuser.

Description

Staff members of psychiatric programs act as "straight" role models for participants. The nurse acts as a female (usually) role model and a representative of the straight, or non-drug-using, society. Female addicts observe the nurse's behavior and responses and, in some cases, may emulate her behavior.

Nursing Approaches

In general, the nurse reflects straight values but not necessarily society's negative viewpoint toward the drug abuser. By her approach, attitude, and behavior, she can dispel many of the stereotyped beliefs the resident has toward the straight world. An honest and nonjudgmental manner on the part of the nurse helps to reinforce similar behavior in the program participant. It is therefore very important that the nurse not reinforce drug-using behavior through her mode of dress, speech, or covert behavior. Perhaps the most important aspect of this component is the need for the nurse to know herself, i.e., understand her inner feelings and achieve self-awareness about the image she projects to others. In this respect, the nurse is in a state of continual learning about herself just as the drug abuser is in a similar position.

Component

Provide for follow-up care or transition into another treatment program.

Description

After the patient has completed a psychiatric program and achieved a desired degree of readjustment, he may be discharged to his home or seek entrance into a long-term rehabilitation program.

Nursing Approaches

1 The nurse will relay her observations to the other team members on the patient's readiness for discharge or transfer. Often this is done in the multidisciplinary conference during which the care team pools information before deciding whether or not the person is ready for discharge. The feelings and attitudes of the resident toward this decision are an integral part of the decision-making process.

2 When the recovered drug abuser is discharged to his home, the nurse can implement follow-up measures via home visits, telephone contact with him and his family, or make referrals to the public health nurse.

SUMMARY COMMENT

Psychiatric treatment for drug abusers requires the intense involvement of the entire treatment and care team. It is important to remember that the nurse also may maintain a one-to-one nurse-patient relationship with certain patients in need of more intensive therapy. A nurse may carry a specific caseload of patients, depending on the program's design and her education and experience.

The interventions and treatment components presented in this chapter are intended as guidelines for the nurse contemplating or actually working with the drug abuser. Different nurses will undoubtedly develop variations in these approaches as well as create new ways to meet individual needs.

REFERENCES

Alley, Frederick D., and Calvin Simons: "Narcotic Detoxification and Rehabilitation Service," *Hospital Management,* **110**:64–67, October 1970.

Berzins, Juris I., and Wesley F. Ross: "Experimental Assessment of the Responsiveness of Addict Patients to the 'Influence' of Professionals Versus Other Addicts," *Journal of Abnormal Psychology,* **80**:141–148, October 1972.

Brink, Pamela J.: "Heroin Addicts: Patterns of Behavior During Detoxification," *Journal of Psychiatric Nursing and Mental Health Sciences,* **10**:12–17, March–April 1972.

Brink, Pamela J.: "Nurses' Attitudes Toward Heroin Addicts," *Journal of Psychiatric Nursing and Mental Health Sciences,* **11**:7–12, March–April 1973.

Childress, Gwendolyn: "The Role of the Nurse with the Drug Abuser and Addict," *Journal of Psychiatric Nursing and Mental Health Sciences,* **8**:21–26, March–April 1970.

Dambacher, Betty, and Karen Hellwig: "Nursing Strategies for Young Drug Users," *Perspectives in Psychiatric Care,* **9**:200–205, September–October 1971.

Huey, Florence L.: "In a Therapeutic Community," *American Journal of Nursing,* **71**:926–933, May 1971.

Levine, Stephen, and Richard Stephens: "Games Addicts Play," *Psychiatric Quarterly,* **45**(4):582–592, 1971.

Russaw, Ethel H.: "Nursing in a Narcotic-Detoxification Unit," *American Journal of Nursing,* **70**:1720–1723, August 1970.

Watson, Deena D.: *National Directory Drug Abuse Treatment Programs, 1972,* U.S. Government Printing Office, Washington, 1972.

Chapter 16

Nursing Care of the Drug Abuser in the Community

The community nurse's role in the care of drug abusers covers three basic areas: school health nursing, industrial nursing, and public health nursing. Nurses working in other community based positions include those in the physician's office and innovative drug or free clinics. The community nurse can make vital contributions to the overall treatment, care, and rehabilitation of drug abusers.

THE ROLE OF THE SCHOOL HEALTH NURSE

Because abusers of illicit drugs are frequently adolescents and young adults, the school health nurse will have numerous opportunities to confront the problems of drug abuse. Many of these children and teenagers attend school while abusing drugs. In fact school environments are often the prime drug supply sites for the student abuser.

As recognition of the pervasiveness of drug abuse into every ethnic and age group continues, school health nurses will need to acquire the knowledge, interest in, and ability to fulfill a vital role in the identification, treatment, and rehabilitation of the young drug abuser. Components of the nurse's role in the school setting are numerous and include interaction with students, faculty, family members, and community.

Knowledge of Drugs

Before the nurse can help in identifying school drug abusers and abused drugs, she must acquire a working knowledge of the actions, side effects, and adverse reactions associated with the abused substances. Such understanding based on valid and substantial information allows her to accurately assess drug abuse and related problems—physical and psychological. In addition, she should make every effort to keep up-to-date with the trends in drug usage and variations in methods of use.

When new drugs or new combinations of known drugs are being used on school grounds, the nurse should determine the nature of the change and investigate the extent of use among students. It is vital that she not assume an inquisitorial role in identifying student drug abusers or the specific drug involved. Her approach must convey caring and respect for the feelings and beliefs of the students, not preoccupation with "turning in" drug abusers. Over time, each school nurse will devise methods that are comfortable yet succeed in gaining the students' trust and confidence.

Verification of Drug Abuse

When the conduct of a student seems erratic or unusual, the classroom instructor may consult the nurse in an effort to determine the cause of the behavior. The nurse will then meet with the student to gather firsthand information, both physical and psychological. (She may also identify potential or existing drug abusers during routine health screening.) The assessment process includes observation of physical status and includes the following: general physical appearance, hygiene, condition of skin, reactivity of pupils, reflex response, gait, tremors, and central nervous system depression.

Students who are under the influence of drugs at the time of the meeting must be made to understand that referral to a physician or hospital may be required if physical responses are severely depressed. If the response is mild but the student's ability to protect himself from gait instability is limited, it is necessary to implement protective measures. In some cases, it is sufficient to keep the student in the health center; in others, the parents may be called to take the student home. In the latter instance, the parents must be carefully instructed to observe for increased central nervous system depression, bizarre behavior, or other unusual responses. When circumstances permit, the nurse can seek verifying information from the parents about the student's drug abuse behavior. Often parents will deny the existence of the problem to others but will respond to the sincere, caring approach of the nurse. Special effort should be made to convey a nonjudgmental attitude in these interactions. The cooperation, not the hostility, of the parents is absolutely necessary in the care, treatment, and rehabilitation of adolescent drug abusers.

Psychological assessment can be carried out through several channels: parental observations of changes in behavior, data obtained about classroom behavior from teachers, or direct observation and interaction with the student. If the student is so involved in drug abuse that his life is endangered by possible overdoses or binges, the nurse may also receive information from concerned friends. In general, student peers will not "squeal" (inform) on drug-abusing friends. The nurse should look for such behaviors as erratic attendance patterns, poor scholastic performance of previously academically successful students, inability to pay attention in class, changes in peer group associations, avoidance of former friends, an exaggerated antiestablishment-antiauthoritarian viewpoint, and overt boasting of drug-abusing behavior.

Straightforward inquiries will often elicit straightforward student responses. The nurse can then concentrate on related topics: How often are drugs used? How many different drugs are used? Are they taken alone or with others (people or drugs)? What administration method(s) is used? Do the parents know about the behavior? If so, what is their reaction? How long have drugs been abused? What are the student's feelings about drug abuse? Answers to these and many other similar questions aid the nurse in understanding the student's problem.

Counseling Student Drug Abusers

The school health nurse is in a unique position within the school: she is not responsible for teaching, grading, or discipline. In seeking the nurse's help with health problems or coming in contact with her during health screening, the student may voluntarily discuss drug-dependence problems. Students identified as drug abusers by the school nurse may also respond favorably to nurse-initiated interaction. In either case, the nurse acts as a counselor to the student and becomes involved with his problems, fears, and feelings. The aspect of more formalized treatment is integrated into counseling sessions.

When counseling the student, the nurse should establish a relaxed, accepting, open atmosphere. In some cases, communication is facilitated if the nurse integrates contemporary vocabulary or slang into her conversation. It must be remembered, however, that the student is not interacting with a peer, and so studied attempts at sounding like one are quickly judged as condescending and phony behavior. In encouraging the student to talk about his problems—family, peer, boyfriend or girlfriend, job, grades, etc.—the nurse should strive to pinpoint underlying problems that contributed to or led to drug abuse or dependence. Problems that to the nurse may seem insignificant or trivial can often appear overwhelming to the student and trigger an episode of drug abuse. For example, the adolescent who fears academic failure and subsequent parental pressure of discipline may "tune out" with drugs when he receives a low grade. Or, the young girl whose boyfriend breaks up with her may turn to drugs as an escape from emotional hurt and disappointment.

Once problem areas are identified, the nurse then tries to help the student devise alternative problem-solving approaches that are realistic and compatible with available resources. Often it helps the student to gain perspective if he realizes that other people have similar problems, feelings, and anxieties. As the nurse helps the student identify problems and appropriate responses, she carefully evaluates his involvement with and dependence on drugs. Referrals to treatment agencies and other professionals are sometimes necessary in order to ensure that the student will receive the care and attention required to overcome drug abuse.

Initiation of Referrals

Students who need comprehensive care cannot be adequately treated in the school health center due to limited resources, equipment, and personnel. In such cases the nurse makes referrals to the family physician, local treatment programs, or community self-help groups, many of which are geared specifically to the needs of adolescent drug abusers. True drug dependence that involves physical dependence requires skilled and knowledgeable controlled withdrawal or drug substitution therapy.

Besides professional treatment referrals, the nurse may also encourage the student to seek additional supportive resources in people he respects and values: friends, family members, clergymen, teachers, or any other person the student mentions. When feasible or requested, the school nurse may make the initial contact, in person or via telephone, with the person on behalf of the student.

The overall goal of referrals by the school health nurse is to induce the student to get treatment. These referrals must convey a supportive, accepting, and honest attitude. If the student suspects that he will be "busted" (arrested) because of admitting drug abuse, his confidence in the nurse and other health professionals will decline rapidly. Required reports of drug abuse activities and referrals to school administration officials must be done in a routine, low-key manner indicating that a *health* problem has been identified, not a *moral* problem.

Involvement of Family Members

Parents or guardians of students who abuse drugs must be included in the counseling and decision-making process in terms of treatment, care, and rehabilitation. In many cases, such involvement is mandatory when the abuser is a legal minor and consent must be obtained prior to initiating referrals. Counseling sessions with parents alone or parents and students sometimes disclose additional problems within the family that should be referred.

Depending on the school nurse's responsibilities and personal desires, it is often possible to make visits to the students' homes. The purposes for such visits can include escorting students home when under the influence of drugs, discussing drug abuse health problems, and initiating follow-up care. Family members frequently appreciate the nurse's interest, which can engender trust and confidence in her as a health professional concerned for the well-being of the family as well as the drug abuser.

Education for Drug Abuse Prevention

As the only health professional in the school (in most cases), the school health nurse has a responsibility to inform students, parents, faculty, and administrators of the hazards of drug abuse and the availability of treatment. The nurse may accomplish this objective through seminars, classes, and individual discussions that emphasize prevention and precaution, not scare tactics. The latter are rarely effective with potential or actual drug abusers and tend to polarize viewpoints in a negative direction. Audiovisual media, graphic art, and other materials may be helpful in pointing out the serious dangers involved.

It must be emphasized that the educational aspect of the nurse's role is an ongoing one. The "one-shot" approach—for example a student assembly or brief yearly education program—is not sufficient to meet the need for continued exposure to such information.

THE ROLE OF THE INDUSTRIAL NURSE

Although not as widespread, or perhaps as widely recognized, as alcoholism, drug abuse in industry has become a serious problem. Employees tend to abuse nonnarcotic drugs such as marijuana, barbiturates, and stimulants. The abuse patterns may be one of on-the-job drug ingestion when physical dependence has developed or abuse mostly after working hours or on weekends. In either instance, these employees may exhibit behavioral changes that have a direct impact on work performance.

Heroin dependence is difficult to maintain and conceal when the user is employed. The frequent need to "fix," obtain drugs, and portray normalcy is usually not compatible with the structured employment situation. Those people who can sustain opiate abuse and keep their jobs have been able to establish a consistent, dependable source of supply and at the same time control the physical dependence. In general, preemployment screening succeeds in excluding obvious drug abusers. Unfortunately, such screening also succeeds in rejecting recovered drug abusers as well.

The role of the industrial nurse in relation to employee drug abuse and alcoholism overlaps. It must be remembered, however, that while the purchase of alcohol is legal, the purchase, possession, and use of heroin, marijuana, and other drugs are illegal. This difference greatly affects employment performance and opportunities.

Education on Drug Abuse

The industrial nurse may be responsible for conducting employee, supervisor, and administrator educational programs on drug abuse. All levels of the organization must be included. Educational methods can include audiovisual materials (films, slides, and tapes), seminar discussion groups, formal teaching sessions, poster campaigns, or periodic workshops. In each case, the nurse may be wholly responsible for the organization, implementation, and evaluation of the program. Information on signs and symptoms of drug abuse should be presented in clear and understandable terms applicable to the nonprofessional and non-health-field-oriented person.

The educational responsibilities of the industrial nurse include community teaching. In some cases, an employee will request information on drug abuse problems that exist or are suspected within his family. The nurse can provide specific data as well as suggest additional sources of community support and information. Because the nurse in an industrial setting is often viewed as the major source of health-related knowledge, it is imperative that she know and understand the actions, side effects, patterns, and adverse reactions associated with the major abused drugs so that she can disseminate information to employees as well as participate in community-oriented public education program.

Recognition of the Drug Abuser

In the course of her work, the industrial nurse has many opportunities to contribute to the identification of the employee drug abuser. Often she works in a consulting capacity with the employee's supervisor in verifying behavior patterns that are indicative of drug abuse. Some changes in behavior include the following:

1 Increased tardiness and absenteeism. When drug users "trip out," they lose their sense of time and will therefore often be late or fail to report to work if under the influence of drugs. Barbiturate abusers may not be able to "get started" in time to arrive at work promptly.

2 Erratic work performance. Fluctuations in work output and quality that represent a noticeable change from usual performance may be indicative of drug abuse. The person who becomes exceedingly hyperactive and speeds through the work while neglecting quality may be abusing stimulants. The listless employee who seems unusually relaxed or unconcerned about his job or who frequently daydreams or nods may be using hallucinogens or barbiturates. It should be emphasized that erratic job performance can be sporadic, occurring at frequent intervals, or rarely. The employee may not be truly dependent on the drug.

Nevertheless, the use of the drug during working hours may adversely affect his performance to the extent that it harms himself or other employees.

3   Mood changes. Employees may exhibit unusual mood changes related to the effects of the drug or the requirements of obtaining it. When physical dependence has developed, tolerance increases, necessitating increased amount of total drug intake. If the drug is difficult to obtain or expensive, the employee may borrow money from friends, take out a loan from the employee credit union, or steal industrial goods that can be resold. These efforts soon cause the employee to isolate himself from his peers, although concerned friends may seek help in his behalf. Obvious mood changes while on the job should be rapidly identified and validated to prevent accident and subsequent physical injury.

4   Changes in physical appearance. Uncharacteristic neglect of personal hygiene, disheveled clothing, when coupled with overt evidence of needle tracks on the skin, point toward drug abuse behavior. Employees who reach the stage of dependence in which such obvious changes occur will often quit their jobs, or be fired. These changes appear as drug abuse reaches more nearly chronic proportions and are usually only one factor in the decision to fire the employee.

Counseling the Employee Drug Abuser

The industrial nurse's counseling of the suspected or verified drug abuser closely parallels that discussed in Chapter 8. Certain aspects of the counseling process for the employee, however, deserve elaboration here.

The employee who abuses illicit drugs is subject to arrest and criminal prosecution. He must be made aware of this possibility and its impact on his life and his family's life. Drug abusers generally do not respond to scare tactics, and so the nurse must present information in an open, straightforward manner, trying not to play the role of authoritarian. Precaution in this regard is especially important because of the nurse's neutrality within the company or business. If the employee suspects that the nurse is "passing judgment," her effectiveness as a counselor will be hampered.

The drug-abusing employee must also realize that his behavior will generally be less tolerated than that of the alcoholic. Social values, attitudes, and stereotypes of what drug abusers do and who drug abusers are continue to dominate many industrial work situations. Until these negative feelings are countered with valid information on the problems leading to drug abuse and its true characteristics, the employee must realize that he will very likely be discharged, turned over to the legal authorities, or both. Legal implications for the employee and the employer must be considered in the nurse's counseling session.

Reinforcement of Treatment and Rehabilitation Programs

The drug abuser who enters a treatment program and participates in rehabilitation may be able to return to his former job. Although not a common practice, some large companies are implementing retraining programs and cooperative programs that permit the drug abuser to continue employment while being treated. The employee who is adhering to a methadone maintenance program and who is progressing in the rehabilitation process should be given the opportunity to return to work or find suitable employment. The industrial nurse should reinforce rehabilitation treatment goals for these employees as well as encourage company managers to implement drug abuse programs when there is an identified need.

Employees who return to work while undergoing treatment or following treatment may benefit from and appreciate the nurse's interest in their progress. Providing a "listening ear" that the recovered drug abuser can use while at work becomes an important aspect of the nurse's role. Depending on the company's policies and the program's needs, the industrial nurse may be responsible for periodically monitoring the employee's response to medication as well as identifying any problems he may have in relation to his job.

THE ROLE OF THE PUBLIC HEALTH NURSE

Casefinding and Referrals

Nurses working in the community have many opportunities to detect drug abusers. As the public health nurse (PHN) enters the homes of families in need of health care, she can note clues that point to drug abuse. In many cases, parents or siblings will ask her what can be done. When overt requests are made, she can make referrals to community agencies, counsel the drug abuser, and work with the family to help them understand their role in the problem. In seeking to identify the drug abuser, the PHN can focus on the same indicators discussed in Chapter 8 in relation to the alcoholic.

The drug abuser may feel relatively free to discuss his problems with the PHN because her community health care role is accepted and respected. When he indicates a desire and readiness to undergo treatment, the PHN is in an ideal position to make referrals to community based drug treatment programs. For this reason, it is vitally important that the PHN have adequate knowledge of her community's treatment and rehabilitation resources.

Counseling on Drug Abuse

Both the abuser of drugs and his family can benefit from counseling by the public health nurse. In addition to providing supportive counseling on treatment resources within the community, the nurse can serve as a source of unbiased information on the characteristics of drug abuse. Family members may request this information, or the nurse can offer it when she realizes that a family member is especially susceptible to drug abuse because of his environment or socioeconomic status.

When a family member, either child or spouse, is drug-dependent, the other members frequently need an avenue of expression for their feelings. The PHN can fulfill this need by encouraging them to discuss their fears, anger, and frustrations stemming from the drug abuser's behavior. For example, when the drug is expensive, the dependent person may steal money and resellable household objects in order to buy it. If the family income is severely cut as a result of such behavior, family members tend to reject the drug abuser, often turning him out of the home. The nurse can help the family to secure financial assistance when needed by making referrals to social service agencies. She cannot dissolve emotional reactions to the behavior of the drug abuser, but she can encourage their expression and accept the family's need to ventilate their feelings.

Another important aspect of the PHN's counseling role is of an educational nature. Just as the spouses or children of alcoholics hold many stereotyped beliefs about alcoholism, so do family members hold prejudicial and biased beliefs about drug abuse. The nurse can help correct misinformation and distortion, thereby encouraging a more realistic understanding of the problem.

Although the causes of drug abuse have not yet been clearly identified, the nurse can aid the family in concentrating on behavior that may have contributed to the development of drug dependence. Such open interaction is possible only after the nurse has established a trusting and accepting relationship with the family. These discussions can help the family realize the impact of their behavior on other family members. When deep-seated, complex problems become evident, the nurse should make referrals to other professionals who specialize in family counseling. In this instance, she facilitates efforts to help the entire family through a potential or an existing crisis situation.

Initial efforts to encourage the drug abuser to seek treatment may not be successful. The public health nurse must realize that drug dependence is probably one of the most challenging health problems she will ever face. It may be necessary to develop varied interventions and approaches to the problem using available community self-help organizations, former drug abusers, as well as professional treatment sources, to stimulate the person's entrance into a treatment and rehabilitation program.

Methadone Maintenance Program Responsibilities

The community or public health nurse is frequently a member of the methadone maintenance program staff. The program may be a part of the hospital outpatient clinic or located in community clinics. Regardless of the location, the nurse has a number of responsibilities.

Dispensation of Methadone The nurse is generally responsible for dispensing the prescribed methadone dose to the program participants. Each time the drug is dispensed, the abuser verifies his identity and takes the medication in the presence of the nurse, who maintains accurate written records according to federal, state, and program regulations and guidelines.

Recording Response and Progress Because the nurse has daily, consistent contact with the drug abuser, she can observe responses to the medication and progress within the program. Accurate notes should reflect unusual behavior changes as well as specific behavior changes indicative of the person's increased ability to assume more responsibility.

Obtaining Urine Specimens As previously stated, the nurse may be responsible for the supervised collection of urine specimens before dispensation of methadone. She must take precautions that the person does not turn in a false specimen, and thus it is often necessary to actually observe the collection process.

Counseling the Drug Abuser In her daily routine the nurse has continual opportunities to interact with the program participant. By her nonjudgmental and open attitude, the nurse conveys interest in the person and his problems. Often just listening helps to reduce anxiety in the person who is trying to learn non-drug-oriented coping behaviors and alternative problem-solving methods. A more in-depth discussion of nursing approaches applicable to the counseling situation is given in Chapter 15.

Health counseling and screening may also be a responsibility of the nurse in a methadone maintenance program. Preliminary evaluation of complaints of illness or disability may be conducted by the nurse before referral to the physician.

Participation in Group Sessions Depending on the resources of the methadone program, group therapy sessions may be conducted during the day or in the evening. Participants may be required to attend the sessions as one facet of the overall treatment framework. The nurse often serves as a cotherapist or co-group leader in these sessions. Basically, the group therapy setting seeks to help the drug abuser learn new coping behavior and problem-solving methods through a dynamic sharing and learning process. The nurse concentrates on facilitating group interaction and recognizing manipulative behavior that blocks progress. (Refer to Chapter 15 for further information on nursing interventions applicable to the group therapy setting.)

Observing for Drug Abuse While on a methadone maintenance regimen, the opiate addict will not respond to injected heroin. For this and other reasons, the addict may periodically abuse other drugs while on the program—especially barbiturates and alcohol. Urine specimens will reveal such episodes. The nurse should be aware that these practices are relatively common and subsequently observe for physical manifestations of drug abuse. Certain methadone maintenance programs will dismiss addicts who chronically abuse other drugs. When alternative abuse occurs, it is a definite signal that the person is not coping well without illicit drug intake. The nurse's observations are verified and reported to other staff members, and appropriate disciplinary action is taken, or changes in approach are made to counter the detrimental behavior.

INNOVATIVE COMMUNITY NURSE ROLES

In recent years, nurses working in the community have developed extended roles, some of them concentrating on the drug abuse problem. Certain nurses with advanced preparation at the master's level have established private practices that focus on providing services to referred patients and persons seeking nursing care. The evolution of this role is just beginning. It is hoped that such practitioners will eventually be able to have an impact on the recovered drug abuser's problems of transition between treatment program and reentry into the community.

Nurses working in the free clinic or drug clinic setting have much contact with drug abusers who either seek specific crisis intervention services and basic health care or assistance in controlling or ceasing drug-dependent behavior. In this environment, the nurse assists with health screening and makes specific referrals for follow-up care or definitive therapy when needed. As a volunteer or staff member at the clinic, she also participates in counseling sessions, rap sessions, and therapy sessions. Because the atmosphere is generally casual, relaxed, and unstructured, the drug abuser often feels free to use the clinic's services and communicate with staff members. Thus the nurse has an ideal opportunity to interact with the drug abuser in a nonthreatening, low-keyed manner. Because of the nurse's professional medical and nursing knowledge, she is often responsible for teaching staff members basic cardiopulmonary resuscitation measures that are vital when an overdosed drug abuser is brought to the clinic.

By working in the drug abuser's environment, the nurse can acquire an indepth understanding of the problems leading to and resulting from drug abuse. The challenge of devising relevant nursing interventions for identified problems is enormous but one many nurses actively seek.

SUMMARY COMMENT

The evolving and innovative nursing roles in working with drug-dependent people in the community offer a major avenue of hope for effective delivery of health care services to these people. Such creative nursing role development is to be applauded and encouraged, for it provides a realistic solution to one of the most destructive and pervasive public health problems in modern society.

REFERENCES

Caskey, Kathryn K., Enid V. Blaylock, and Beryl M. Wauson: "The School Nurse and Drug Abusers," *Nursing Outlook,* 18:27–30, December 1970.

"Drug Abuse in Industry," *Selected Reference Series,* ser. 6, no. 1, July 1973, National Clearinghouse for Drug Abuse Information.

Hine, C. H.: "The Role of the Industrial Nurse in the Detection and Prevention of Drug Abuse," *Occupational Health Nursing,* 17:15–17, April 1969.

Krome, Ronald L. et al.: "The Role of the Registered Nurse in Methadone Maintenance Programs," *Michigan Nurse,* 44:5–7, September 1971.

Pearson, Barbara A.: "Methadone Maintenance in Heroin Addiction," *American Journal of Nursing,* 70:2571–2574, December 1970.

Ramer, Barry S.: "Is Methadone Enough? The Use of Ancillary Treatment During Methadone Maintenance," *American Journal of Psychiatry,* 127: 1040–1044, February 1971.

Snider, Arthur: "Corporate Junkies," Chicago Daily News in *Honolulu Star-Bulletin,* p. D-2, November 6, 1972.

Part Three

Rehabilitation and the Changing Role of the Nurse

On the health-illness continuum, rehabilitation is an ongoing process essential to the eventual achievement of wellness. Although rehabilitation generally is emphasized following acute illness or trauma, in reality it begins with initial treatment. Since this is especially so with alcoholics or drug abusers, it is necessary to implement specific nursing interventions while first caring for these patients. In many cases, it is these first efforts that set the tone for further rehabilitation achievements.

The role of the nurse in rehabilitation programs will vary, or be limited by the current emphasis of nursing practice as well as by the goals of different programs. For example, the nurse's role has been more clearly defined with rehabilitation of the alcoholic than with drug-dependent persons. Current and future trends of nursing practice, education, and research, however, hopefully will precipitate more intensive involvement of the nursing profession in the rehabilitation process for alcoholics and drug abusers.

Rehabilitation must be viewed as the beginning for the alcoholic or drug abuser . . . the beginning of a new, drug-free life. The nurse can contribute one of the most important elements to this beginning: *hope*. With full recognition of the challenges, potential disappointments, and frustrations associated with the rehabilitation of alcoholics or drug abusers, the nurse can become a key source of hope to anyone trying to overcome self-destructive behavior.

Chapter 17

Rehabilitating
the Alcoholic

The literature on alcoholism discusses just about every aspect of the condition in great depth—except rehabilitation. Generally this topic is squeezed in with information on treatment regimens, but never fully treated as a specific and vital area of concern to health professionals. In this chapter the nature and significance of rehabilitation is explained and the role of the nurse in rehabilitation of the alcoholic is discussed.

DEFINING REHABILITATION

In this book, rehabilitation of the alcoholic is defined as the process through which the alcoholic requires the ability to live without alcohol while rebuilding a meaningful self-image and assuming a purposeful position in society. It must be remembered that the alcoholic might not have had these abilities before the development of alcoholism. He might never have experienced fulfilling interpersonal relationships or employment. If such is the case, rehabilitation will entail acquiring new behavioral skills, not the awakening or recovery of previously attained abilities. Alcoholics who at one time did experience satisfying relationships and self-actualizing activities may become rehabilitated when these abilities are rekindled. In essence, then, rehabilitation is more than recovery and abstinence. It is a new way of living with intrapersonal insight and a respect for oneself and life itself.

PHILOSOPHY AND GOALS OF REHABILITATION

The philosophy of a particular alcoholic rehabilitation program will in large part determine its goals. In programs where their main goal is the removal of physical and psychological alcohol dependence, the underlying philosophy may be that alcoholism is (1) a symptom of underlying intrapsychic conflict, (2) a disease in itself characterized by identifiable symptomatology, or (3) a behavioral problem for which the alcoholic can assume responsibility and control. No philosophy is wholly right or wrong, but it should be appropriate to the varying needs of different alcoholics. As a result, health professionals must realize that lack of success need not always be attributed to the patient himself. It might also be attributed to the program's approach.

Goals are a necessary component of any rehabilitation program because they point to desired outcomes for the alcoholic and the health professional. They exemplify hope and a belief that the alcoholic *can* be rehabilitated. Goals should be realistic and based on comprehensive understanding of the dynamics and characteristics of alcoholism. Unrealistic goals designed in such a way as to "program" the alcoholic's failure succeed only in perpetuating self-negating, self-defeating beliefs the alcoholic might hold toward recovery. The following goals are realistic and reflect the belief that rehabilitation is an ongoing dynamic process that can take place in a variety of ways.

Goals of Rehabilitation

Abstinence The basic goal is total abstinence from alcohol. Some programs emphasize total, permanent abstinence and consider rehabilitative efforts to be a failure when the alcoholic has a relapse, but most programs concentrate on short-term abstinence that will lead eventually to permanent abstinence. In these programs, relapse is viewed as a temporary setback. Other programs emphasize decreasing episodes of intoxication in those persons who are not able to maintain complete abstinence. In general, a realistic goal is to aim for eventual permanent abstinence through incremental steps of short-term success.

Self-Awareness In order for the abstinent alcoholic to succeed in daily living without alcohol, it is necessary for him to gain an ever evolving self-awareness of his emotional limitations and strengths. Once he is aware of personal stress and anxiety points, he can develop non-alcohol-oriented behavioral responses. Self-awareness is attained gradually and involves family members also.

The spouse and children of the alcoholic need assistance in recognizing their behavior and how it may contribute to the perpetuation of alcoholism.

Self-awareness is a long-term goal in terms of degree or depth of sensitivity achieved. It is also a short-term goal in the sense that the alcoholic first gains a superficial self-awareness that becomes expanded as he progresses through the rehabilitation process.

Problem Solving As the alcoholic seeks self-awareness and is helped to achieve it, he is also guided in developing constructive problem-solving methods rather than resorting to alcohol when life problems and stresses become intolerable or uncomfortable. A major goal, then, is the development of realistic problem-solving techniques and the strengthening of healthy coping mechanisms. The alcoholic can accomplish this goal over time by making day-to-day progress.

Family Stabilization Rehabilitation is not complete until the family of the alcoholic becomes involved in the process. Once the alcoholic has undergone treatment and has begun to participate in rehabilitation, the spouse and children must become engaged in their own rehabilitation, for it is currently recognized that the alcoholic is not the only afflicted member in the family. The spouse frequently reinforces alcohol-dependent behavior or is dependent on the spouse's alcoholic behavior for his or her own need fulfillment or repression. For these reasons, it is important that the spouse and adolescent children (at least) participate in separate or joint rehabilitative efforts. When members of the alcoholic's family gain self-awareness and acquire healthy problem-solving abilities, stability and unity can hopefully be reestablished or perhaps established for the first time. As with the previously discussed goals, the stabilization of the family unit is a long-term goal with incremental steps leading to final attainment.

Career Development The alcoholic (man or woman) frequently requires assistance in identifying career goals, refocusing on or reorienting to past employment, or training and retraining for job placement. Rehabilitation efforts help the abstinent alcoholic meet his career goals by equipping him with marketable skills and self-confidence and by motivating him to recognize personal areas of strength. The availability of such rehabilitation services will depend on individual program resources and intent.

The alcoholic woman who does not seek employment also requires assistance in her career development—the career of homemaker and mother (when applicable). A healthy reorientation to domestic responsibilities, areas of satisfaction, and ways to occupy leisure time become vitally important.

The key to establishing goals for alcoholics is realism—a realistic attitude toward the needs of the alcoholic and the dynamics of alcoholism. Goals should not be inflexible; that is, they should not prevent the person's progress but further it by establishing a desirable and attainable outcome.

CHARACTERISTICS OF ALCOHOLIC REHABILITATION PROGRAMS

Rehabilitation should start with the initial admission of the alcoholic, whether in a general hospital, a detoxification unit, or a psychiatric setting. Some treatment facilities do try to initiate rehabilitation during the acute stages of treatment, but the majority do not. In reality, rehabilitation *can* start with hospital admission. For example, as the nurse cares for the alcoholic in the hospital, she can initiate rehabilitation through (1) verbally interacting with him, (2) identifying the degree of insight he has into his illness, (3) interacting with his spouse or family to determine their needs, (4) communicating with staff on assessment findings, and (5) seeking guidance from rehabilitation specialists on how best to facilitate the transition of the impatient alcoholic to the community rehabilitation setting.

Private and publicly financed rehabilitation programs have increased during the past decade partially from increased federal and state financial assistance. Prominent locations are general hospitals, publicly supported psychiatric hospitals, privately supported treatment and rehabilitation centers (e.g., the Salvation Army), halfway houses or quarterway houses, and the outpatient clinics.

Services Provided

Programs can be extensive or concentrate on selected areas of concern. For example, programs for poverty level alcoholics and their families provide services that have special relevance to the problems of the poor. Middle-class or financially secure alcoholics may not require the same services but will benefit from a different type of program. To meet the differing needs of their patients, programs may offer various combinations of the following services.

Residential Accommodations Many programs require the alcoholic to live in the program's residential facilities. Residential programs provide intense treatment, separation from external sources of stress, and a secure environment in which the alcoholic can work toward goal attainment. Payment for residential rehabilitation is usually voluntary when public financing is available; that is, the resident pays what he can afford and the supporting agency makes up the difference.

Detoxification Some programs provide comprehensive care and treatment of the alcoholic from the time of his discovery through completion of the program. Most rehabilitation centers, however, are not equipped or staffed to provide this service and receive patients on transfer from the hospital after detoxification.

Education An integral part of rehabilitation is learning about the dynamics and characteristics of alcoholism: how it develops, why it may develop, who becomes an alcoholic, how the family responds to and reacts to alcoholism, and physical problems associated with the illness. Approaches to education can include daily or scheduled lectures, seminars, films or slide presentations and discussion, or informal seminars arranged in case-study fashion in which the alcoholic presents his own history (or a hypothetical case is presented) followed by an in-depth discussion of the common problems illustrated by the real-life example and possible solutions.

Alcoholics Anonymous The alcoholic may participate in AA meetings on an optional or compulsory basis. Many programs depend heavily on AA while others offer it as an option only. AA meetings may be conducted at the rehabilitation center or in the community. Program residents are sometimes required to attend community AA meetings as a means of establishing community relationships. These supportive relationships can then provide a degree of continuity when the person returns to the community.

The spouse and children of the alcoholic are frequently encouraged to attend Al-Anon and Al-Ateen meetings to gain insight into their own problems as well as those of the alcoholic. Meetings are sometimes held at the rehabilitation center but are more commonly held in the community.

Group Meetings Daily or several times weekly, scheduled group meetings may be held in which the alcoholic's presence is required. These gatherings may be led by a professional therapist, an alcoholic counselor, or a program staff member. The alcoholic is stimulated to face his problems, who he is, who he can become, and how he can achieve realistic goals. Staff members can be active group participants who refocus group interaction, help to identify and articulate problem areas, and facilitate interpersonal communication. In some cases, the staff member may take a passive role and simply observe interactions and identify any problems that need in-depth rehabilitation efforts.

The design and goals of group therapy sessions in the rehabilitation setting often parallel those in the psychiatric setting and are in fact patterned after or an extension of such groups. In the carefully planned and coordinated treatment and rehabilitation sequence, activities carried out or initiated in the psychiatric or general hospital are continued, as needed, in the rehabilitation facility. Thus alcoholics who have experienced group therapy or encounter therapy in one program can continue to grow and gain self-awareness in the rehabilitation environment.

Self-Government Resident self-government meetings are a part of some programs. The residents elect representatives and work together to establish or recommend policies to govern their behavior and interpersonal relationships. These meetings allow the alcoholic to express leadership potential, exercise independent self-expression, and gain a degree of personal satisfaction and self-confidence. Some programs, however, do not include a self-government component because it is felt that the alcoholic must concentrate on intrapersonal self-development and awareness, not superficial group activities that may allow him to camouflage his problems.

Work Assignments The resident is usually held responsible for the physical maintenance of his immediate living environment. In addition, he may be assigned various other tasks that contribute to the overall upkeep of the rehabilitation facility. These work assignments help him pass time, provide fulfilling activities, stimulate a sense of responsibility and self-respect, and encourage a feeling of capability in accomplishing specific tasks.

Occupational Therapy When financial and staff resources permit, many programs offer occupational therapy services through which the patient can relearn former skills or acquire new ones. In some residential programs occupational therapy is much emphasized. The alcoholic learns a trade or skill that can be used within the rehabilitation facility. One notable example is the Salvation Army, where remodeled and reconditioned articles are sold to the public and the income used to defray the costs of operating the rehabilitation center.

Recreation Therapy There is a growing realization that one of the alcoholic's problems is an inability to use leisure time in a healthful, relaxing fashion. Recreation therapy encourages him to learn new approaches to the use of leisure time, i.e., to develop hobbies and recreational interests that can be used when he leaves the program. Also, the rehabilitation facility itself serves as a locus for recreational activities, which may include games, sports, intellectual discussions, artistic endeavors, etc.

Disulfiram Therapy As a rehabilitation option and to reinforce abstinence, the alcoholic may elect to participate in a disulfiram (Antabuse®) medication regimen. Many programs do not offer this alternative but, rather, only non-drug-oriented rehabilitation. In programs that function largely on an outpatient basis, disulfiram therapy may provide valuable support to alcoholics who are not residing within the facility.

Job Counseling Vocational counselors or other program staff members help the alcoholic in finding employment before he leaves the facility. In some cases, release or discharge from the program is contingent upon having a job. The counselor works with the resident to determine his interests and capabilities before he contacts potential employers. The alcoholic frequently requires job counseling and placement assistance because of past poor job performance and erratic work patterns.

Transition Assistance As the resident prepares for reentry into the community, he often needs help in making the transition between living in the facility and on his own in the community. To meet this need, the program may include the full- or part-time services of a social worker or community outreach worker whose role includes coordinating follow-up care, arranging for living accommodations within the community, helping the recovered alcoholic get financial assistance, and communicating with community agencies that will offer the alcoholic supportive assistance once he leaves the program. In some situations, these functions are fulfilled by the nurse or other staff member. In either instance, transition assistance is often indispensable in bridging the gap between the protective environment of the rehabilitation program and the community.

Halfway Houses Some programs operate halfway houses that function as an intermediate residence for the alcoholic reentering the community. Advantages of the halfway or quarterway house include (1) small number of residents (usually no more than fifteen or twenty), (2) individualized attention in a comfortable, homelike environment, and (3) location in the community that the resident hopes to reenter as a contributing member.

Follow-up Plans Depending on the community's resources, the staff may initiate follow-up care after the alcoholic has left the program. Follow-up may include referrals to day care centers, mental hygiene clinics, Alcoholics Anonymous, the public health nurse, or other social service organizations. Periodic return visits to the facility can be on a scheduled or spontaneous basis and can provide an ideal opportunity to evaluate the alcoholic's progress.

Staffing of Rehabilitation Programs

The staff of an alcoholic rehabilitation program is multidisciplinary. Different programs will have varying combinations of the following professional staff members: nurses, physicians, psychologists, representatives of the clergy, psychiatrists, social workers, and occupational and recreational therapists. In addition, nonprofessional counselors, volunteers, and recovered alcoholics make major contributions to the program.

The alcoholism counselor is a relatively new member of the rehabilitation team. Generally, he is a nonprofessional, sometimes a recovered alcoholic, who has received special education and training in the many aspects of alcoholism. He works with the patient individually as well as in the group interaction setting. Professional staff members often rely on the counselor's special insight and interest in the alcoholic and his knowledge of the problems that arise in interacting with alcoholics.

Length of Rehabilitation Programs

Programs range in length from as short a period as ten days to one or two years. The method used to implement the program over a specified period of time will vary and may include in-residence program participation and extended outpatient or day care activities. Programs that provide services to large numbers of patients may have a minimum residence requirement of four to six weeks after which the alcoholic may become an outpatient or day center participant for several more months.

The length of the program is influenced by the program's definition of rehabilitation. If the definition centers on short-term, intensive therapy and not long-lasting recovery, the program will tend to be short. Programs with the goals previously enumerated are longer, since time is necessary to aid the patient in attaining self-awareness and the ability to live an alcohol-free life.

Rehabilitation Program Participants

Some programs are limited to either all men or all women, especially to men only. This restriction may be based on a belief that mixed populations create an overly complex situation in which the unique needs of each sex are hard to meet or it may result from past problems with mixed residents. Several programs have found, however, that with adequate staff and facilities, the mixed population promotes an aspect of resocialization that is impossible in programs where members are all of one sex.

Alcoholics from poverty-level socioeconomic groups and minority ethnic or racial groups are rarely members of rehabilitation programs. This situation may be due to restrictive admission procedures or criteria or to a lack of understanding of the special problems that these groups have. Some programs, however, are designed especially for poverty-level, skid-row alcoholics, but they face an uphill challenge because of the chronic problems presented by these people (e.g., high relapse rate, lengthy alcohol dependence, lack of personal resources).

Rehabilitation "Success" Rates

Statistics on "success" are not available for all programs because it is very difficult to define success. Does it mean total abstinence? Decreased episodes of intoxication? Increased self-awareness? Changes in attitude toward drinking? Changes in family responses or behavior toward the alcoholic? Continued employment? These and other questions must be clarified when statistics on the success of a program are presented.

Criteria consisting of improved intrafamily relations and few or no drinking episodes have resulted in success rates ranging from 20 to 67 percent. Success in achieving complete abstinence for one year or more is perhaps as low as 2 percent or as high as 58 percent.[1,2,3,4,5]

Determining success rates is beneficial in that it guides program revision and expansion. Careful delineation of the measurement criteria adds validity to success rate statistics. Nurses, other health professionals, and care givers who work with alcoholics in a rehabilitation center should thoroughly scrutinize statistical data that imply success or failure and keep in mind the specific goals of their programs.

Possibly the major characteristic of alcoholism rehabilitation programs is diversity—diversity in goals, philosophy, staff composition, and client population. Variety of this kind is desirable when it enables the diverse needs of different client populations to be met. It is undesirable, however, when it results in the needs of certain alcoholics being overlooked or denied.

Alcoholic Rehabilitation in Industry

Industry has for many years recognized the negative influence of alcoholism on production capabilities. It is estimated that anywhere from 3 to 5 percent of the employee population are problem drinkers or alcoholics. To combat the detrimental effects of alcoholism for both the employee and the employer, many large companies have instituted company-sponsored rehabilitation programs. These often include extensive in-company educational programs for all employees, periodic workshops for increasing individual awareness of alcoholism and the behavior associated with it, and periodic updating and reinforcement of previously presented information. In addition, supervisory personnel are encouraged to refer suspected alcoholic employees to the industrial health center for treatment.

Industrial programs seek to retain the alcoholic employee, not terminate employment. The person is viewed as a valuable, experienced worker who will not lose his job if he demonstrates willingness to undergo treatment and follows through with entrance into treatment. Once he has undergone detoxification and initial therapy, he often can return to work and continue treatment as an

---

[1] Vernon E. Johnson, *I'll Quit Tomorrow*, Harper & Row, New York, 1973, p. 2.

[2] Raymond M. Glasscote et al., *The Treatment of Alcoholism: A Study of Programs and Problems*, The Joint Information Service of the American Psychiatric Association and the National Association for Mental Health, Washington, 1967, p. 41.

[3] Shirley E. Cooke, "Project Rehab: A Progress Report," *Maryland State Medical Journal*, 21:85–86, June 1972.

[4] Milan Tomsovic, "A Follow-Up Study of Discharged Alcoholics," *Hospital & Community Psychiatry*, 21:95, March 1970.

[5] Albert N. Browne-Mayers, Edward E. Seelye, and David E. Brown, "Reorganized Alcoholism Service," *Journal of the American Medical Association*, 224:233–235, April 9, 1973.

outpatient. Knowing that he will have a job after detoxification can motivate him to seek help.

The success rates for industrial programs tend to be high, ranging from 55 to 72 percent.[6,7] Such high rates may be attributed to (1) the employer's support of the employee and active interest in his success, (2) the employee's understanding that admitting his alcoholism will not result in the termination of his job, and (3) the employee's realization that failure to get treatment and regain control of his behavior can mean the loss of his job. Some industrial programs use alcoholism counselors as well as nurses, physicians, and other professional health workers.

Industry is more and more conscious of the pervasiveness of alcoholism among workers. The cost to industry of alcoholic employees in terms of lost work hours, decreased effectiveness on the job, danger to employees' physical safety, and lower productivity runs into billions of dollars per year. As a result, companies are motivated to continue to develop and implement alcoholic rehabilitation programs.

ROLE OF THE NURSE IN THE REHABILITATION SETTING

The alcoholism rehabilitation setting may or may not include the nurse as a staff member. When the nurse is a staff member, her role often will include many of the components discussed in Chapter 7. In addition, she makes several other contributions that further the rehabilitation goals. Roles often overlap in the rehabilitation setting (as they do in other settings), and thus, the nurse's role may reflect more or less of the traditional nursing action components.

Health Teaching

One of the nurse's most important roles is that of health teacher. Generally she is the primary health teacher. Both the alcoholic and his family need to be encouraged to learn or relearn healthful dietary patterns as well as the importance of physical self-care.

Coordinating Rehabilitation Activities

The nurse is very often a coordinator of activities for program participants. She may be responsible for organizing recreational activities, scheduling therapeutic

[6] Ralph E. Winter, "One for the Plant," *Maryland State Medical Journal*, 19:99, January 1970.
[7] Robert R. J. Hilker, Fern E. Asma, and Raymond L. Eggert, "A Company-Sponsored Alcoholic Rehabilitation Program," *Journal of Occupational Medicine*, 14:771, October 1972.

group sessions, making initial arrangements for transition into the community, and interviewing prospective or new residents. The coordinator position carries with it leadership responsibility and requires a high degree of perceptiveness and sensitivity to the needs of the alcoholic. When coordinating resident activities, the nurse works closely with other program staff members.

Evaluating Progress

Another important function of the nurse is evaluation of the alcoholic's behavior and personal growth in group therapy, his understanding of his illness and its permanent limitations, his degree of attitude change toward the nature of his illness, and his level of insight into the implications of alcoholism for future living. Information is gathered through personal observations in direct interaction with the alcoholic and through passive observations made of his behavior during the daily activities of the program.

An important aspect of the evaluation process is assessment of the spouse's or family's progress in rehabilitation. The wife or husband of the patient is encouraged to accept counseling or participate in group therapy while he progresses through rehabilitation, so the nurse often has many opportunities to interact with the family member(s) and therefore to assess their progress. In making an evaluation, she considers members' level of understanding of the illness, the implications for future relationships, and their depth of insight into their own attitudes and responses to the alcoholic.

Evaluations are shared with other staff members in an ongoing process so that staff approaches can be modified to correspond to the needs of the patient.

Counseling

Counseling the alcoholic and his family is frequently part of the nurse's role in rehabilitation programs. She may implement one-to-one or group interaction to guide the alcoholic or his family to recognize the nature of alcoholism and its impact on the individual and the family unit. The counseling process is long-term, often initiated with admission to the rehabilitation program and continuing on an outpatient basis. The relationship the nurse builds with the alcoholic and his family serves as a source of support and caring concern during rehabilitation. By her open, nonjudgmental approach she helps the patient learn self-acceptance and, over time, regain a sense of self-respect. The counseling process should be paced to meet the alcoholic's responses while at the same time challenging him to gain insight and reject past self-destructive, manipulative behavior.

Health Assessing

The alcoholic usually views the nurse as a health expert. When he complains of physical discomfort or has symptoms of illness, the nurse is often responsible for assessing the problem and determining initial interventions. Alcoholics who have had previous histories of physical dysfunction may require continuing follow-up assessments to ensure that the prescribed treatment regimen is being followed.

In addition to these basic aspects of the nurse's role in the alcoholic rehabilitation program, she may also (1) serve as cotherapist in group therapy sessions, (2) be responsible for gathering follow-up data after the alcoholic has left the program, (3) conduct in-service education and orientation programs for new staff members, or (4) be jointly responsible for community education programs.

SUMMARY COMMENT

Rehabilitation of the alcoholic and his family requires the multidisciplinary resources of professionals and nonprofessionals. Guiding and stimulating the abstinent alcoholic to regain a sense of well-being, self-awareness, and self-acceptance is a challenging assignment and one in which the nurse plays an integral part. Specific nursing methods in a rehabilitation setting correspond closely to those discussed in previous chapters (see Chapters 5-8). Nurses who work with alcoholics in a rehabilitation program generally develop personalized approaches that are comfortable for them and that are effective in achieving goals. It must be remembered that the nurse experiences personal growth and development just as the alcoholic does. At times this experience is unpleasant but it is also fulfilling.

REFERENCES

Bosma, Willem G. A.: "Training Professionals for Meeting the Needs of Alcoholics and Problem Drinkers," *Maryland State Medical Journal*, 22:102–104, October 1973.

Bosma, Willem G. A.: "Training Professionals for Meeting the Needs of Alcoholics and Problem Drinkers," *Maryland State Medical Journal*, 22:84–87, November 1973.

Clyne, Robert M.: "Pitfalls in a Rehabilitation Program for the Alcoholic Employee," *Industrial Medicine and Surgery*, 40:34–37, September 1971.

Cooke, Shirley E.: "Project Rehab: A Progress Report," *Maryland State Medical Journal*, 21:82–87, June 1972.

Dunn, John: "Northwestern Wisconsin Alcoholism Project," *Rehabilitation Record*, 12:24–29, September–October 1971.

Glasscote, Raymond M. et al.: *The Treatment of Alcoholism: A Study of Programs and Problems*, The Joint Information Service of the American Psychiatric Association and the National Association for Mental Health, Washington, 1967.

Hilker, Robert R. J., Fern E. Asma, and Raymond L. Eggert: "A Company-Sponsored Alcoholic Rehabilitation Program," *Journal of Occupational Medicine*, 14:769–772, October 1972.

Johnson, Vernon E.: *I'll Quit Tomorrow*, Harper & Row, New York, 1973.

Lister, Leonard M.: "Inpatient Alcoholic Rehabilitation Care," *Maryland State Medical Journal*, **20**:33–36, May 1971.

McCourt, William F.: "How You Can Really Help the Alcoholic," *Medical Insight*, 36–48, March 1971.

Mellon, Lawrence J.: "How Boeing Handles Alcoholism," *Industrial Medicine and Surgery*, **38**:317–323, October 1969.

"Nursing Home Plan Includes Alcoholic Rehabilitation," *Modern Nursing Home*, **28**:51–53, February 1972.

Skelley, Thomas, and Gregory March: "Rehabilitating the Alcoholic," *Rehabilitation Record*, **12**:23–24, September–October 1971.

Winter, Ralph E.: "One for the Plant," *Maryland State Medical Journal*, **19**: 97–99, January 1970.

Chapter 18

Rehabilitation of the Drug Abuser

With the increasing acknowledgment of the scope and extent of drug abuse has come recognition that traditional approaches to rehabilitation are incompatible with the nature of the problem and ineffective in teaching drug abusers new, non-drug-oriented behavior patterns. In an attempt to meet the challenge of drug abuse rehabilitation, innovative approaches have been devised in recent years. The methods used rely heavily on the individual program's definition of rehabilitation.

DEFINING REHABILITATION

It is neither feasible nor reasonable to define rehabilitation in limited terms when the process is applied to the needs of the drug abuser. For example, if rehabilitation is defined only in terms of drug abstinence, heroin addicts being maintained on methadone would not be rehabilitated. If it is defined as successful reintegration of the abstinent drug abuser into society, people who are living productive lives within the Synanon lifestyle are not rehabilitated. In order to take into account the various methods currently being used, the following definition is offered: Rehabilitation is the process by which the drug-dependent person acquires the ability to alter his lifestyle and drug-oriented belief system, learn non-drug-oriented approaches to problem solving, and understand and control his behavior. Besides encompassing the common aspects of rehabilitation, this definition permits whatever flexibility is necessary. The broadness of the definition allows it to be applied to the rehabilitation of sedative, stimulant, hallucinogen, volatile substance, and narcotic abusers. It is the degree or depth of the rehabilitation process that will vary in relation to each drug of abuse.

GOALS OF REHABILITATION

The philosophy of a particular program will determine its goals and how they are achieved. If a program bases rehabilitation on the belief that drug dependence is the result of unresolved intrapersonal psychological conflict, the program may emphasize a psychiatric approach. If drug dependence is believed to be related to environmental pressures, a structured, in-residence approach may be emphasized.

Prescribed goals should point toward desired outcomes, whether drug abstinence or change in lifestyle. Unreasonable or seemingly unattainable goals succeed only in "turning off" the drug abuser, who is usually present-oriented, not future-oriented. All goals should be flexible enough to meet the individual needs and capabilities of the drug abuser. Some programs will often delineate subgoals that lead to attainment of the main goal.

Rehabilitation Goals

Drug Abstinence   Most programs require drug abstinence as a prerequisite to acceptance, with the exception of methadone programs. Although the drug abuser can usually maintain abstinence while in the structured program environment, continued drug-free living after leaving the program is fraught with difficulty and frustration. As a member of a rehabilitation program, the drug abuser is helped to learn to withstand the pressures to return to drug use. In many cases, the goal is not attained initially or is never attained. Achievement of continued drug abstinence remains the ultimate goal for anyone who seeks a totally drug-free life.

Lifestyle Alteration   One means of ensuring that the drug abuser will be able to sustain abstinence is to demand or encourage alteration in lifestyle. Such a change is particularly important for persons who are physically dependent on barbiturates or opiates. Both dependencies require a continuing supply to prevent withdrawal. The constant need to hustle for money to purchase drugs usually leads the addict into a drug subculture. The heroin addict in particular finds it necessary to closely associate with other drug users and resort to criminal activities in order to maintain steady drug supplies.

Attitude Change   The rehabilitation program will also try to develop attitude changes within the drug abuser. If the person is to be able to eventually maintain abstinence on his own and learn new methods of interaction with others, he must first change his attitudes. Three areas of attitude change are emphasized:

1 *Attitude change toward self.* Drug abusers often have very little self-respect and self-confidence. The depth of such feelings will vary with the person's personality, the drug of abuse, and the behavior necessitated by or associated with the drug. A primary subgoal, then, becomes to produce an attitude change toward the self by fostering feelings of self-worth, self-confidence, and self-acceptance with a corresponding deemphasis on past behavior and emphasis on present and future accomplishments.

2 *Attitude change toward other people.* Some drug abusers have a negative or hostile attitude toward "straight" people (non-drug users). These feelings can be translated into apathetic or manipulative responses during interaction with non-drug abusers or other drug abusers. Through various approaches the drug abuser is helped to understand other people and to become more sensitive to their needs so that he can successfully reenter society.

3 *Attitude change toward society.* An antiestablishment, antiauthoritarian "rip-off" attitude is not in itself a block to rehabilitation. But blind adherence to such attitudes prevents insight into motivations and personal feelings. Changing the drug abuser's negative attitudes toward society becomes a necessary prerequisite to promoting deep personal understanding. It is important to remember that such a change does not imply shaping the drug abuser into a proestablishment mold. Emphasis is on helping him to objectively evaluate the pros and cons of society rather than rejecting the whole because some of the parts are faulty.

Personal Development   In helping to achieve abstinence, most programs encourage new, non-drug-oriented behavior patterns and attitudes. The drug abuser is required or stimulated to acquire mature and responsible behavior. Progress in personal development may be continually measured by performance in the rehabilitation setting. The ultimate goal is the evolution of personal characteristics, attitudes, and behaviors that will support a drug-free lifestyle and an ability to interact with other people.

Vocational Development   Drug abusers who are employed usually don't require as much vocational counseling as those who are chronically unemployed. An unskilled drug abuser with minimal formal education needs extensive vocational training or counseling. The program may require participation in training programs to prepare the person for job placement when he is ready. For those who begin to abuse drugs before completing school or before they reached employable age, the job-related knowledge and skills or counseling received during rehabilitation is their first exposure to the requirements, responsibilities, and satisfactions of employment.

Reentry into Society Most rehabilitation programs have the ultimate goal of returning the drug abuser to society as an abstinent, potentially productive contributor. A notable exception is the Synanon program, which concentrates on the development of an alternative, non-drug-oriented lifestyle within the boundaries of the program. Graduates of Synanon may leave the program or remain in the community. For very practical reasons, preparation for reentry into society has to be a major goal of any program. (It would neither be reasonable nor possible for rehabilitation programs to become custodial institutions for drug abusers.)

Program Development Goals

Most programs have certain goals that facilitate program enrichment but are not related to the achievement of specific rehabilitation goals for the drug abuser. Among the most important of the program development goals is evaluation. Many programs are implemented without an adequate evaluation plan that would guide revision and modification of approaches. After several years of operation, the program finds it necessary to determine how effective its methods are and, at that time, devise an evaluation plan. To prevent such a problem, most programs currently integrate evaluation methods into their overall plans.

Adequate follow-up is a second program development goal. Many programs emphasize statistical follow-up measures that focus on data, not people. Other programs seek to determine whether the rehabilitated drug abuser has adjusted to drug-free living. Most programs use a combination of both approaches.

A third program development goal is community education. Once the community learns more about the nature of drug abuse and the rehabilitation program's design and intent, greater cooperation and community involvement can be achieved. Providing information to the public is important. The input of community members helps to ensure that the purposes of the program are being met for both the drug abuser and the community.

REHABILITATION OF THE NONNARCOTIC DRUG ABUSER

People who abuse or become dependent on stimulants, barbiturates, hallucinogens, or volatile substances present a challenge to health professionals. Traditional rehabilitation approaches tend to be used. These methods rely heavily on psychotherapy to handle the underlying problems that either led to or resulted from drug abuse. Long-term psychiatric care in the group or in a one-to-one situation, family therapy, or inpatient hospitalization may be successful in producing a drug-free lifestyle.

Certain types of drug abuse seem to be self-limiting. For example, adolescents who abuse glue, paint thinner, or other volatile substances may spontaneously stop the practice after entering young adulthood. In such cases, abstinence may not be emphaiszed in the program. Persons dependent on amphetamines may require psychotherapy or the prescription of antidepressant drugs. Abusers of hallucinogens can also benefit from psychotherapy. Often, however, psychotherapy is ineffective for members of the counterculture. One-to-one psychotherapy or intensive counseling may help the hallucinogen abuser integrate his drug experiences so that he can return to his former lifestyle or acquire an alternative one.

It is hoped that the trend toward devising treatment methods for heroin addicts while neglecting the rehabilitation of other drug abusers' problems will begin to reverse itself now that governmental agencies and professional health workers recognize the pervasiveness of nonnarcotic drug abuse in this country.

In summary, the rehabilitation of the nonnarcotic drug abuser at any age is done within a traditional framework of psychotherapy, group therapy, or family therapy. Vocational rehabilitation is seldom part of the program but after achieving abstinence, the individual may receive vocational counseling from a publicly funded agency. Programs designed to meet the unique needs of various drug abusers are uncommon. The goals presented in the previous section pertaining to attitude changes, personal development, abstinence, and reentry into society, however, can be applied to the psychotherapeutic framework.

REHABILITATION OF HEROIN ABUSERS

The treatment of heroin abusers has received great attention, considerable financial support, and creative input during the past two decades. In large part, this has been due to the tremendous amount of publicity given to the criminal and sensational aspects of heroin dependence. Unfortunately, this publicity has not served its purpose entirely but has succeeded in creating considerable fear of drug abusers in general. However, one beneficial aspect of this heightened interest is that it has led to concentrated efforts toward devising new methods in the treatment and rehabilitation of heroin addicts.

Many well-known programs use similar approaches, modifying them where necessary to meet specific program objectives or addict needs. Most programs aim at the goals previously mentioned, and although the paths chosen to reach these goals may vary, the ultimate outcomes are similar. As each of the approaches is discussed, their success rates will also be given.

Civil Commitment Programs

Traditionally, treatment and rehabilitation of drug abusers has taken place in institutional environments. Drug-dependent persons were committed to the programs by civil authorities, progressed through the institutional process, and were discharged to return to their prior lifestyle and usually to drug dependence. Recent changes in civil commitment programs, however, have endorsed more therapeutic environments for rehabilitating drug abusers, specifically heroin addicts.

The best known of these programs is the Clinical Research Center in Lexington, Kentucky. Many large civil commitment programs located in other states have patterned their rehabilitation procedures after the Lexington center. A brief description of this program will illustrate the civil commitment program approach to the rehabilitation of drug abusers.

The Clinical Research Center The revamped rehabilitation program at Lexington now consists of four evaluation and treatment services and an autonomous self-help unit called Matrix House. (The basic components of the Matrix House approach are discussed in the following section on Residential Therapeutic Communities.) The drug abuser is committed through petition to the U.S. Attorney closest to his home. The petition can be initiated by the addict or a relative. In addition, narcotic abusers charged with or convicted of federal crimes may be committed to the Center. They are committed for a minimum six-month stay followed by community aftercare for thirty-six months. Aftercare and follow-up are arranged in the drug abuser's home location.

Each of the four evaluation and treatment services (Excelsior House, Numen House, YOUnity III, Ascension House) are therapeutic communities that use confrontation approaches, group psychotherapy, vocational assignments, recreational and occupational therapy, and educational activities. General health care and maintenance services are also provided. Concepts from many disciplines and other rehabilitation programs are used by the individual units to meet the needs of the residents. The goals closely parallel those previously discussed and include (1) developing the inner resources and abilities of the drug addict, (2) instilling a sense of responsibility for self and others, (3) teaching vocational skills, and (4) teaching how to relate to other people. Each service uses slight variations in similar approaches to achieve goals, and the staff is composed of both professionals and nonprofessionals.

After leaving the in-residence center, the person returns to his home, where he undergoes aftercare. He is usually assigned to a counselor who is associated with a community rehabilitation agency. If the person should relapse into drug-dependent behavior, he can be readmitted to the Lexington facility for another six-month, in-residence stay. As of 1970, 87 percent of the addicts in aftercare were drug-free 80 percent of the time and 13 percent were completely drug-free.[1]

Other programs use similar methods including halfway houses, which allow for more supervised aftercare. The degree of supervision will vary according to financial resources and the goals of the program. Some programs include periodic urine specimen checks for drugs during the aftercare period. The length of time devoted to in-hospital residence and aftercare can be influenced by the narcotic abuser's criminal record. For example, the narcotic abuser committed following a felony or misdemeanor in California has a seven-year program commitment.[2]

In general, the civil commitment approach seems to meet a societal need to periodically remove criminal addicts from circulation. The programs also meet an identified need for many drug abusers who are unable to benefit from other types of noninstitutional rehabilitation. Until more community-based programs are organized and granted more extensive financial support, the civil commitment approach will continue to be necessary.

Residential Therapeutic Communities

One of the more promising outlooks in the rehabilitation of narcotic-dependent persons is that represented by the residential therapeutic community. The forerunner of these programs is Synanon, which was established in California in 1958. Most, if not all, of the therapeutic community programs have either patterned themselves after Synanon or modified Synanon procedures to meet their own specific goals.

Synanon   The Synanon method consists of (1) isolating the drug-dependent person from his drug-oriented environment, (2) thoroughly changing his lifestyle, (3) providing self-help in overcoming the dependency on drugs, (4) developing his inner strengths, (5) engendering a drug-free value system and attitude toward life, and (6) stimulating self-responsibility and maturity. Peer interaction is the vehicle through which these goals are accomplished. Synanon programs are organized and administered by ex-drug abusers. Professional assistance mainly for health problems is sought as needed.

Synanon is more than a program. It has evolved into a communal lifestyle followed by drug abusers seeking rehabilitation as well as non-drug users who seek the challenge of living in an open, expressive climate. Addicts who have progressed through the program frequently stay within the Synanon

---

[1] *Lexington: The Clinical Research Center*, U. S. Government Printing Office, Washington, 1971, p. 18.
[2] Roger E. Meyer, *Guide to Drug Rehabilitation: A Public Health Approach*, Beacon Press, Boston, 1972, p. 57.

environment or go on to become staff members of Synanon-like programs in other locations.

Admittance to Synanon is based on a "talk your way in" system; that is, the prospective resident must convince staff members that he is capable of functioning within the limitations of the program. Once admitted, however, he is free to leave at any time. First the new resident undergoes detoxification by "cold turkey"—without receiving any discomfort-relieving medications. After the acute withdrawal symptoms are over, he is given a menial work assignment. If he demonstrates personal growth and maturity, the work assignment and his status improve. The work assignments foster the development of responsibility and are necessary to the actual operation of the program.

Synanon has evolved one of the most effective approaches to interpersonal communication and the stimulation of self-growth: confrontation therapy, or "the game." The addict is daily confronted by his peers with his immature and self-destructive behavior. The group therapy setting provides an environment in which peers use attack methods to break down his drug-oriented belief systems while at the same time helping him recognize and learn healthy responses to life's daily frustrations and problems. However, he is also encouraged to freely express his feelings, problems, and hostilities to the group. Confrontation can take the form of violent verbal attack, challenge, and criticism. Physical violence is strictly prohibited. If a particular person is the subject of potentially overwhelming verbal attack, the confrontation is diverted by group members who then focus on the interaction process.

A rigid system of discipline is consistently enforced. A resident who violates rules or behavioral regulations is subject to various types of disciplinary measures that are dealt with in the group setting. He is challenged to assume responsibility for his behavior, which has been pointed out by a peer, and to ensure that similar behavior does not recur. For example, using street language and boasting about past drug-oriented exploits are deemed rule infractions. These behaviors are considered immature and are therefore prohibited.

The length of stay within a Synanon program is unlimited. The ex-addict can stay in the program indefinitely as a staff member or as a resident of the Synanon community. Because rehabilitated addicts can remain within the Synanon community and because physical discharge or departure is not the major goal of this approach, it is not possible to accurately evaluate the success of Synanon in traditional terms. For example, approximately half of the addicts participating in Synanon programs eventually become staff members. If the focus of rehabilitation is to produce drug-free living and a productive, meaningful life, the people who remain in Synanon and work with other addicts can be considered rehabilitated.

Other Therapeutic Community Programs Several other therapeutic programs have evolved in the last decade or so. Some of the well-known ones are

Phoenix Houses, Daytop Village, Odyssey House, Matrix House, and numerous state-sponsored programs. The techniques used include confrontation therapy, peer pressure and support, development of introspective insight, and encouragement of mature behavior and responses to life's problems and challenges. These programs are patterned after Synanon but have these significant differences:

1 *Time limit.* The resident stay can range from nine to thirty months or more. The Synanon program has no such limitation. A time limit may motivate an addict to make progress in order to be ready to meet the challenges of a drug-free life.

2 *Staff composition.* The staff can be dominated by nonprofessional ex-addicts. However, professionals may also be on staff or act as consultants for specific problems. Professionals may be responsible for the organization of group therapy. These programs seem to value the professional as someone who has a vital contribution to make to the rehabilitation process.

3 *Method of support.* Most of these programs receive all or the majority of their financial support from community, federal, or state agencies. As a result, they are required to collect data on goal attainment.

4 *Program emphasis.* Reentry into society is emphasized as the ultimate goal of rehabilitation. Several of the programs operate community halfway houses where the senior program residents are sent for a time before returning to everyday life.

5 *Drug violation detection.* In many programs, urine specimens are collected and analyzed periodically. When violations are found, which is seldom, disciplinary measures are taken that can range from peer reprimand to discharge.

Admittance to the programs closely parallels that of Synanon but also includes court referral of drug abusers in lieu of prison sentences. Resident populations tend to be of different ethnic backgrounds, sex, and age. Some programs hesitate to accept adolescents because of the ego-threatening encounter techniques used. The young adolescent has usually not developed an identity structure strong enough to withstand the pressures inherent in therapeutic community treatment.

The success of the therapeutic community is measured, in most cases, by whether permanent, complete drug abstinence is achieved. Thus, the success rate is low. If partial abstinence or extended periods of abstinence characterized by independent, productive living were considered criteria of success, the rates would probably be higher.

Because no program meets the needs of all kinds of drug abusers, various programs have evolved to deal with specific age groups. The young adult or adult person often does well in the structured therapeutic community previously discussed. The adolescent, on the other hand, may benefit more from a program with a less ego-threatening atmosphere. Programs for the adolescent may have a religious orientation such as Teen Challenge or emphasize the development of individual and interpersonal responsibility.

Day Care Programs Perhaps the best known of the day care programs is Reality House in New York City. Group therapy is the major vehicle used to achieve drug abstinence and mature, responsible behavior. Groups are either led by professionals or by combinations of professionals and ex-addicts, according to the current phase of rehabilitation. As the person learns to understand and express his motivations, he progresses to a higher level of responsibility within the program. Vocational counseling is included in the level progression, and all activities are carried out during the day. Only a small segment of the drug abuser population responds well to the day care treatment, but it is appropriate for some narcotic abusers who might not accept other types of rehabilitation programs.

Methadone Maintenance and Rehabilitation

Methadone is used in certain rehabilitation programs. (A discussion of methadone treatment and the role of the nurse is included in Chapters 13 and 16.) While the addict is being maintained on methadone, he participates in group therapy designed to aid him in living without heroin. Some programs begin gradual, controlled withdrawal from methadone after the person has been rehabilitated. Other programs simply offer methadone maintenance as an alternative reinforcement of regular rehabilitation services.

PROBLEMS IN DRUG ABUSER REHABILITATION

Rehabilitation is often impeded or destined for failure because of problems inherent in the program itself, to society's view of the ex-addict, or to the drug abuser's personality.

Early Onset of Drug Abuse

A significant number of drug abusers begin their habit early in life, sometimes as young as 8 or 10 years of age. Children this young have not yet learned responsible behavior patterns, and their drug dependence may prevent normal personality maturation to the extent that they never learn how to have a healthy relationship with others. When these people enter a rehabilitation program, they may challenge and frustrate the staff members.

Day-to-day contact with the immature, manipulative, and defensive drug abuser may cause skepticism among care givers. At the same time, the drug abuser begins to realize that in order to succeed in maintaining a drug-free life, he must foresake his former behavior patterns—a very unsettling thought as far as he is concerned. The threat of losing his current identity may serve as the primary stimulus to leave the program prematurely.

Personality Weaknesses of the Drug Abuser

Many of the personality traits of drug abusers, especially narcotic abusers, are not acceptable to society as a whole: an inability to trust and depend on others, express feelings and thoughts, and form healthy interpersonal relationships; dishonesty and manipulative behavior. These drawbacks are tackled in the rehabilitation setting but are very difficult to counter.

Lack of Constructive Public Education

Although some drug abuse educational programs depict realistic aspects of the problem, many do not. Many of the fictionalized television programs play up the sensational aspects of drug abuse—crime, drug supply routes, international smuggling operations, etc. Although these presentations do help to make the public aware of the problem, they do not always do so from the public health point of view.

Professional education on the many aspects of drug abuse is superficial at best. As a result, many health professionals who might be able to contribute to the rehabilitation of the drug abuser either have no preparation to do so or have accepted many of the stereotyped, negative attitudes toward people who abuse drugs.

It would seem, then, that public and professional education should stress the realistic, factual aspects of the problem, and sensationalism should be avoided. More extensive dissemination of information on available treatment facilities and ways for the individual citizen to assist in fighting drug abuse is greatly needed.

Follow-up and Reentry Deficits

Rehabilitation programs that include follow-up care are few. Thus drug abusers who do not have the support of lay organizations, such as AA for the alcoholic, often return to their habit. Although there is a Narcotics Anonymous organization, it is not as widespread or as well-known as AA. The lack of follow-up care represents a major obstacle to long-lasting success in rehabilitation. This is not to imply, however, that follow-up care ensures abstinence. It does imply that adequate follow-up could increase the total number of drug-free days per rehabilitated drug abuser.

Common reentry problems include (1) the inability of the ex-addict to function within a group of citizens not all whom accept him and (2) failure to find suitable employment. Many employers hesitate or refuse to offer jobs to ex-drug abusers. Not being able to find fulfilling careers can be so frustrating and stressful to an ex-addict that he may return to drugs. Besides the problem of finding employment, he may not be able to benefit from vocational counseling if it is not geared to his capabilities and limitations and if there are not enough opportunities in the community.

Lack of Industry Involvement

Industry has taken a responsible and active role in uncovering alcoholics and rehabilitating them. Unfortunately, its involvement in the rehabilitation of ex-drug abusers has not been extensive. The lack of industry-sponsored jobs and job rehabilitation programs for ex-addicts seriously limits their chances of becoming productive members of society. Several large companies are developing programs, and hopefully they will demonstrate not only the economic benefits of industry involvement but also indicate to those seeking rehabilitation that employment opportunities and alternatives do exist.

THE NURSE IN THE REHABILITATION SETTING

The philosophy of the program will in large part determine whether or not the nurse will have a role in the rehabilitation process. Some programs include nurses on the staff but tend to restrict their role to the evaluation and care of tangible health problems or illnesses. Involvement in therapeutic nurse-patient relationships on a one-to-one basis or in the group setting is not part of the nurse's role in such programs.

The nurse's limited involvement may be due to several factors:

Limited Nursing Roles Rehabilitation programs that are staffed by ex-drug abusers and health professionals (psychologists, psychiatrists, physicians) are generally of the therapeutic community type. In these programs, nurses have occasionally assumed supervisory or administrative roles, but on the whole responsibilities tend to be confined to the care of health-related problems, health education teaching, and administering medications.

With programs in institutions or hospitals, including methadone programs, the nurse's role is more extensive, as discussed in Chapters 15 and 16.

Negative Attitudes toward the Drug Abuser Nurses are often not free from negative, stereotyped societal attitudes toward drug abusers, although such attitudes can be overcome by factual information and personal contact with patients. Nevertheless, many nurses find it extremely difficult and frustrating to work with drug abusers, and stereotyped attitudes are reinforced by the patient's behavior. A large measure of patience and an understanding of the dynamics of drug-dependent behavior, however, may enable the nurse to control these negative attitudes and derive both personal and professional satisfaction from her work.

Lack of Drug Abuse Education A nurse's hesitation to care for drug abusers in a rehabilitation setting might also be due to a lack of education on the subject. Schools of nursing generally devote limited, minimal attention to the various aspects of drug abuse—physiological responses and related considerations, nursing assessment of needs, and appropriate interventions. Ongoing professional education programs in the community, when they exist, tend to serve only nurses working with drug abusers. As a result, those who might contribute but are not currently doing so may not be receiving the necessary background information and encouragement. Refresher courses and supervised experience with drug abusers in rehabilitation settings are either nonexistent or minimal.

Extensive educational programs on drug abuse will not erase the hesitancy many nurses have to work with ex-addicts. They can, however, increase the professional interest of nurses in creating and assuming a more involved and concerned role in rehabilitation programs.

Lack of Professional Communication between Nurses Nurses who have succeeded in implementing new and effective ways of dealing with drug abuse have not communicated with other interested nurses about their accomplishments. The nursing literature on this topic is scant. Yet it is important for nurses who have had some success to share their experiences with other nurses through professional publications, workshops, or other means.

SUMMARY COMMENT

Rehabilitation of drug abusers is an absolute necessity if these people are ever to assume a meaningful and contributing role in society. Currently there are several approaches that have had a degree of success: civil commitment programs, therapeutic community programs, and methadone maintenance programs. Each employs similar methods with variations according to its philosophy and the people served.

The rehabilitation process can start with hospital admission and be continued in an organized program until the patient can reenter the community drug-free. The role of the nurse in this process can begin with hospitalization or detoxification, be continued and expanded in the psychiatric setting, and be reinforced in the community by public health, industrial, and school nurses. It is hoped that nurses interested in drug abuse will begin to carve more active roles for themselves in rehabilitation programs and thereby enhance the effectiveness of these programs.

REFERENCES

Ball, John C.: "On the Treatment of Drug Dependence," *American Journal of Psychiatry,* **128**:873–874, January 1972.

Batiste, Curt G., and Lewis Yablonsky: "Synanon: A Therapeutic Life Style," *California Medicine,* **114**:90–94, May 1971.

Cancellaro, Louis A.: "New Treatment Concepts at the NIMH Clinical Research Center, Lexington, Kentucky," Wolfram Keup (ed.), *Drug Abuse Current Concepts and Research,* Charles C Thomas, Springfield, Ill., 1972.

Deissler, Karl J.: "Synanon: How It Works, Why It Works," in Paul H. Blachly (ed.), *Progress in Drug Abuse,* Charles C Thomas, Springfield, Ill., 1972.

Glasscote, Raymond M. et al.: *The Treatment of Drug Abuse,* The Joint Information Service of the American Psychiatric Association and the National Association for Mental Health, Washington, 1972.

Katz, Charles J.: "Drug Abuse Rehabilitation Program for Youth," *Rocky Mountain Medical Journal,* **67**:57–60, July 1970.

Kaufman, Edward: "A Psychiatrist Views an Addict Self-Help Program," *American Journal of Psychiatry,* **128**:846–852, January 1972.

Kaufman, Edward: "Reality House, A Self-help Day-Care Center for Narcotic Addicts," in Wolfram Keup (ed.), *Drug Abuse: Current Concepts and Research,* Charles C Thomas, Springfield, Ill., 1972.

Lexington: The Clinical Research Center, U.S. Government Printing Office, Washington, 1971.

Meyer, Roger E.: *Guide to Drug Rehabilitation: A Public Health Approach,* Beacon Press, Boston, 1972.

Reeder, Charles W. et al.: "Vocational Rehabilitation of the Hard-Core Addict," *Rehabilitation Literature,* **34**:11–14, 20, January 1973.

Rosenthal, Mitchell S., and D. Vincent Biase: "Phoenix Houses: Therapeutic Communities for Drug Addicts," *Hospital & Community Psychiatry,* **20**: 26–30, January 1969.

Schoolar, Joseph C., G. Michael Winburn, and J. Ray Hays: "Rehabilitation of Drug Abusers—A Continuing Enigma," *Rehabilitation Literature,* **34**:327–330, November 1973.

Scott, Donald, and Harold L. Goldberg: "The Phenomenon of Self-Perpetuation in Synanon-Type Drug Treatment Programs," *Hospital & Community Psychiatry,* **24**:231–233, April 1973.

Sitomer, Curtis J.: "Rehabilitation Center Helps Addicts," Christian Science Monitor Service in *The Sunday Star-Bulletin & Advertiser,* Honolulu, August 5, 1973. p. C-12.

Walls, Richard T., and Stephen P. Gulkus: "What's Happening in Hard-Drug Rehabilitation?", *Rehabilitation Literature,* **34**:2–6, January 1973.

Weppner, Robert S.: "Matrix House: Its First Year at Lexington, Ky.," *HSMHA Health Reports,* **86**:761–768, September 1971.

Yablonsky, Lewis: *The Tunnel Back: Synanon,* The Macmillan Company, New York, 1965.

Chapter 19

Future Trends

The interest in alcohol and other drug abuse problems is increasing yearly, and health professionals now realize that a multidisciplinary plan for treatment, care, and rehabilitation is essential. As important members of the health care delivery team, nurses must identify goals, determine appropriate interventions, and acquire the ability to thoroughly evaluate and revise plans of care. Further development of current and future trends in nursing education, practice, and research should help facilitate the nurse's abilities in these areas.

NURSING EDUCATION

Different schools of nursing tend to provide different kinds of information and clinical learning experiences related to alcoholism and drug abuse. Some schools have a sophisticated curriculum specifically designed to prepare the nurse to assume an active role in the care of persons with drug-dependence problems. The majority of new graduate nurses, however, have received minimal preparation and often feel unqualified to give nursing care in this area. Yet revision in nursing education on alcoholism and drug abuse is necessary because ever increasing numbers of drug-dependent persons are entering the health care delivery system.

As a means of initiating and reinforcing new educational trends, nurse educators may want to consider the following:

1 *Specific background content.* In nursing schools, the classroom discussion of alcoholism and drug abuse should not be confined to a single lecture. The often complex facets of these problems cannot be adequately covered in one lecture. The use of learning modules, programmed instruction, and other independent student-learning methods may help in providing adequate information. The coordinated use and involvement of community resource persons who have expertise in drug abuse and alcoholism can also be of much value.

Nursing students at all levels should receive instruction on alcoholism, drug abuse, and appropriate nursing care interventions. The depth of the content will vary, of necessity, with the type of nursing program. Undergraduate as well as graduate curricula should include the subject of drug dependency. At the graduate level emphasis should be placed on applied research and development of new roles. A graduate school option of specializing in drug abuse nursing must also be considered.

2 *Clinical experience.* In order for nursing students to gain experience in handling drug abusers, clinical components should be planned as integral parts of drug abuse education. Numerous settings may be used to provide such experience.

The hospital environment affords many opportunities for students to learn about drug dependency. The emergency room of the general hospital could be used for observation and assessment experiences, as well as nursing care experiences for the senior students. Graduate students might also use this location for identification and implementation of new nursing roles and approaches. The general nursing unit and the detoxification unit can acquaint students with the various withdrawal and overdose phenomena, initial rehabilitation efforts, and the diverse complications of drug dependency. In-hospital psychiatric nursing units can serve as ideal sites for the development of interaction skills in less hectic surroundings. All in all, the general hospital is a good place for nursing students to gain experience in caring for the alcoholic, the drug abuser, and their families.

3 *Community resources.* Most of the large, urban communities have alcoholism and drug abuse programs. Schools of nursing located within a reasonable distance from such programs might seek to coordinate student-learning experience at such facilities. The halfway house, therapeutic community, and neighborhood drug clinic, for example, could provide stimulating experiences in observation and assessment. Lengthy assignments to these facilities would not be necessary for undergraduates. The goal would be to expose students to available community resources and, in turn, make them aware of what they can contribute.

Learning experiences in the area of public health nursing might include supervised observation or interaction with alcoholics and drug abusers in their own environments. Students could assist with health screening in free clinics or with casefinding during an assigned public health rotation.

4 *In-service education.* Nurse educators serving as in-service instructors or directors within the hospital also have much to contribute. Ongoing orientation to hospital policies and programs, periodic workshops or seminars, and introduction of new nursing care techniques and treatment methods are some of the topics that can be covered by the in-service educator. The multidisciplinary health team approach lends itself to the hospital setting. Nurses, physicians, psychologists, dieticians, social workers, and other health professionals all can learn from one another and contribute to the attainment of team goals.

5 *Continuing education.* Nurses who are currently caring for alcoholics or other drug abusers may periodically seek or require updating of their knowledge. In order to provide appropriate continuing education for practitioners, the educator should carefully and thoroughly assess the care requirements of the patients receiving nursing services.

Perhaps the most important aspect of nursing education, regardless of the location, is to cover not only the most publicized types of drug abuse but also the dynamics of various drug dependencies, pharmacology of the drugs, goals for nursing care, and current as well as innovative procedures. Emphasis should be geared to the community's major drug abuse problems with the realization that certain types of drug dependence are not as visible as others (for example, barbiturate abuse) but may nevertheless require intensive nursing intervention.

NURSING PRACTICE

Nurses have long been caring for persons with drug-dependency problems. Increased recognition of the prevalence of drug dependence and stepped-up efforts to provide adequate health care to these people have led to greater contact between nurses and drug abusers. At the same time, nurses in many locations are beginning to express specific interest in learning about drug abuse and identifying relevant implications for nursing practice. In response to this interest, certain changes in nursing practices have come about. Among the most significant of these has been the development of new nursing roles, many having considerable potential impact for the care received by drug-dependent people.

The Clinical Specialist

The clinical specialist position has been evolving over several years, and some nurses functioning in this capacity have directed attention primarily to alcoholics or people with other drug abuse problems. Both in an institutional setting and in the community, the clinical specialist may be in a position to provide guidance to nursing personnel in identifying and solving these people's problems.

Amplifying awareness of individual patient needs and common characteristics of the drug abuse patient in general is another important aspect of the clinical specialist's role. The leadership skills and the ability to function as a role model are further components of the position. For example, nurses can learn new techniques from the clinical specialist and apply similar methods to their own patients.

Continued development of the clinical specialist's role in providing and facilitating the care received by the alcoholic or drug abuser is a promising trend. As more nurses seek practice in this specialty, it is hoped that the quality of care will correspondingly improve.

Independent Nursing Practice

Within the last couple of years, several nurses with advanced academic preparation at the graduate and post-graduate level have set up independent nursing practices within their communities. A basic purpose of this independent practice has been to provide specialized care for persons seeking a one-to-one nurse-patient relationship. The potential benefit of this type of practice to drug-dependent persons has neither been evaluated nor measured. Ideally, however, it would give the nurse an opportunity to provide care on a consistent, long-term basis while attending to related health care teaching.

Family Therapy

Nurses who recognize the significance of family dynamics and how they relate to the treatment and rehabilitation of the alcoholic or drug abuser may choose to specialize in family therapy. Generally, the nurse prepared for and interested in this field would implement the role within an institutional setting or as part of a community based treatment program. She might function as cotherapist, group leader, or nurse therapist responsible for a selected number of families. Graduate and postgraduate academic preparation in nursing or a related discipline is usually a prerequisite. Again, since drug dependency has now been recognized as a major, unique health problem, greater numbers of nurses may seek the necessary preparation to practice family therapy. In reality, the family of the alcoholic or drug abuser requires planned intervention and guidance in the resolution of deep-seated problems. Without such intervention, comprehensive and long-lasting rehabilitation will not be possible.

Extended Nurse Roles

Nurses in family therapy and independent practice may be described as functioning in an extended nurse role. In addition to these two roles, however, many nurses are moving existing practice into previously unexplored directions.

(One of the best-known examples of the extended role is the pediatric nurse practitioner.)

Nurses who recognize the impact of drug dependence on the ability of health professionals to deliver care have the opportunity to create innovative extended modes of practice. For example, a nurse might design an extended role from a hospital setting to the adjacent community, acting as a health care coordinator. In this capacity, she can engage in limited casefinding, coordinate the person's entrance into the care system, and provide follow-up care after he leaves the institutional setting. To further ensure continuity of care, this nurse can make periodic visits to her hospitalized clients.

Many variations of the extended role concept are possible. Individual nurses who identify a potential area of patient need should be encouraged and supported in the identification and implementation of the role. With such involvement, perhaps some of the confusing problems so often encountered by nurses working with alcoholics or drug abusers might be alleviated.

NURSING RESEARCH

To date, research on drug abuse and alcoholism has been minimal. If nurses are to devise interventions and techniques to meet the specific needs of persons with drug-dependence problems, it will be necessary to conduct some exploratory and experimental research. Descriptive and exploratory studies might aid in identifying nurses' values and attitudes toward drug abusers and alcoholics. Equally important is research on the *patient's* values and attitudes toward care givers, the care received, and where it takes place.

Other studies could center on currently used nursing actions as they apply to the care of the alcoholic or drug abuser in the hospital, psychiatric, and community setting. Such information, whether in quantitative or descriptive terms, would serve as vitally needed baseline information that could indicate areas in need of experimental research. For instance, studies of this nature could be directed at implementing new nursing methods with a specific group of patients while continuing to use traditional interventions with a similar group. Controlled evaluation at the end of the experimental period would yield comparative data to determine the effectiveness of both new and traditional techniques. Research findings from descriptive and experimental studies might then be applied to the appropriate areas of nursing practice and education. Thus the quality of nursing care administered to and received by the alcoholic and drug abuser, as well as family members, could be progressively improved while simultaneously increasing the nurse's professional satisfaction and interest in caring for these often challenging patients.

It must be emphasized that all nursing research does not have to be patterned after a strict academic model. Nurses are in daily contact with drug-dependent persons. They can gather important data on common care problems, interpersonal behavior patterns, or patient responses to different nursing actions.

Regardless of the methodology employed, however, the results of research must be shared with other practitioners working in similar situations. Research should be communicated in easily understood terms so as to encourage nurses in various areas of practice to use research findings. In this way, important new knowledge can be applied to everyday practice.

SUMMARY COMMENT

Continuation of current and future trends in the development of drug abuse nursing will rely on education and research and how each is applied to practice. Trends in education, research, and practice must be both encouraged and supported by the nursing profession. As shown in Figure 19-1, the exchange of ideas among the three fields of practice is interrelated and interdependent. Thus, nurses in each field of practice have much to contribute to the perpetuation and increase of interest in nursing alcoholics and drug abusers.

Figure 19-1

Index

Withdrawal syndrome:
  in drug dependence, 110, 134, 135,
    146-147, 157, 171-172, 193
  newborn, 116-117, 173, 176-178,
    186-188, 193, 200, 210-213
  nursing care for, 209-213
  symptoms of, 175-176, 185-187,
    200-202, 210-213

Withdrawal syndrome:
  treatment for, 168-169, 175-178,
    185-188, 202, 209-210, 223,
    271
Work assignments (for patients), 84,
  228, 232, 256, 269, 271
World Health Organization, 11, 110